THE UPPER ROOM

Disciplines

2018

UPPER
ROOM BOOKS®
NASHVILLE

AN OUTLINE FOR SMALL-GROUP USE OF DISCIPLINES

Here is a simple plan for a one-hour, weekly group meeting based on reading *Disciplines*. One person may act as convener every week, or the role can rotate among group members. You may want to light a white Christ candle each week to signal the beginning of your time together.

OPENING

Convener: Let us come into the presence of God.

Others: Lord Jesus Christ, thank you for being with us. Let us hear your word to us as we speak to one another.

SCRIPTURE

Convener reads the scripture suggested for that day in *Disciplines*. After a one- or two-minute silence, convener asks: What did you hear God saying to you in this passage? What response does this call for? (Group members respond in turn or as led.)

REFLECTION

- What scripture passage(s) and meditation(s) from this week was (were) particularly meaningful for you? Why? (Group members respond in turn or as led.)
- What actions were you nudged to take in response to the week's meditations? (Group members respond in turn or as led.)
- Where were you challenged in your discipleship this week? How did you respond to the challenge? (Group members respond in turn or as led.)

PRAYING TOGETHER

Convener says: Based on today's discussion, what people and situations do you want us to pray for now and in the coming week? Convener or other volunteer then prays about the concerns named.

DEPARTING

Convener says: Let us go in peace to serve God and our neighbors in all that we do.

Adapted from *The Upper Room* daily devotional guide, January–February 2001. © 2000 The Upper Room. Used by permission.

THE UPPER ROOM DISCIPLINES 2018, ENLARGED-PRINT EDITION

© 2017 by Upper Room Books®. All rights reserved.

Upper Room Books website: books.upperroom.org

Cover design: Left Coast Design, Portland, Oregon

Cover photo: © SusaZoom / Shutterstock.com

At the time of publication all websites referenced in this book were valid. However, due to the fluid nature of the Internet some addresses may have changed, or the content may no longer be relevant.

The week of March 19–25 first appeared in The Upper Room Disciplines 2003. The week of November 5–11 first appeared in The Upper Room Disciplines 2000. Reprinted and used by permission.

Writers of various books of the Bible may be disputed in certain circles; this volume uses the names of the biblically attributed authors.

ISBN: 978-0-8358-1625-0 (print, enlarged-print edition)

For quick access to the scriptures recommended in this book, visit **BibleGateway.com or Biblica.com**

Printed in the United States of America

CONTENTS

FOREWORD

I just returned from a vital-church immersion experience in South Korea. I spent some time with the Bupyeong Methodist Church. Prayer is at the heart of the discipleship experience at the Bupyeong church. Can you picture hundreds of people gathering at 5 A.M. every day (including Sundays) to pray in a corporate worship service? Can you hear the sanctuary filled with passionate singing and vocal prayer as the sun begins to rise? If you ask those in attendance about their faithful participation, they respond that they believe the daily discipline of prayer enhances their relationship with God. Many would argue that the key to the revival movement in South Korea is the daily discipline of fervent and vibrant prayer.

You hold in your hand a key to your spiritual growth. *Disciplines* is a tool that allows you to attend to the reading of scripture, prayer, and devotion on a daily basis. Systematic, devotional use of scripture is essential for spiritual development and growth. It helps keep our faith alive.

All living things grow, but not all things grow constantly. Many plants grow in spring and summer, begin to go dormant in late fall, and remain dormant during the winter. We sometimes experience seasons in our life when our faith seems dormant. The good news is that some changes occur *only* in dormancy. Roots deepen in fall and winter. The same is true in our lives. It's especially important to practice the daily discipline of scripture devotion in our seasons of winter. When we engage in daily spiritual formation, we deepen our roots for the next spring's growth and fruit. We also grow our capacity to handle any season of life.

The habit of daily devotion through spiritual formation helps us grow to spiritual maturity. Eugene Peterson's *The Message* captures how we do this in very practical terms.

So here's what I want you to do, God helping you: Take your everyday, ordinary life—your sleeping, eating, going-to-work, and walking-around life—and place it before God as an offering. Embracing what God does for you is the best thing you can do for him. . . . Fix your attention on God. You'll be changed from the inside out. . . . God brings the best out of you, develops well-formed maturity in you. (Romans 12:1-2)

We will always offer excuses for not having enough time for daily devotion and scripture formation. But if we are honest, we admit to making time for things that matter most to us. I have two children. My son decided he wanted to take piano lessons. My wife and I signed him up and bought the practice books. He faithfully attended lessons and practiced every day. Then his commitment to practice time started to wane. After a few months he decided he'd had enough and wanted to quit. We wouldn't let him quit until he completed the year. My son didn't become a concert pianist, but he learned a valuable lesson: We grow by making commitments. There is power in our commitments.

In fact, for anything that's important in our lives, we're going to have to make a commitment. So, why not challenge yourself to experience a more personal and intimate relationship with God through the use of this daily devotional?

I pray that this volume of daily devotions will provide you with what you need to make a fresh start in Christ, while adding value and meaning to your spiritual journey. I believe God's highest desire for us is to be in relationship with God through Jesus Christ and for that relationship to deepen day by day.

—JUNIUS B. DOTSON
General Secretary (CEO), Discipleship Ministries
The United Methodist Church

God Our Redeemer

JANUARY 1–7, 2018 • STEPHEN B. CHAPMAN

SCRIPTURE OVERVIEW: The beginning of the New Year reminds us of God's love for all peoples through the celebration of Epiphany. Isaiah uses imagery of a wedding and a garden to declare that the beauty arising from Israel will go to all nations. The psalmist praises the Lord on behalf of everything and everyone on the earth, including men and women from all peoples. Paul proclaims that Christ fulfills the expectations of Israel; he is the open door for all to become children of God. In Luke, Simeon and Anna speak prophetically over the infant Jesus in the Temple, declaring him the light to the Gentiles. God's promises made in love are fulfilled in love.

QUESTIONS AND THOUGHTS FOR REFLECTION

- Read Isaiah 61:10–62:3. How are you daily becoming Zion, a person of justice?

- Read Psalm 148. How does your connection to God connect you to creation?

- Read Galatians 4:4-7. How confident are you that God listens to your prayer?

- Read Luke 2:22-40. When have you experienced sacrifice as gain rather than loss?

Associate Professor of Old Testament; Director of Graduate Studies, Graduate Program in Religion, Duke Divinity School.

NEW YEAR'S DAY

As one year turns to the next, we naturally reflect on the passage of time. The seconds tick away and are gone. Each moment of our lives is finally temporary. The space between the future and the past is so thin that sometimes it threatens to disappear. So what is the point of another day, of today, of this new year?

Time is God's gift to us in two ways. Time's persistent prodding prevents us from fruitless nostalgia, from getting stuck in the past. With God's help, we check our watches, calendars, and phones and then say to ourselves and each other, "What's next?" The passage of time gives us a farther horizon and keeps our focus ahead of ourselves. Time also presents us with constant opportunities for a fresh start, a do-over, a chance to amend our ways and reconcile ourselves with those we may have hurt or offended. Time *does* heal wounds. Time reminds us how the mercies of the Lord "are new every morning" (Lam. 3:23).

But there is still more. The Bible portrays for us how God encompasses even time. God is "the Alpha and Omega, the beginning and the end." At the origin of all things, God was there, active and alert. (See Genesis 1:1.) At the end of time, God will still be there. God's creation will be renewed and transformed, and death and sorrow will be gone for good. The ending to the Bible's story of time is strikingly not about how we will finally go up to God, but how God will come down to us, to dwell (or "tabernacle," as the Greek puts it) among us. And every second that passes brings us nearer to that glorious day.

O Alpha and Omega, our rock of ages past and hope for years to come, make your home with us and dwell among your people throughout this coming year. Amen.

Faith sometimes leads believers to focus on spiritual realities to the neglect of earthly cares. The psalmist never does so. For the psalmist, a vital awareness of God reminds believers of the spiritual significance of their everyday lives and their kinship with every living creature. Modern people tend to think of the "spiritual" as one thing and the "worldly" as another, likewise the miraculous and the ordinary. However, the psalmist holds them both together, rejoicing in their interconnection. All life, all creation, is a single tapestry or web as seen through the psalmist's eyes. Even the sky "pours forth speech" (Ps. 19:2) on a daily basis, proclaiming God's glory.

As sensible people, we view such ideas skeptically or purely poetically. Yet the psalmist insists that the sun and the moon do offer God praise, that the living creatures of the sea and land also praise God, and that the birds and trees and hills truly praise the Lord's name. This is more than metaphor. The psalmist understands all creation as God's handiwork. The world is a mighty choir of voices, each one honoring its Creator in its own way but joining all the other voices in glorious harmony too. All things in creation provide holy testimony to God, both by a kind of speaking and also by doing, by fulfilling their appointed roles established by God in the beginning. Even "fire and hail, snow and frost" have their divinely mandated parts to play. Moreover, the gathering of a people lies at the heart of God's work in creation. Only as part of the vast sweep of God's cosmic drama of redemption does our human vocation become plain.

Creator God, in you all things live, move, and have their being. Raise up a horn for your people once more, that we may join in the chorus of praise being sung all around us. Amen.

If I forget you, O Jerusalem, let my right hand wither!" (Ps. 137:5). This verse recalls the importance of the city of Jerusalem within the Bible. Christians focus so much on God's universal presence that we can struggle to consider any one place as holier than another. Yet the Bible centers on Jerusalem as the origin and goal of God's redemptive work. Jerusalem, or Zion, is special to God, God's own city. In verse 10, rather than the prophet or individual worshiper speaking, Zion itself speaks, looking ahead to the hour of its salvation. Like a fertile garden, Zion will one day bear the fruit of righteousness. Beginning in chapter 62, God responds by announcing that the time of vindication is at hand "for Zion's sake."

So this is a good day to pray for the peace of Jerusalem, the modern city that regularly features in the news. Jerusalem's violence is a scandal. A faithful Christian presence in Jerusalem deserves prayers of support, even as prayers of repentance acknowledge Christian complicity in the bloodshed. Jerusalem is a real place, and God cares for Jerusalem in a unique way.

However, the poetic name "Zion" reveals that, for Isaiah, Jerusalem is already a symbol as well as a site. The people of God are also Zion. Each believer is Zion too, not in whole but in part. Over and over, scripture witnesses to the connection between holiness and righteousness. The way to become Zion, a people capable of receiving God's favor, is to be a community without "robbery and wrongdoing." God loves justice! This affirmation is just as remarkable (and challenging) today as it was in ancient Israel. Where do you see injustice in the world? How are you prepared to intervene on behalf of justice?

O God, we pray for the peace of Jerusalem. Grant us the courage to live justly and promote greater understanding. We know you bless peacemakers. Amen.

As we age, we can become obsessed with the past, how things used to be. But Simeon looks forward to the deliverance of Israel. His mindfulness of God's promises and hopefulness of present fulfillment allow him to recognize God's messiah in the baby Jesus.

Simeon takes the child in his arms and blesses him, praising God for Jesus' true identity as "a light for revelation to the Gentiles and for glory to your people Israel." Simeon knows the future will not be easy for this child. He does not romanticize the future any more than he romanticizes the past. Still, the fulfillment of God's long-standing promises gives rise to thanks and praise. The eighty-four-year-old prophet Anna has never left the Temple because she too looks for a sign that God is prepared to act anew in the lives of her people. Once she sees Jesus, young as he is, she cannot stop speaking about him.

The story about Jesus' parents presenting him at the Temple (Luke 2:22-24) sets the stage for all that follows. As was the custom, Jesus' first Temple visit requires a sacrifice. How fitting that a sacrifice accompanies the one who will one day become Israel's sacrifice! Indeed, the sacrifice of the two turtledoves prompts Simeon to see Jesus for who he is. Today we tend to think of a sacrifice as losing something. For the Bible and for God, sacrifice instead means giving.

Jesus' parents give turtledoves to God as a sign of their joy. Simeon and Anna give thanks that their lives have finally brought them consolation. God gave an only begotten Son to all of us, Jew and Gentile, because God so loved the world.

We thank you, O God, for the precious gift of your Son Jesus Christ, our living sacrifice. Amen.

In modern life, time has become primarily a quantitative measure. "How much time is left?" we ask. Yet we also talk about having a bad time or a good time, which suggests that time possesses a qualitative dimension as well. Paul writes of the "fullness" of time when God sent Jesus Christ, who fulfilled Jewish law and, by fulfilling it, opened up the opportunity for non-Jews to enter into the family of God, to become God's children by adoption.

Many Christians today overlook what an incredible gift it is to be a Christian. Perhaps we take for granted our standing before God and our ready access to God's mercy and blessings. Paul describes Gentile Christians as heirs to God's promises. But we are heirs, he writes, by adoption. In a profound way, then, God is not our "natural" Father. So how much more precious is it that we too can cry out "Abba" and feel confident that God listens to us?

With our inclusion in God's people, it is not only we who are redeemed but time itself. The Bible tells us that time was not simply ticktocking along throughout the many centuries prior to Jesus' birth, nor is the time between Jesus' day and our own lacking in significance. God has a plan for the world, and God is working it out. Even when we struggle to find signs of God's activity or when we encounter the all-too-frequent tragedies in this fallen world, we can remain confident that God is God. Time itself is God's own creation. One day all will be made plain to us, and, as adopted heirs of God's promises, nothing "in all creation, will be able to separate us from the love of God in Christ Jesus our Lord" (Rom. 8:39).

Abba, thank you for making us part of your family, for making us part of your plan for the world. Amen.

EPIPHANY

Tradition holds that Paul wrote Ephesians while imprisoned in Rome. His experience as a prisoner underscores the contrast between bondage and freedom found throughout his teachings. It also establishes a contrast between isolation and community, between individual believers and the church. Here in Ephesians, Paul reminds his Gentile Christian audience that they are not only heirs to God's promises but "fellow heirs, members of the same body, and sharers in the promise."

We often focus on the shortcomings of the church. How imperfect and all too human it appears! Many of us know people who have been terribly wounded by a church experience, which may have soured them on the Christian faith altogether. Yet this very fragile institution, Paul insists, retains cosmic importance. The church is the culmination of history and the fulfillment of creation, he writes, because it is in and through the church that God's plan, hidden for ages, can now be revealed. The church imparts the wisdom of God's creation. The church is the final stage of God's "eternal purpose" in Christ.

For all its imperfections and faults, the church of Jesus Christ remains holy and blessed as God's chosen vessel and best strategy for a world brimming with hostility and distrust. The church's task is to identify God's wisdom "in all its rich variety" and make it known. Yet we are unaccustomed to thinking of the church as being in the "wisdom business." How can local churches be more explicit and more diligent in seeking God's wisdom? And how can they confront the principalities and powers of our day with God's wisdom in all its rich variety?

O God, source of all wisdom, help your church seek knowledge,
that it may share your truth with the world. Amen.

BAPTISM OF THE LORD

As Paul travels through Asia Minor, modern-day Turkey, he encounters a group of twelve disciples who know of John the Baptist but not Jesus. Because they have never heard of the Holy Spirit either, they are probably Gentiles. (Jews would have known about the Holy Spirit from Israel's scriptures; see Psalm 51:11.) Paul explains to them how John's baptism was preparatory, signaling repentance, but also looking ahead to Jesus, the one who was to follow after John. Paul baptizes the disciples in Jesus' name. They receive the Holy Spirit and prophesy and speak in tongues together.

However, one of Paul's initial questions to them is revealing. Paul does not ask "In whose name were you baptized?" but "Into what then were you baptized?" Baptism, for Paul, is not simply a symbolic act performed in Jesus' name that hopefully yields spiritual results. Baptism is a sacred act of mystical union, in which the baptized are united with the Holy Spirit. So these willing disciples in Acts 19 are baptized "into" the Holy Spirit as well as "in" Jesus' name. Christians sometimes wonder whether the Holy Spirit is somehow inside them or perhaps visits them in particular moments. Paul's understanding is the reverse: Christians baptized in Jesus' name are now "in" the Holy Spirit. The Holy Spirit holds the power, not us. Our efforts to pursue God's will and accomplish spiritual tasks do not depend for their success on our occasional appeals to the Holy Spirit for assistance. Our successful efforts depend on whether we recall our baptism and our uniting with the Holy Spirit, God's active presence in the world. The question is not whether the Holy Spirit dwells in us, but whether we dwell in the Holy Spirit.

Holy Spirit, help us to remember our baptism. We strive to live and work and rest within you all our days. Amen.

Discipleship's Transforming Power

JANUARY 8–14, 2018 • ANNE MATHEWS-YOUNES

SCRIPTURE OVERVIEW: We read the stories of Samuel and the calling of Jesus' disciples in John, and it is easy to feel jealous. God spoke so directly into their lives that they should have had, it seems to us, full and unwavering confidence in their calling. Didn't they have an unfair spiritual advantage over us? However, the psalmist reminds us that God knows and sees us individually just as well as God knew Samuel and Jesus knew his disciples. God has plans for us, even if they are revealed in less obvious ways. The reading from Corinthians is quite different in its message. Perhaps we can at least recognize that even if we never hear God's audible voice, through scripture God still provides guidance for our lives.

QUESTIONS AND THOUGHTS FOR REFLECTION

- Read 1 Samuel 3:1-20. In what ways do you remain responsive to hearing God's voice?
- Read Psalm 139:1-6, 13-18. What sense of God's involvement in your everyday life do you have?
- Read 1 Corinthians 6:12-20. How do you remind yourself of the spirit–body connection?
- Read John 1:43-51. When have you allowed prejudice to affect your decision about a person's competency?

President, E. Stanley Jones Foundation, Metropolitan Memorial United Methodist Church, Washington, DC.

We need a prophet badly. . . . "The word of the LORD was rare in those days; visions were not widespread." While young Samuel appears unprepared to hear from the Lord, it seems no one has heard from God lately. The challenge for young Samuel is to determine that it is God, not his mentor Eli, who is calling him. Three times the Lord calls to Samuel; each time Samuel runs to Eli. With Eli's dulled spiritual sensitivity, he does not perceive who is calling. The third time is the charm. Eli realizes the Lord is calling Samuel. Only then does he provide the young boy with a suitable response.

Not all of us expect to hear from the Lord. We hear what we are conditioned to hear. We make mistakes at times because we fail to listen or to understand the messages we receive. Sometimes through fear or impatience we block out the messages altogether. We can recall instances of missed or garbled communications in our personal and professional lives—sometimes with painful consequences.

Though Samuel misunderstands God's call to him, he remains responsive to the persistent voice. The elder Eli offers some sage advice to his protégé, using words to this effect: "When you hear the voice again, listen carefully and engage it." Samuel follows the advice only to hear bad news for the house of Eli. Message received, message delivered. Eli acknowledges this word from the Lord. We too would do well to slow down, listen intently, and seek to hear what our initiating God is saying to us.

May I never forget that it is you, God, who takes the initiative. Teach me to slow down, listen more intently, and seek understanding before acting on what I think I have heard. May I be open and receptive to your calls to me. Amen.

Who wants to hear bad news? A parent finds a child standing in the kitchen next to an empty cookie jar with crumbs on his shirt. The parent asks, "Who ate all the cookies?" Looking bewildered, the child responds, "I don't know." Perhaps the parent responds with punishment for lying. Another parent might approach the situation differently by creating a safe place for the child to describe what happened.

Samuel receives bad news about Eli from the Lord, but he avoids interacting with his mentor, Eli. Perhaps he hopes the Lord's message is not real and that he can forget about it. However, Samuel trusts Eli and has enough confidence and courage to deliver the bad news. He delivers all of it, leaving nothing out. Eli accepts the consequences of what he has heard, saying, "It is the LORD; let him do what seems good to him."

These verses convey many lessons. Perhaps we learn the importance of creating safe places for people to share bad news. Perhaps we can focus on developing the internal confidence and courage necessary to deliver bad news. Maybe, like Eli, we can learn to ask for the bad news, be strengthened to receive it and gracious enough to acknowledge our identity as God's children even in the face of such news.

Samuel models responsiveness and obedience to God's word; Eli submits to that word. May we remain obedient to the message we have heard from the Lord and accept the consequences of acting on it.

O Holy One, who bears all news, good and bad, may we be willing to seek and to deliver bad news when necessary. Teach us to do so with compassion and care. Amen.

The psalmist speaks of God's complete knowledge of him: The Lord knows what the psalmist will say before he says it, what he will do before he does it. The psalmist uses the words *I, me,* and *my* to speak of his close relationship with the great God of creation. "You . . . are acquainted with all my ways." Yet, how can this sense of intimacy with God possibly be true?

How do we square those words with the dark nights of our soul? How do we take comfort from those words in our sleepless nights? Why does the Lord seem far removed when we say certain things and take certain actions?

Our challenge in understanding the psalm's message may arise because we hear the message from a human perspective. From our point of view, this intimacy with God does not seem possible. Yet when we hear the psalmist's words and seek to internalize them, we find ourselves drawn into the possibility of relationship with the Creator of the universe.

For all our misplaced arrogance about how no one could be worse than we, God has seen much worse—God has seen *our* worst. God *knows* us and chooses to be in relationship with us. The Hebrew Bible describes a rhythm of life between God and people in which we are and are not in relationship with God. This scripture affirms God's persistent desire for relationship no matter what we have said, no matter what we have done. The next move is ours.

O Holy One, remind us of your presence and your willingness to understand, to accept, and to forgive us, even when we find it impossible to understand, accept, and forgive ourselves. Teach us again that the power of your love comes as a most welcome gift of your grace. Amen.

The nature of relationship with God is deeply personal. This is not a relationship between a philosophical construct and humanity in general. The relationship exists between the Creator of the universe and individual humans. "Your eyes beheld my unformed substance. In your book were written all the days that were formed for me, when none of them as yet existed."

God engages in our daily lives, and we can encounter God's presence in our everyday experiences because we belong to God. The psalmist reminds us that God knows who we are and, more importantly, God knows whose we are. We cannot begin to imagine the many ways that reinforce such a strong and enduring connection. Nor can we realize how much God cares for each person. The phrase "joined at the hip" does not even begin to explain this intimate connection.

Because God created us with the freedom to accept or reject relationship, we may freely choose to live beyond a connection to God. But God remains connected to us even, and especially, when we feel far removed from divine grace and mercy. Our freedom does not include our ability to deny who we are and from whence we came: We are God's.

Since we belong to God, we can affirm that all humankind belongs as well. How comforting it is to know the extent and power of God's love for each of us and God's commitment to be in relationship with all of us as we both know and are known by the Divine! As we experience the reality of God's love, we can now affirm that we do not want to escape God's love.

Dear God, give me the grace to know, even on those days when you seem far away, that you made me with intent and love. I now want to draw on your love with grateful abandon. Amen.

What connects the body with the spirit? What happens when we drive a wedge into life between the sacred and the secular, between the spiritual and the material? Paul discovers that his brothers and sisters in Corinth hold some mistaken ideas about the material order. Their resulting behaviors are way off the mark. They live as if their spirituality can remain sacred and intact no matter how they behave. They fail to realize the sacred nature of the material side of life. As a result, they take some serious missteps. The time has come for a stern (but loving) message, and Paul offers it. I would welcome Paul giving us that same message.

God created both the material and the spiritual and affirms both as good. While I may exercise my freedom to do all things, I can choose to affirm God's promises and conduct myself in a way that pleases God. What I do with my body, what I eat or how I act, is not separate or irrelevant to my spiritual nature. The connection between spirit and body matters: God will raise our bodies just as he raised Jesus' body. God redeems our lives and that of creation. We are not our own but Christ's, and we are to live fully out of our integrated selves.

Paul calls his flock to task because they do not understand or believe the powerful integration of life between the material and the spiritual. His words serve as a pertinent reminder to us as we "glorify God" in our bodies!

Lord Jesus, thank you for the gift of an integrated life. We acknowledge that your grace affirms the material and the spiritual aspects of our lives. May we honor that gift. Amen.

"Can anything good come out of Nazareth?" Nathanael gives voice to his prejudice, a prejudice that could have closed down a fruitful avenue in his future. How often have we allowed past events to influence our current assumptions, which then hinder future possibilities? How many times have we let our prejudice predict the future? Haven't we all—in our hearts, if nowhere else—concluded that someone won't amount to much because of background, race, family, or our own contempt?

We've heard a lot about implicit bias lately. For example, we might say and believe in our racial neutrality, but scientific studies show that racial bias remains pervasive and invisible to the persons who suffer from it. We all have biases; we all risk discriminating on the basis of these judgments, despite our best intentions.

Philip chooses not to argue. Instead he invites the doubter to "come and see." He cleverly undercuts Nathanael's prejudice by inviting him to see for himself. Often we, like Nathanael, simply need to see for ourselves. Jesus expands our vision, allowing us to see life and others with "new eyes." Life, in all its fullness and abundance, overwhelms our prejudice.

Following Jesus changes everything. It does not matter where we have come from; it only matters where we are going. We accept the invitation to "come and see." See what came out of Nazareth, the place where Jesus began his healing ministry. Jesus of Nazareth—the world's savior and our own.

O Holy One, teach me to recognize your presence in settings and among people that surprise me. Help me remove the blinders of prejudice. I yearn to see the world as you do and to embrace life as you do—with love and compassion. Amen.

Discipleship's Transforming Power   27

Philip has heard Jesus' call to "follow me" and witnesses to Nathanael. Philip does not find Nathanael's dismissive comment about Nazareth off-putting. Instead, he invites Nathanael to "come and see." Philip turns a potential personal "upset" to a "set up." Jesus takes over and addresses Nathanael, which may have been the biggest surprise of Nathanael's life. Jesus already knows Nathanael, and that makes all the difference.

What does it feel like to be recognized—sought out and fully seen by God who knows our needs—at the very moment we feel inclined to go another direction? Jesus' knowledge of Nathanael shocks him. He realizes that being known by Jesus is both undeserved and unmerited. He feels compelled to testify, "You are the Son of God!" His profession of faith is more extensive than Philip's witness to him.

Imagine what happens to us when Jesus calls us to follow him. He knows us and the secrets of our hearts. He knows our weaknesses, inadequacies, and doubts. Yet he invites us into an intimate relationship with God by becoming his disciples.

John's Gospel emphasizes the decision of accepting or rejecting Jesus. Nathanael, an Israelite without deceit, chooses to accept Jesus and receives his promise of seeing "greater things than these" and "heaven opened and the angels of God ascending and descending upon the Son of Man."

Jesus calls us to follow, and we decide. Following him requires a daily commitment; our obedience brings transformation. We follow with our hearts and our lives, settling only for God's fullness of life.

O Holy One, I am so blessed that you already know me. Help me see the greater things that you have in store for me. Give me courage to ask others to "come and see." Amen.

Living into Trust

JANUARY 15–21, 2018 • ADRIENNE SPARROW TREVATHAN

SCRIPTURE OVERVIEW: Things are not always as they seem. To Jonah it appears that the people of Nineveh are beyond hope, so he runs away rather than going to preach to them. God has other plans; to Jonah's surprise, the Ninevites turn to God. To our eyes, social standing and wealth may seem to divide people into different classes; but the psalmist declares that in God's economy, all are equal and will be repaid the same. Paul echoes the theme of the temporary nature of all things in this life; they should not be our source of security. Jesus opens his ministry in Mark by proclaiming that God is breaking into history to overthrow what has been accepted as the way things are. Sometimes God's perspective is not our perspective.

QUESTIONS AND THOUGHTS FOR REFLECTION

- Read Jonah 3:1-5, 10. When have you experienced God's call to a task you would have preferred not to undertake? What happened? What did you learn about God?

- Read Psalm 62:5-12. When have you experienced God as refuge and fortress? How do you actively embody God's hope and offer it to others?

- Read 1 Corinthians 7:29-31. How lightly do you hold your job, your relationships, your possessions, given the passing nature of the present age?

- Read Mark 1:14-20. When have you heard Jesus call to you to follow? How did you respond?

Associate minister of education and administration at Holy Covenant United Methodist Church, and administrator at Berry United Methodist Church in Chicago, Illinois.

For God alone my soul waits in silence." The psalmist offers healing for the world-weary soul. In the midst of an uncertain and violent world—if we are still, we may hear the psalmist's voice urging us to trust in God. The opening two verses of the psalm bear a striking resemblance to verses 5 and 6 of today's reading. Verses 3 and 4 lay out the problem facing the psalmist: He feels assailed, battered, and surrounded on all sides by people who pay lip service to God while deceiving others. Nothing less than pouring out his heart before God will do as he affirms the unshakable foundation of his life. His images of God are more than metaphors meant to be stitched onto a pillow: *rock, salvation, fortress, refuge*. They are strong, trustworthy. In verse 8, he reminds the members of his community to trust in and to "pour out [their] heart before [God]."

Often church people foster the idea that we can separate our theology—our words and beliefs about God—from the struggles and pain in our lives. For the psalmist, our trials may be the very place where we develop an authentic relationship with God—a relationship in which we experience God as refuge and place of solace. We may find ourselves asking, "How long?" as does the psalmist in verse 3. How long must we remain in a situation of abuse? How long will people delight in falsehood? We face the rawness of our emotions and the pain of our economic or political realities and discover the ultimate rest and security that come in trusting God. In the midst of trials and trouble, we calm our soul. In the silence, God calls us into relationship, and we move from where we are to where God longs for us to be. When we become vulnerable, God can use us.

Strengthening God, empower us to pour out our hearts and lives before you as we trust in your protection. Amen.

The psalm moves from placing full trust in God to a painful acknowledgment of our own human frailty. Whether rich or poor, powerful or disempowered, "human beings are nothing but a breath" (v. 9, CEB). The psalmist strongly contrasts humanity's limitations with God's goodness. We wonder then about a person's ability to effect change or make any difference in the world. If placed on the world's scales, even a breath of air is weightier than a single person. Rather than placing our confidence in wealth or power, we trust in God's power to redeem situations. The psalmist takes comfort in the vastness of God's steadfast love.

We may be tempted to list the ways that others have wronged us or failed to live up to their potential as children of God. As humans we instinctually compare ourselves to others in an attempt to measure worth. We easily forget our call to take comfort in God's strength and goodness rather than to despair over others' actions. God holds in the balance both power and love, maintaining a tension between autocratic authority and sentimental, passive love.

"Power belongs to God, and steadfast love belongs to you, O Lord." God remains faithful even if we are a mere breath in creation. When we focus on the goodness and fullness of God, we move from pointing our fingers to raising our hands in awe—a transformation made possible only by God.

Pardoning God, help us see and know the fullness of your love. When we are tempted to measure others by our own understanding of what is right, convict us. Empower us to be people who seek comfort in your love. Amen.

Living into Trust

As an act of grace, the story continues with God's word coming to Jonah a second time. God's response not only frees Jonah from his predicament but reminds Jonah who he is and what he is called to do. Verse 1 refers to Nineveh as a "great city"—one of the larger cities in the Old Testament—with a population of more than 120,000. Trying to convert a city this size is no small feat.

We can only imagine what Jonah is thinking his first day of travel. Has God's grace stunned him? Is he still working through his anger? Or does he graciously accept his role in bringing healing, even to the Ninevites?

Remarkably, the Ninevites take Jonah's words to heart. They "believed God." They don't necessarily believe the messenger or the message; they do believe that Yahweh will follow through on the threat that their city will be overthrown. They receive that word with sincerity—an amazing turnaround—and disaster is averted. "God changed his mind."

In setting Jonah on this course, God believes that the Ninevites can change, and the Ninevites bank on God's willingness, in freedom, to change the judgment. "They proclaimed a fast, and everyone . . . put on sackcloth." The story conveys a powerful testimony to God's grace.

How often would we, like Jonah, prefer that people get what's coming to them? Yet God gives Jonah and the Ninevites another chance, and God's freedom and responsiveness offer us that same second and third opportunity.

Compassionate God, thank you for second and third chances.
Thank you for using even us. Amen.

Mark's account of Jesus' life is one of the more dramatic Gospels. In some scripture versions, Mark uses the word *immediately* about forty times throughout the Gospel. When John the Baptist is arrested, Mark wants to make it clear that Jesus follows in the tradition of John. "The kingdom of God has come near." Jesus begins to call people to repentance and belief. Repentance—turning in a different direction—comes first in Mark's story. Not only does it link Jesus' message to John's message, but it demonstrates that repentance is the faithful response to God's reign.

We can easily skip over this call to repentance, especially if we've heard this story many times before. We'd prefer to focus on these brave disciples, leaving the lives they've known to pursue a new adventure—not to mention that repentance isn't something the church always does well. How do you call people to repent without shaming them or making them feel guilty? How do you recognize sin in your life and find your way to grace? Repentance is often not immediate at all. But it's hard to follow if you're going in the wrong direction.

Jesus sought followers who would willingly reorient themselves to a new way of living. Jesus' invitation to Simon and Andrew to "fish for people" creates a metaphor they understand; fishing has been their life. Maybe fishing for people will free them from the rigors of their vocation. "Immediately they left their nets and followed him." Simon and Andrew trade their lives of security to follow the path of risky discipleship.

Empowering God, help us reorient our lives so that we can respond wholeheartedly to your call to follow. Amen.

James and John quickly leave their father with the nets and the boat; scripture offers no commentary on their father's feelings. Mark's sense of urgency in moving the story forward doesn't allow the reader to dwell too long on family members. Action is always immediate. Even if Zebedee doesn't understand Jesus' meaning when he calls Zebedee's sons to leave everything behind, Zebedee is there when Jesus sees some trait or characteristic in them that merits his invitation. Sitting in the boat mending nets after a long day's work, Zebedee may hope he has prepared his sons well enough for life's opportunities.

Jesus meets the two men where they are, both physically and vocationally. He comes to their setting. He does not seek out government officials or people who will elevate his status. He approaches fishermen who have spent their entire adult lives perfecting skills on the water. Nothing about their lifestyle is easy or predictable; perhaps that makes them ready for a life of discipleship. Jesus issues the call to discipleship not as a blind following but as a choice to use experiences, skills, and culture for God's glory.

This is good news for us because God calls us to follow and learn in our varied vocations. Jesus calls us to transform our world by living in justice and compassion, using the skills we have developed and the language we know. Only then can we meet people where they are. Our experiences, stories, and culture shape us so that when we face a new challenge or calling, we can step forward with confidence—immediately.

Life-giving God, may we use everything we are to follow you. Thank you for the experiences that have shaped us; be with us as we grow in your grace. Amen.

For those in healthy marriages or with material "creature" comforts, this passage can seem harsh or unwieldy. Why would Paul disregard the importance of a healthy relationship or the opportunity to rejoice over God's provision?

Paul believes that Christ's return is imminent. The "old age" of strict adherence to the law has passed; believers now live at the beginning of the "new age" of Jesus. Paul advises those followers who live in the in-between time.

Paul encourages individuals to remain in the same social system as they were when they first accepted Christ—even, and including, those with a lower social standing. American history has shown the dangers of this passage when taken to its extreme: an affirmation of oppressing minority groups and keeping those deemed socially unworthy beneath those with authority. But as New Testament scholar Richard B. Hays explains in *Interpretation: A Bible Commentary for Teaching and Preaching*, Paul's "immediate pastoral concern is to set his readers free for wholehearted service of God wherever they find themselves located in the present time" (123).

In light of Christ's return, "the present form of the world is passing away." Social systems and roles hold no value in God's new order. Paul emphasizes the priority of commitment to God in light of God's reign. We acknowledge our ties to roles, relationships, and possessions but avoid *overattachment* to any of these. We pledge our allegiance to God and God alone.

Creating God, create within us a sincere desire to serve you in every aspect of our lives. Strengthen us to align our priorities with yours and to do so with conviction. Amen.

The image of God as refuge is powerful. At its core, a refuge is any space that provides safety and shelter from danger or chaos. But as followers of Christ, we do not always find ourselves in safe or sheltered situations. Depending upon where we live or what we are exposed to daily, our need for a place of shelter is a very real concern. Can we talk about God as refuge or fortress when we are not safe ourselves? If we are safe, can we tell those in dangerous settings that God is their refuge too?

The psalmist answers with a resounding yes. To understand God as shelter and place of safety implies that we ultimately rest in God rather than in the circumstances of our lives. We then live in such a way that we become the embodiment of God as shelter and refuge for those who are unsafe or in danger. What would such embodiment look like? It could entail making a space at your table for a child who comes home to an empty house after school. Perhaps a neighbor with limited means would appreciate a meal. It could be as simple as taking time to speak with friends and neighbors about their issues or concerns.

As we work to embody a safe space of refuge for others, we begin as does the psalmist: in silence before God. But we do not stay in a place of silence. The psalmist reminds us that our trust and deliverance comes from our relationship with God. Once we find our hope in God alone, we share it authentically. We affirm God as hope, rock, salvation, fortress, deliverance, honor, and refuge. We move from the sacred space of silent reverence and anticipation and begin to embody hope for others. We learn that God is indeed a refuge for us all.

Sheltering God, move within my life as a refuge and place of hope. Help me to find my rest in you. Amen.

The Word in Our Heart

JANUARY 22–28, 2018 • SCOT P. MCCLYMONT

SCRIPTURE OVERVIEW: This week's readings center on God's authority. In Deuteronomy God promises to raise up a prophet to guide the people, and God warns the people not to listen to voices that do not speak for God. The psalmist overflows with praise for God's great works. God is powerful and awesome, yet gracious and merciful also. Paul instructs the Corinthians to place the rights of others before their own rights. A person's conscience may allow him or her to exercise freedom in Christ; however, with this freedom comes responsibility. We must surrender our own rights, if necessary, for the good of others. In Mark's Gospel, Jesus shows his power over the forces of darkness: even the unclean spirits recognize and obey him.

QUESTIONS AND THOUGHTS FOR REFLECTION

- Read Deuteronomy 18:15-20. To whom or to what setting do you turn when you yearn to hear God's voice?

- Read Psalm 111. How willing are to you to immerse yourself in life? in your worship setting? What causes you to simply dip your toe in? What would help you make a fuller commitment?

- Read 1 Corinthians 8:1-13. When have you been conscious of another's limitation in some area and intentionally chosen to avoid a certain behavior?

- Read Mark 1:21-28. Jesus calls James and John from their fishing nets. He takes them as they are exactly where they are. Where have you sensed a call from God? How did that call change your vocation or avocation?

Pastor, 4 The World Ministries, a nondenominational church, Smyrna, Delaware; professional musician, active in addiction recovery.

How often have we yearned to hear God's voice? The Israelites desired such instruction. Yet, Moses reminds the people of the time God spoke and the divine was made manifest in their midst. Their response: "If I hear the voice of the LORD my God any more, or ever again see this great fire, I will die." God proposes a mediator: a prophet like Moses.

During my hospital chaplaincy, I visited a patient who was experiencing spiritual distress. When I skimmed the chart, I learned the patient was deaf and preferred sign language but could read lips. With no interpreter available, I planned to use my basic signing skills to open a line of communication. I walked into the room confident that I could communicate with the patient. It did not go as I had expected; I could not understand the patient.

Time after time, God's people fell away from God's instruction, so God established a line of prophets like Moses who could continually bring God's word to the people. Unlike my situation with the patient in the hospital, God always finds a way to communicate with us.

God speaks, exhausting every measure to tell us of God's love and care. As the Bible unfolds, we begin to realize that this is a love story on an infinite scale between God and God's people. Are we listening and responding to God's voice?

God, I know you speak, but sometimes I find it difficult to hear what you are saying. May I listen with more than my ears so I may respond by following you with all that I am. Amen.

It always gives me pause when someone begins a conversation with, "The Lord told me to tell you. . . . " More often than not, the speaker follows the statement with a criticism or complaint disguised as a "word from the Lord." God speaks to all of us, but today's passage tells us that God grants authority to some voices over others.

In the verses leading up to today's reading (vv. 9-14), God notes the voices and practices that the Israelites are *not* to heed, specific practices such as divination and soothsaying. God grants no authority to those who practice these activities.

Instead God promises to establish a line of prophets like Moses, authoritative communicators of God's word to the people. These are the prophets to whom God calls the people to listen. They have the authority to hold both the people and other religious leaders accountable to God.

As Christians, we understand Jesus as the culmination of this line—a prophet who not only speaks the word of God but *is* God's Word. We read the Bible through the lens of Jesus. We believe Jesus is the fulfillment of scripture and thus brings to us the full word of God.

When we express skepticism about someone's "word from the Lord," we can look to Jesus as the prophet who showed us everything we need to know about God. We follow the example and heed the words of Christ. We need not turn to horoscopes or fortune-tellers for truth; God gave us a line of prophets and an ultimate prophet to bring us God's word.

God, guide us by the truth of your word. Help us discern what comes from you. When we are tempted to follow practices that do not come from you, guide us to Christ—your Word and our Savior. Amen.

The word *authority* can mean different things based on several factors. If you are young, you might think of a teacher or parent as an authority. You may hold high regard for the government; government officials serve as authorities. Others may consider authority in the abstract—anything to which they adhere, including laws and commands. As Christians, we believe God and God's word—written or living—is our highest authority. Today's reading emphasizes Jesus' authority.

Jesus enters the synagogue on the sabbath and begins teaching. Mark does not mention the content of Jesus' teaching; instead he emphasizes *who* teaches and *how* he teaches.

The first dialogue in the passage highlights *who* teaches that day—Jesus of Nazareth, the Holy One of God. The unclean spirit recognizes that Jesus' authority stems from God. Jesus rebukes the spirit, which leaves the man, albeit violently. Then, the people recognize *how* Jesus teaches—with authority. They do not yet recognize Jesus as the Son of God; they simply acknowledge his authority. Its source puzzles them, and they begin to ask, "What is this?"

Jesus' divine authority portrayed in this scene, along with the questions the people in the synagogue raise, prompt us to consider the sources of authority in our own lives. Who has authority in my life? Is it the living Word of God, Jesus Christ? Do I look to the Bible for guidance or to the latest *New York Times* self-help best seller? God grants authority to the written word of the Bible and the living Word of Jesus Christ. We look to both for authoritative and trustworthy guidance.

God, I give you full authority over my life. Lead me, guide me. Be the Lord of my life, this day and every day. Amen.

Each time we read the Bible, it can speak to us in a new way. I have preached on today's reading many times in my thirteen years of ministry; each time God reveals a different aspect—a new revelation to me.

As I read this passage again, I focused on verse 27: "A new teaching—with authority!" But Jesus' teaching is nothing new. He teaches the words of the prophets, the scriptures, and the traditions people already knew. The authority with which Jesus teaches—and the presence he brings as the incarnate Word of God—creates fresh meaning and gives new life to God's word.

Newly planted churches love to use the word *new* on their websites and advertisements. *New* church, *new* community, *new* and relevant preaching, *new* ways of worship, *new* approaches to singing praise—a *new* way to experience God. But the Bible's message does not change. A new building, new songs, or new lights cannot make the gospel—God's good news of salvation in Jesus Christ—better or more relevant.

Jesus helped his followers see God in a new way, all the while proclaiming the old-yet-ever-new story of God's steadfast love. Through our life experiences, we come to understand aspects of the Bible that we may not have noticed before. The living Word of God has the authority to help us experience God in new ways. That is nothing new, but a new life is ours when we choose to embrace it.

God, may we bypass the latest fads to develop ways to know you better—through the firm foundation of your word and our relationship with the living Word, Christ Jesus. Amen.

Paul discusses consuming meat sacrificed to idols from two perspectives: knowledge and love. This issue concerned the Christians in Corinth in particular, but Paul's guidance deals with more than food. His message reveals his hopes for Christian care and concern within community.

Paul acknowledges that many believers know idols do not exist. However, some people in Corinth, even some believers, may consider food sacrificed to an idol as sacred. This could raise issues in the community as to whether eating this food is idolatrous. Paul tells the people in Corinth that knowledge is not bad—in fact, knowledge helps them make moral decisions, like knowing they can eat this meat.

In this week's passage from Deuteronomy, we learned that God grants more authority to some voices than others. Paul teaches that love holds more authority than knowledge in Christian communities. It is good to be knowledgeable, but it is better to love others—especially if knowledge may cause them to stumble in their faith.

Paul tells us to err on the side of love. Though he does not fully develop this point until later in the letter, Paul mentions love in the first sentence of the section—even before explaining his stance on the issue at hand. Paul calls for the kind of love that builds communities, love for those with whom we share life and faith. Paul's deep commitment to supporting others in their faith brings him to state boldly that he will never eat meat again if it makes someone stumble in his or her faith.

It is not only what we know that leads us to Christ. How we love and support one another helps us live well and leads others to God.

Lord, make me aware of my actions so that I do not become a stumbling block to anyone's faith in you. Amen.

I had a drinking problem for nearly two decades before I became a pastor. Through my faith in Christ, I am now strong enough not to drink when others around me are doing so; but this is not the case for many who struggle with alcohol addiction. Being around alcohol can cause them to stumble on their path to recovery, so I try to know who around me struggles with addiction and avoid placing them in situations where there is alcohol.

Paul addresses this very problem in today's passage. As people of faith we know that everything comes from God; we do not know God any less and are not any less known by God if we have a drink, utter a curse word, or listen to secular music. As faith leaders, though, we are called to consider what might harm others—those who struggle with addictions or who believe these things do not come from God. Might a new believer stumble if he or she saw a church leader at a bar having a drink, heard the choir director curse, or witnessed the pastor rocking out to secular music? These behaviors may not obstruct our faith, but they could get in the way of others' faith.

Out of consideration and love for believers who hold differing views, we consciously choose to avoid behaviors that we know would cause others difficulty. Preserving the fragile fabric of community becomes a top priority. "Love builds up."

God calls us to value Christian community above our own desires and actions; we then choose to live in such a way that we always build up one another.

Almighty God, may I remain humble in love for all your children. May I rely not only on what I know but also on what I know of the other and the love of Christ. Amen.

The first Sunday in February each year, I participate in the annual Polar Bear Plunge for Special Olympics Delaware. Each year I plunge my whole body into the forty-degree Atlantic Ocean while others only dip their toes and run back up the beach. Full submersion is not required, but I feel that those who do not jump in miss out on the full experience.

Today's psalm helps us understand the benefits of fully immersing ourselves in God. The psalm focuses on God's great works, which reveal God's goodness and authority. The works and workings of God reveal a God who is "gracious and merciful," "holy and awesome." We find out who God is by looking carefully at what God has done in our midst.

The psalmist expresses his enthusiastic gratitude: "I will give thanks to the LORD with my whole heart, in the company of the upright, in the congregation." How often do we gather with our faith community and just dip our toes into our worship of God? I don't mean this in a physical way—those who lift their arms or dance to praise God are not necessarily more immersed in thanksgiving than those who sit quietly. I do wonder how often we simply go through the motions of worship rather than entering fully into thanksgiving with our whole hearts. Our worship is most honest when we acknowledge God's goodness and mercy with our full selves, worshiping God with all we are and doing so together with our siblings in Christ.

Ask, What keeps me from worshiping God with my whole heart? What keeps me from fully worshiping God in the company of my siblings in Christ? Give thanks for God's authority in your life and for congregations that offer a place of Christian community to worship with your brothers and sisters in Christ.

Lord, grant me the strength to release what hinders me from a full relationship with you and my congregation. Amen.

Imagining Now

JANUARY 29—FEBRUARY 4, 2018 • JUDY SKEEN

SCRIPTURE OVERVIEW: What is the ultimate source of our strength? All the authors for this week come to the same conclusion: True strength comes from the Lord. Isaiah asks his audience: Who is like God? God never grows weary and provides unfailing strength to those who wait for God. The psalmist praises God as the one who lifts up those who are beaten down. It is not those with human strength who are truly mighty but those empowered by God. In Corinthians, Paul states that he has laid down any form of his own strength so that the gospel may advance. Jesus heals many in Mark as a demonstration of his power over the physical world. Thus, God's power is not just a metaphor but a reality.

QUESTIONS AND THOUGHTS FOR REFLECTION

- Read Isaiah 40:21-31. When has your focus on past events or ones yet to come caused an inability to perceive God's work in the present?

- Read Psalm 147:1-11, 20c. What part of your life bears witness to humanity's desire for winners and losers? How can you help others see God's desire for wholeness?

- Read 1 Corinthians 9:16-23. What behaviors are you willing to take on or give up "for the sake of the gospel"?

- Read Mark 1:29-39. What intrigues you about the pattern of concealment and revelation in Jesus' life that Mark's Gospel portrays?

Professor of religion at Belmont University, Nashville, Tennessee, with educational experiences in biblical studies, pastoral care, and spiritual formation; finds deep recognition of God's power to make whole in the company of four-legged creatures these days as well as two-legged creatures.

The people of Israel had to adjust their understanding of what God was up to when the Babylonians took them into exile. They felt abandoned by God. Now the prophet asks them to remember and reframe their experience so they can live in confidence and hope in the face of restoration and more change. When we face what stands before us, we see the problems and we feel the current pain. When our religion prepares us to deal only with the past and the future, we find ourselves limited in what we can see in the present.

Isaiah relays the good news that the end of exile is in sight, although the people cannot see it yet. The rulers of their exile have not yet spoken of their freedom to return home, to make new choices for their lives. The voice of Isaiah reminds them of experiences they have known and can build on: God is powerful and gracious. God who created still holds creation. God can free them and bring them home.

Isaiah reminds the people that God who is praised is also the creative Spirit who tends to details of creation. This Creator God is the basis of their confidence. The prophet asks the people to remember and ponder what they once knew about God's action in their lives and to reconsider how they build on their trust in God. Their life experience has changed their understanding of what it means to be the people of God.

We find ourselves looking back, standing on a certainty we built in the past. News of change is not always welcome; tools, maps, and constructs may not hold.

Creator, who imagined us all and tends us still, give us strong footing to stand with you through change and into an abundant future. Give us strong hands and hearts to dream this future with you, a place where we all can know your grace and power. Amen.

Isaiah poses many questions, questions that are spoken out into the world, pointing to that which can't be contained in a single answer. Can we link remembering to imagining into the future? The voice of Isaiah reminds the people in exile that God remains steadfast from Creation forward. God holds the corners of the curtain that encompasses everything, the creative force that makes the place for all creatures to live.

Who is the One in power? The One who reduces those who rule some segment of creation to passing seasons or even to the rubble of a single storm. We see power wielded each day in systems, institutions, relationships, a single life. We grant power to others because of title and position. We grant power to others believing if they love us, choose us, we won't have to struggle so much. We look to human systems of power to rescue us, to do for us what we don't know how to do.

"Have you not known? Have you not heard? Has it not been told you from the beginning? Have you not understood from the foundation of the earth?" The One with lasting power is the One with lasting creativity and imagination. The One who brought all to life sustains their living and holds the corners of their dwelling places. This One can give and take away power as swiftly as a winter storm. The One who created still rules over all; earth's rulers will fade like straw, blown about and blown away by the wind.

Gracious God, forgive us for thinking we are in charge. And forgive us for not doing what we can when we can. We hope in you and ask that you entrust to us the work of seeing and sharing, of being conduits of your creative power in a world full of hurt. Amen.

Do you remember working to learn the right answers so when the questions were asked you could raise your hand and speak the answer, receiving acknowledgment for being a good student? Try this one: Who is God to be compared with? What answers might the exiled Israelites have been hearing in their place of foreign captivity? The stars and the moon? The thunder and the lightning? Are the forces of the universe to be feared and served?

The voice of Isaiah sounds strong and clear: No one compares to God, the powerful Creator who dreamed up the stars and the moon. Look to the night sky and take comfort. The One who made those beautiful lights cares for the world and all that is in it. God has named the stars, tends them, sends them on their journeys, and knows they are all in their place. The stars bear the witness of humans, whom he compares to grasshoppers and sprouts that live briefly and are blown away. The stars tell the glory of the One who put them there.

When we walk through the world without seeing, with our heads down, we miss not only the incomparable and powerful but the broken and lowly. Walking with the Creator we discover a rich witness in creation as to the imagination and power within our reach.

Can we become students again, students in the classroom of creation? Might the questions posed each day by the change of seasons and the witness of faithful rhythms be good companions for our majestic and brief journeys? What is concealed in plain sight by the One who imagined and brought all into being?

Creator of night sky vistas and daytime dreams for peace, grant us the vision to see our now and our next, knowing there is none other but you and no other to whom we would entrust our future. Amen.

At work in the world is a force of wholeness. It can be unseen and misunderstood, overlooked and discounted. At the heart of the created order resides the heart of the Creator who remains unimpressed by displays of power, unmoved by haste.

Over time human culture has created a split between winners and losers. We laud the skills of strength and speed and associate the qualities of weakness and patience with those who are bound to lose.

The psalmist assures us that God views these qualities differently. Caring for the weak and those who have taken a beating in life is not contrary to being powerful. God's greatness is in the company of God's compassion, and both are strengthened by this tension. God manifests power in caring for the needy, those deemed insignificant or uncountable. God knows, names, and tends all of these. Power and compassion create a stronghold as a result of living in tension. The strength of the mighty is built upon the faithfulness of those who have known heartbreak and still stand, still seek, still hope—and still know fear.

The psalmist calls for praise born of hope and reverence. The ability to see what is right in front of us is a survival skill. When given so many pathways to distraction and patterns of becoming numb to heartbreak and tragedy, a life of praise for God is a life lived between what is and what can be. When we bring our imagination and our brokenheartedness to God, we are welcomed to a partnership of wholeness-making. We stand in the company of all those created and cared for by this praiseworthy God.

Praise to you, O God, for creating us to walk together and to care for one another. Show us yourself; quicken us to see our partnership with you in bringing wholeness to all life. Amen.

The hidden way of God is the way of becoming whole. How do we reconcile a biblical witness of God's own self being revealed with the Son of God working to keep things quiet? This tension of concealment and revelation shows up in the very first chapter of Mark's Gospel. (See Mark 1:24-26.)

In today's passage, Jesus heals Simon's mother-in-law, who immediately returns to her kitchen chores. So many people follow Jesus that he stops at sundown, not to pray but to expel demons (whom he forces to keep quiet) and to make whole the demon-possessed. He silences those who might speak something it is not yet time for. The next day, with morning prayer interrupted, Jesus proclaims the nearness of the kingdom of God and teaches about the wholeness this reign brings.

We read of a seeing and a knowing. Many gather and witness the healings. Jesus silences some because of what they know of him. His teaching and healing activity cultivates curiosity in the people watching and in the readers of the story. When we refocus to see this tension, we also can see a pattern of the life lived in private and the life lived in public view. Does one pattern offer a clue to the other?

Does the need for concealment somehow relate to what cannot be seen until eyes are opened? Might the curiosity and spectacle block the true seeing of the majesty and wonder of a God who can imagine wholeness coming in human form at the hands of a human being who didn't arrive as expected but rather came in vulnerability and in poverty?

God of light, shape in us the patience to see clearly, to allow our curiosity to become imagination, so that we may welcome the wholeness in ourselves and in others. Amen.

Have you ever walked away from a tense conversation wondering what caused you to get so worked up? Something was at stake for you that surprised you and caused a defensive reaction. You felt unprepared.

Throughout First Corinthians, Paul addresses issues that arise and create barriers to the gospel of Christ. Paul makes clear what he has chosen and what has chosen him. Because he has been chosen, he feels compelled to address what stands in the way of the message being made clear.

In today's passage, Paul points directly to the question of his financial support as an apostle and revisits the question about food sacrificed to idols. He abdicates his own life patterns; his relationship to the law has been reoriented by the law of Christ. There is in him this unrelenting defense of the law of Christ. He did not choose this, and he is not getting paid for this.

Because Paul has been claimed by the gospel of Christ, he is now an athlete building stamina to address whatever stands in the way of the message so that all may come to Christ. His defense also points us toward a way to take pleasure in our calling, the proclamation of coming wholeness. He feels the strength of being entrusted with this obligation and wants to be in on it.

"Do you not know? Have you not heard?" (Isa. 40:21). Just as the voice in Isaiah 40 calls us to remember our foundation, Paul calls us to remember why none of the window dressing matters. An important issue is at stake: becoming whole or stalling out.

Grant us the stamina of the athlete, the vision of the mystic and the soul of one who lives to please you, the praiseworthy God of creation and imagination. Amen.

Questions abound in Isaiah 40: Have you been paying attention? Who is like God? The questions continue in these verses: "Have you not known? Have you not heard?" In other words, how clearly do we see what is right in front of us?

The voice of Isaiah echoes the voice of God in the story of Job. There is the witness of nature to the care and company of God. There is the witness of nature to the vast and utter power of God. There is the call to look up, lift your head, and see what is about you. Look back and remember what you learned from the beginning. Dust it off and add to it what you have learned since then. It all adds up to a life lived in the company of all God's creation. A life of community and heartbreak—and a brief life at that.

When we consider power in this context, we might expect fear and hope to pale in the sight of it; but power is being shown by care for those whom God acts on behalf of. God's attention does not come and go. It stays where it has always been, and it brings restoring power to the young and the strong. God's restoration comes for those who respond in hope to God's beckoning and wholeness-making actions.

To wait on the Lord is to be able to see, or to wait to see, believing that which is not only unseen but unfathomable when looking at what is right in front of our eyes. The cycles of the earth, the strength of the eagles are all reasons to be hopeful, to live in expectation, to practice imagination.

Compassionate God, when life rocks us and threatens to erase our memories of your good and faithful provision, grant us enough memory to know that you are with those who mourn, those whose hearts are broken, and those who turn to you for hope and meaning. Amen.

Waiting for the Light

FEBRUARY 5–11, 2018 • MATTHEW B. GASTON

SCRIPTURE OVERVIEW: In the week leading to Transfiguration Sunday, the texts all deal with holy, transforming light; but they also speak to the awkwardness of waiting for and finally experiencing that light. Elisha's is a stop-and-go pilgrimage before he sees the chariots of fire. Our psalmist proclaims the march of the sun across the sky while also waiting for the eschatological arrival of God's justice for God's people. Paul empathizes with the believers in Corinth who are having to wait and work to "give the light of the knowledge of the glory of God." Jesus leads Peter, James, and John up a mountain where they wait and are terrified by the cloud of glory that overshadows them.

QUESTIONS AND THOUGHTS FOR REFLECTION

- Read Psalm 50:1-6. If your life was like the sun arcing across the sky from sunrise to sunset, where in the daytime arc are you right now? What justice would you like to take part in creating before your life sets in the west?
- Read 2 Corinthians 4:3-6. In what areas of your life do you feel blinded to the light God wants to shine there?
- Read 2 Kings 2:1-12. Think of a time you have felt most blessed by God. How long did you wait for that blessing? Was it worth the wait?
- Read Mark 9:2-9. Recall your last "mountaintop" experience with Christ. How would you describe it? How did that experience change you?

Lead Pastor, First United Methodist Church, Plano, Texas.

Today is my birthday and, like every day since I turned thirteen, I will put in my contact lenses in order to see clearly. I have astigmatism. The prefix, *a* means "without." *Stigma* is the Greek word for "point," so an eye that is "without point" is one that does not allow light rays to meet at a single point of focus, resulting in objects looking fuzzy. Greater clarity results with corrective lenses, of course, but clarity results too with greater light. What I find hard to read by an indoor light is easy to read in the sunlight.

Our psalmist frames the lives of God's people "from the rising of the sun to its setting." Between the sun's rising and setting, that great light brings into sharp relief the reality of our lives. Have we spent more of our resources, thoughts, and actions in the service of God and others or in serving ourselves? It is an important question because God seeks always to form us more in God's image.

God comes as judge seeking righteousness for our lives and our lives with one another in this world across which God's light shines brightly, bringing all things into sharp focus.

Today, like most days, I will prayerfully take inventory of my life with thanksgiving. I shall ask where I need God's light to shine brightly in my life so I can see more clearly what God needs me to see in others' lives—so that I can serve God and neighbor. This will be my sacrifice of praise.

O Morning Sun, help me see more clearly so I may act more nearly to your heart's desire. Amen.

As a child, I was both terrified and tantalized by *The Wizard of Oz.* The Wicked Witch of the West scared me, but I loved Glinda, the Good Witch of the North. I adored Munchkins and loathed flying monkeys. Yet the greatest juxtaposition for me came at the end of the movie when our fearful but undaunted band meets the great and powerful Oz. They are mesmerized as the great Oz blasts fire and bellows thunder—at least until the smallest of the group, Dorothy's little dog Toto, pulls back the veil on the elderly man working the machinery generating the illusion. "Pay no attention to that man behind the curtain!" roars Oz. But it is too late; the ruse is up. That which was hidden is now seen for what it truly is—a magnificently manufactured lie.

From 2 Corinthians 3:12 forward, the author uses the word *veil* in several ways: A veil hides the glory of God shining in Moses' face. The Israelites' minds are veiled from seeing the power of God behind the covenant. Those who know Christ have unveiled faces.

In today's verses, the minds of some Corinthians are blinded by "the god of this world." They are persons for whom the gospel is veiled as they stand transfixed by the powerful and much lesser gods of this world. In our context, those gods include alluring and false promises, fake news, two minutes of Twitter titillation or Facebook fame. We indulge our fantasies and have trouble finding our faith. We yearn for a gospel that is authentic, life-changing, and right. We stand in need of someone to pull back the veil so that we can see what is real and, in so doing, find our best and true selves.

Lord, take the veil from my mind's eyes so that I may see you and find myself. Amen.

A pop song came out in 1982 called "Heartlight." The love song was part of the soundtrack of the child-friendly sci-fi movie *E.T. the Extra-Terrestrial*. E.T. is a frail and skittish alien. His heart glows red when he makes a friendly connection with another being, as is the case with a young boy who rescues him and saves him until he can reunite with his own extraterrestrial family. The movie is about love, loyalty, and the willingness to trust what you cannot fully understand.

Paul earnestly desires his Corinthian sisters and brothers to see "the light of the gospel of the glory of Christ, who is the image of God." But to "see" or experience that good news, that gospel, the Corinthians will have to trust the source of Paul's heartlight: the self-giving love of Christ. Paul freely offers this gospel as a slave of Jesus. He knows it is as possible and essential for them to know Christ truly just as it was possible and essential for himself to know Christ when that glory on the road to Damascus blinded him.

All people can realize this possibility because humanity, like Jesus, bears God's image. (See Genesis 1:26.) We are created to "give the light of the knowledge of the glory of God." The Creator designed us to let our heartlight shine for God and for others. We find ourselves willing to love and trust that which we may not fully understand, but we love and trust anyway. Only then does the veil lift to give us a glimpse of glory.

O God of glory, release me from my blindness that I may see you as I seek the welfare of others. Amen.

W ait for it . . . " is a popularly used phrase. It bids our patience to wait for the sake of something more, something better. I have never been good at waiting; I always want to accomplish more in a day than there are hours to do it. I look for the fastest lane, the shortest line, and the earliest start—all in the name of productivity. I would not have done very well as either Elisha or one of the band of prophets who follow Elijah around. Three times Elijah tells Elisha to stay put; two times Elisha tells the band of prophets to stay quiet; and one time Elijah and Elisha are "standing by" the River Jordan. It reminds me of going to worship as a child with my parents and being told to hush and stop wiggling. What is going on here?

In the narrative, silent waiting builds the tension within the story as all parties anticipate Elijah's glorious departure. At a deeper level though, the author/editor may have had the words of the contemporary writer of Lamentations in mind, "The LORD is good to those who wait for him, to the soul that seeks him" (3:25). In Elisha we certainly have a wait-er *and* a seeker on par with Ruth. (See Ruth 1:16-17.) Nothing will deter Elisha from receiving the blessing he seeks from Elijah, even if it means waiting. After all, Elijah himself fervently sought God and failed until he ceased all his striving finally to hear the "still small voice" of God (1 Kings 19:12).

I so want to rush ahead to see the light just over the horizon. But I keep rediscovering that God and I are better served by my choosing to stay both still and quiet and allowing God's holy light to come to me.

O patient God, grant me the patience to wait and listen so that I may hear you speak before I go and do. Amen.

Waiting for the Light

The term *outlier* has come into contemporary use detached from its meaning in Malcolm Gladwell's book, *Outliers: The Story of Success,* which put the word into our parlance. Many equate *outlier* with *anomaly,* but for Gladwell the term is more robust. It refers to extraordinary proficiency attained by ordinary people who have the persistence to put in ten thousand repetitions of their chosen craft. Gladwell's work reinforces the old adage that persistence pays off.

In a culture that increasingly demands instant response and gratification, we can easily forget that the spiritual journey has always been one of dogged persistence. Noah, Abraham, Moses, Ruth—all march across our memories with God-graced determination. Elisha follows a great tradition as he purposefully follows Elijah, convinced that if he remains resolute, he will come to know the blessing of this outlier prophet and the glory of their outlier god. He is not disappointed. Both Elisha and Elijah are rewarded with what they patiently seek. Elijah gloriously meets God, and Elisha receives the mantle of Elijah's prophetic authority. Significantly, both men experience the pure beauty of excellence as they continue together "walking and talking." Persistence pays off.

God is with us for the long haul of our lives. It comes as no surprise that the trek requires determined, watchful waiting on our part along the way. Thanks be to God.

O God of fire and whirlwind, grant us a stalwart spirituality that knows you are the light at the end of our sometimes long tunnels. Amen.

Why is this happening?" is the common question we raise in times of crisis. We desperately want to understand even when we know there are no easy or understandable answers. We rush to do. We send flowers; we cook a meal; we talk too much—anything in our attempts to cope with the anxiety around the great unknown we face.

If Jesus' transfiguration is not enough to shock the three disciples, the sudden appearance in the blinding light of the Hebrew titans Elijah and Moses is enough to completely undo them. Peter freezes and babbles on about a building program. We, like Peter, often find ourselves "terrified" when faced with the Christ standing before us, summoning us to the mission field. And many churches, like Peter, often employ "building projects" as a response. We find ourselves upended from all we knew and with which we were very comfortable.

However, the positive outcome of being upended—even rudely—is that we can end up in a new and life-giving place. A counselor friend reminds me from his practice that instead of focusing on the "why" questions in a crisis, he helps his clients to focus on the "what" questions: What can I learn from this? What can I do differently going forward because of this experience? "What" questions give energy; "why" questions only steal it away.

Peter, James, and John are stuck in the "why" question as they are in most of Mark's Gospel; the disciples are always slow to catch on. In their defense, upending encounters with the Holy will do that.

Recall a time when a shocking sense of God's presence confronted you. What questions arose? What did you do with the answers?

TRANSFIGURATION SUNDAY

Y ou are never the same again." I have heard that statement from parishioners who have encountered utter holiness— the glory of God. Often it comes at the endpoints of life: seeing a first child born or holding her for the first time or being present for a parent's last breath and holding him for the last time. People experience a level of almost frightful awe and wonder over God's nearness in the moment and what it means going forward.

Peter stands speechless in light of the transfigured Jesus speaking with Elijah and Moses. If that light is not terrifying enough, the cloud of Mosaic encounters overshadows them and the voice of God echoes and elevates the declaration made at Jesus' baptism, "This is my Son, the Beloved, listen to him!" No doubt they will. After the theophany, the three disciples can never be the same again.

But what will the change look like? How will they be different? Mark does not tell us; the drama rushes on to the next scene. What we do know is that the disciples receive space to think about it. Jesus orders them to keep their experience confidential until after the Resurrection sometime down the road. For now, each one of them will have to ponder for himself, *What does this mean for me and my life? What can I learn and take with me, even though I will be forever altered?*

If Jesus is transfigured—transformed more clearly into the image of God—then so will we be. This is the Creator's promise confirmed in our baptism. We are yoked to the transfigured Christ who seeks to transform us, one grace-filled encounter at a time. We stand on the cusp of a Lenten season, acknowledging that we too can be gloriously changed forever.

Lord, overshadow us with your presence and your call to listen, ponder, and live a life transfigured for you. Amen.

Lenten Metanoia

FEBRUARY 12–18, 2018 • TOMMIE WATKINS JR.

SCRIPTURE OVERVIEW: The season of Lent is now upon us, a time of inward examination that begins on Ash Wednesday. We search ourselves and ask God to search us, so that we can follow God more completely. This examination, however, can become a cause for despair if we do not approach it with God's everlasting mercy and faithfulness in mind. Although the Flood was a result of judgment, God also saved the faithful and established a covenant with them. The psalmist seeks to learn God's ways, all the while realizing that he has fallen short and must rely on God's grace. For Christians, baptism functions as a symbol of salvation and a reminder of God's covenant faithfulness—not because the water is holy but because God is holy and merciful.

QUESTIONS AND THOUGHTS FOR REFLECTION

- Read Genesis 9:8-17. When in loss have you experienced a new beginning?

- Read Psalm 25:1-10. How do you remind yourself of your covenant with God?

- Read 1 Peter 3:18-22. When have you given up privilege in order to work for justice?

- Read Mark 1:9-15. When did you last hear God speak these words to you: "You are my . . . beloved; with you I am well pleased"?

Associate Rector and Assistant Chaplain at Canterbury Episcopal Chapel and Student Center in Tuscaloosa, Alabama; graduate faculty member of the University of Alabama School of Social Work.

Who of us likes to start over? Noah, his sons, daughters-in-law, and the creatures of the earth start over with God on behalf of all creation. Imagine the angst and fear that might have surrounded them as they began a new life in a totally different manner. I often wonder whether they were angry at God or resentful after all they had been through. Nevertheless, God calls Noah and his family to trust that God will never again destroy the earth by water.

Some of us have experienced loss like Noah, losing almost every material possession. God asks us to trust in God's goodness. We may find it nearly impossible to trust that God will see us through, but through such loss and through beginning again we may experience a metanoia (a change of heart) or a new birth in our relationship with God.

Beginning again makes us vulnerable to God as we trust one more time that God will act in our favor. God establishes a covenant with Noah that extends to all of humanity and creation: God will never again destroy the earth by water. God's covenant includes a reminder both for God and for us of the promise that God has humanity and creation's best interest at heart. Throughout Lent, when we look toward the new beginning that comes on Easter morning, we remember all of God's promises. Even in the vulnerability of loss and new beginnings, we can know that God will remember the covenant God established for us with Noah—a promise to protect us and be with us through new beginnings.

Eternal God, remember your covenant when we are in the vulnerability of new beginnings, and help us remember to trust that you forever have our best interests at heart. Amen.

In today's reading, the psalmist sings a petition for guidance and a change of heart to follow God's paths and to learn God's truth. As the psalmist cries out for forgiveness, understanding, instruction, and humility, we hear an invocation of God's power to liberate the psalmist—and us—from shame and fear.

The psalmist begins the petition by lifting up his or her soul to God, trusting in God as an exercise in humility and vulnerability. The petition then oscillates between admitting faults and reminding God of God's promises of love and goodness. Only when God is mindful of God's mercy, justice, steadfast love, and faithfulness does the bold relationship of our vulnerability before God and petitions for change result in a true metanoia. The final verse of today's passage highlights our responsibilities in keeping divine covenants and decrees, but as we learned in Genesis, God makes promises to us in covenants as well. Part of the praxis of a vibrant relationship with God includes reminding God—as well as ourselves—of the covenants we have made together.

During Lent, we focus on our end of the covenantal bargain—to seek to follow God, to fast from something that blocks our relationship with God. When we acknowledge the behaviors or vices in our lives that separate us from God, we are better able to lift up our souls for change toward following God's paths. God's end of the bargain grants hope in the promise that God's way will ultimately prevail. When we seek to release our sins and shame and humbly follow, God promises that our paths will be those of steadfast love and faithfulness.

Loving God, give us grace to lift our souls to you as we seek the emancipation of your all-encompassing love. Amen.

ASH WEDNESDAY

Lent begins today, as does the forty-day period of fasting. We fast as a spiritual practice with the intention of coming closer to God. We exchange our normal habits for diligent abstinence from any agent that hinders our reliance on God.

For some of us, as the text admonishes, this fast becomes not a way to be closer to God but rather a self-serving way to compete with one another. God recognizes when our fasts serve only our own interests, and God will not be fooled.

Today's reading presents a new type of fasting: one that God initiates and appears to practice in perpetuity. God's fast derives from God's ubiquitous love for all humankind and is exemplified by the Christian values of equality and equity. God makes clear that fasting from material things is not enough. Rather we might fast from our innate internal manifestations of "isms" that block God from our lives and prevent or pervert our carrying out justice.

God's fast, which is particularly interested in loosing, undoing, breaking, sharing, housing, covering, exposing, enlightening, healing, vindicating, and glorifying, yields fruit. What would happen if we adopted God's type of fasting; if we ceased practicing racism, classism, sexism, and exclusionism? What if we, as this passage notes, refrained from pointing fingers or blaming or pursuing our self-centered wills and instead pursued God's will? Perhaps that is the metanoia God invites us into during Lent. This season we can turn our will and eyes from judgment of one another toward love and tolerance for all people in pursuit of deep spiritual change in our lives.

Lord, help me change my heart as I turn from judging others to loving and serving all your children. Amen.

Who likes to suffer? We are rarely willing to suffer for our wrongdoing and even less willing to suffer for doing what is right and just. Set in the context of the full letter, today's passage presents the idea that when we suffer for our conduct in actions of justice, we, like Christ, receive assurance of God's blessing and favor.

Today's reading recalls Noah's survival by his righteousness while weaving together Christ's suffering, Noah's experiences, and baptism. This association results in a link between God's covenant with Noah to have humanity's best interest at heart and the baptismal covenant, which the passage describes as "an appeal to God for a good conscience"—that is, to act righteously—in light of Christ's resurrection.

In our baptism, we vow to respect the dignity and worth of every human being, which charges us to give up complacency and to work for equality and equity for all human beings. In this way, we may suffer along with those for whose rights we fight. This suffering gives us powerful levels of empathy and compassion—spiritual tools that help us undo injustice in our world. Today's reading reaffirms and strengthens God's covenant through Noah: God not only has our best interest in mind; we are baptized into a good conscience that brings us closer to God and may lead us to suffer for righteousness.

The season of Lent and our baptism into new life with and for God compel us to give up our privilege and to become discontented, to see others differently than much of the world sees them, and to work toward justice for the marginalized. Our empathy and compassion empower human rights and social justice movements all over the world, past and present.

Compassionate God, may we be willing to suffer with others for righteousness. Amen.

After Jesus' baptism, the same Spirit who descended like a dove as God proclaims Jesus beloved immediately drives him to the wilderness to be tempted and tested. This is perhaps the only time in the Gospel of Mark that we readily identify with Jesus' experience, which makes us wonder, *Are desert seasons a certainty for all of us so as to draw closer to God?*

Jesus' experience models a way of following God: giving up our self-sufficient ideas so we can perceive God and God's will in new ways. When we willingly release our own power over our lives, we find that God has a way forward for us—just as God promised in the covenant with Noah and the covenant of our baptisms.

As we remember our baptism and other covenants during Lent and begin to look toward Jesus' ultimate sacrifice, we are especially vulnerable to God's power. This first Friday, like all the Fridays to come until Easter, we remember Jesus' willingness to let go of his self-determined will to submit to God's will. The barrenness and void of Jesus' sojourn in the desert and of the desert times in our lives make us humble and compel us to be "all in" for God. As we see Jesus go through this time at the beginning of his ministry, we learn that desert times propel us to new life—the newness in Christ espoused in our baptism. Few of us experience the vulnerability of living in a physical desert, but our desert times require the same humility and willingness to initiate the kingdom of heaven on earth. During Lent we can embody the full reliance on God required in a desert season as we seek to hear and see God anew.

Ever-present God, give us a willingness to go through desert times to be converted to new life in Christ. Amen.

Jesus leaves his hometown of Nazareth in Galilee and journeys through Samaria down into the region where John is baptizing followers. Jesus, an outsider, presents himself to be baptized by John—a process and procedure Jesus no doubt neither needed nor was required to complete. Nevertheless, Jesus experiences baptism like you and I do, and with a similar result—a new life devoted to following God. In Mark's Gospel, Jesus' active ministry begins only after he is baptized.

Jesus' decision to be baptized seemingly signals a new direction in his life. The heavens are torn apart as God confirms that true power exists in a posture of vulnerable humility and a life devoted to following God. Mark invites us, unlike the characters in his Gospel, to hear the words that affirm Jesus' decision: "You are my Son, the beloved; with you I am well pleased." God confirms that to follow we do not use power to manipulate; but by defying expectations, we are transformed into new life.

In baptism, God removes our sin and makes us one with God. Jesus models baptism for us, and every act of baptism lives into Jesus' story—God claims each of us as God's beloved child.

This is indeed good news. God empowers us to do God's will not because we are powerful but because we are followers. Willingness to be transformed by God makes us not susceptible but secure. Truly this is the new kingdom into which we are integrated through Jesus Christ in our own baptism.

Eternal God, make us vulnerable and willing to begin again so that we may love and forgive ourselves and others as you make each of us new though Christ. Amen.

FIRST SUNDAY IN LENT

In today's poetic discourse, David cries out to almighty God for help and assistance. David, who was powerful, invincible, secure, and successful according to human standards, yields all of his societally established power to open himself up to God. Perhaps the most powerful thing we can do as human beings is to ask for help.

Asking for assistance and sharing our personal lives and stories requires a level of humility many of us find difficult. But abiding in the present kingdom of heaven grants an awesome reversal: We know that we need one another as we live our daily lives, yet we need not become dependent on one another. David shows us that honestly confessing our powerlessness and weakness opens us to God. David admits his sinfulness and finds assurance in God's love that frees him—and each of us—from internalized shame. This passage reminds us of God's promises to lead us toward steadfast love and faithfulness, which set us free from the negative thinking of internalized shame.

Perhaps this is the metanoia that we can practice this Lenten season. When we strive for exposure and openness before God, the Holy Spirit empowers us to overcome our own wills and practice living and doing God's will. God delivers us not only from our past sins but also from self-defeating thinking that continues to haunt us. When we ask for help, God will teach us and lead us God's way. We can trust that God loves, leads, and encourages us as we strive to humbly serve the kingdom of heaven on earth.

Empowering God, shame and sin bind us. Remind us of your steadfast love and faithfulness as we seek to follow you. Amen.

Uncomfortable with Grace

FEBRUARY 19–25, 2018 • MARY LOU REDDING

SCRIPTURE OVERVIEW: We cannot earn God's love. Going back to the time of Abraham, God's blessing has been based on faith. God chose Abraham for a covenant not because Abraham was perfect but because he believed God. The psalmist reminds his audience of their ancient relationship with God and expresses the hope that it will continue through future generations. Paul reinforces the centrality of faith in Romans. Following the law was not bad, but no one should believe that following the law could earn God's favor. In Mark 8, Jesus pushes his disciples in their understanding of faith. Trusting God means surrendering everything, including position and reputation. If we value those things more than God, then we are not displaying the faith of Abraham.

QUESTIONS AND THOUGHTS FOR REFLECTION

- Read Genesis 17:1-7, 15-16. No rules, just relationship. How comfortable are you in your relationship with God? Upon what does it rest?

- Read Psalm 22. Which verses are most familiar to you? In what ways does your faith journey live in the interplay of shadow and light?

- Read Romans 4:13-25. How easily do you live in God's grace? In what areas do you find yourself "reckoning" your righteousness?

- Read Mark 8:31-38. When the world asks you who you are, what is your reply?

Former editorial director, *The Upper Room* magazine; author of numerous books.

As a spoiled and somewhat pampered American, I have struggled with the whole idea of Lent. With its call to fasting and self-denial, Lent runs counter to my culture and the media messages that surround me. And I am probably not an outlier in this. Italian journalist Beppe Severgnini observed in his book *Ciao, America! An Italian Discovers the U.S.* that people in the United States are obsessed with comfort, control, and competition. But Lent calls us to surrender control of our impulses to the Spirit and to deny ourselves—to choose to make ourselves uncomfortable.

Lent makes me uncomfortable. I experience this liturgical season as a theological riddle that puzzles me every year. Lent leads us into the most amazing expression of grace we have, to what God has done for us in Christ. We talk about grace as God's unmerited favor; but simultaneously, Lent asks us to *do something* to show our commitment to God. When I consider performance, inevitably I fall into the trap of measurement: Is my Lenten discipline substantial enough? Am I doing it better this year than last? And so on—all the opposite of grace.

This week's scripture passages focus on the tension between grace and performance. They show us the absolute one-sidedness of God's covenant with humanity, alongside the New Testament call to give up everything to follow Christ. I have long believed that the Spirit works in us at the point of our discomfort with people, situations, and ideas. If we turn toward the things that bother us, our unease can become a window to places we need God's grace. Then we choose whether to allow that grace to shape and reshape us. Lent offers us this choice.

What is making me uncomfortable today? What may God be saying to me through my unease?

Uncomfortable with Grace

God's covenant with Abraham was a sovereign act. Over and over in Abraham's story, God takes the initiative, speaking to Abraham apart from any apparent intent by Abraham to seek God. In today's passage, God gives Abram and Sarai new names and opens the door into a different future. God promises to bless Abraham and Sarah and their descendants (and through them "all the families of the earth," Gen. 12:3) before the law, before the Ten Commandments, before the Torah, before any formal Hebrew religion. The covenant God makes with Abraham on behalf of all humanity does not rest on rules. The covenant focuses entirely on relationship.

But we humans like rules, even about relationships; we like to measure ourselves and others. We like to know where we stand, to be able (metaphorically, usually) to check off the boxes for good behavior. But relationship with God is not about measuring and counting; it is about grace. Just grace. You've probably heard the saying, "There's nothing you could ever do that would make God love you more, and there's nothing you could ever do that would make God love you less." That idea makes many of us profoundly uncomfortable.

God invites us into an open-ended relationship that will change the rest of life. Not knowing where a relationship will take us can be unsettling. For some of us, the desire for control, security, and predictability is so strong that any open-ended commitment is frightening, perhaps nearly unbearable (there's a reason I'm not married!). Yet the Lord of the universe invites us: Will you walk with me, relinquishing the need to know where the road leads?

Holy God, the invitation to know you and walk with you is amazing. Help me to risk doing it or to let you help me become willing to risk it. Amen.

Uncomfortable with Grace   71

Peter demonstrates the nearly universal human aversion to pain and struggle—and seemingly even discussion of them. Jesus tells the disciples "quite openly" that he must suffer and die. Peter doesn't want to hear it; he doesn't want his friend to go through these harsh experiences. Who would desire that for anyone they love? But Jesus challenges Peter's statement.

Jesus calls Peter "Satan"—a blistering charge to level at a friend. Then he says that Peter is thinking about the wrong things. Jesus points out that part of our discipleship involves attending to our thoughts. Scripture often mentions this idea, from Psalms and Proverbs to the New Testament. For example, Colossians urges believers to "set [their] minds on things that are above, not on things that are on earth" (3:1), and Paul admonishes the Corinthians to identify every thought that exalts itself against the knowledge of Christ and to take thoughts "captive to obey Christ" (2 Cor. 10:5).

Paying attention to our thoughts takes us deeper than actions, to attitudes and motives. I can easily identify recent thoughts that I know are contrary to what Christ wants for us. Can you? Daydreaming about a bigger house, a fancy car, a more powerful job, great acclaim—all can lure us away from the downward way of servanthood. And we can fall into patterns of looking at people around us negatively and judgmentally rather than honoring each of them as a dearly loved child of God for whom Christ died.

The call to monitor our thoughts is a call to discomfort and to self-control. What might Christ say about where you have centered your thoughts today?

O God, help me center my thoughts on what will honor Christ and enable me to live a life of love and grace, mirroring the grace you show us all. Amen.

I cannot read Psalm 22 without thinking of my friend Andie, whom I met when she was about seven years old. Andie grew up living her faith enthusiastically. She was funny, energetic, and mischievous—a joy to know. Just as Andie finished college, she developed cancer. After treatment she seemed well. But when the cancer returned a few years later, it became obvious that Andie would not win the battle. She died at age twenty-five. In her final months, Andie planned her memorial service. She insisted that Psalm 22 be read in its entirety, and it was.

The psalm moves from a familiar, opening cry of abandonment and despair to a closing hymn of sustained praise and faith in verses 23-31—a monumental journey. Verses 1-22 alternate between anguish and expressions of faith in God's presence and steadfast care. This movement seems a normal part of the spiritual life. Times of hope, expectation, joy, and praise give way to disappointment, doubt, and sometimes the sense of solitary suffering reflected in the psalm's opening. Even Mother Teresa experienced this sense of spiritual bereftness. After her death, the world learned from her journals of a years-long struggle with serious doubt, sometimes doubt about whether God even existed. But she never let doubt keep her from living a life of love and service.

Today's verses affirm that ultimately faith wins. They encourage us to declare to others God's saving deeds. That's what Andie did. Beyond her pain and grief, through this psalm she reminded us that in the extremes of her life, she had found God to be enough. I don't know the person who wrote this psalm, but I did know Andie—and I am grateful for her witness.

Loving God, for your help in the past and your grace promised for today, the future, and life beyond this life, we give you thanks. Amen.

Uncomfortable with Grace　　　　　　　73

God called Abram into a relationship that took Abram from his home and kindred. Abram left Ur not knowing where following God would take him. The call in today's passage is even more sweeping: Jesus calls his followers not only to journey with him but to give up their lives for him and for the sake of the gospel.

Paradoxically, those who do so will not lose their life but find it. This is not a call to mere discomfort or upheaval but to a completely new way of being in the world. Abraham receives a new name; we receive a new purpose and a new identity. Carl Jung said, "The world will ask you who you are, and if you don't know, the world will tell you." When we cast our lot with Christ, we begin discovering who God wants us to be. Each of us finds our true name, our essential identity, in God. (See Ephesians 3:15.) And this life is a fuller life than any we could design for ourselves.

Each day we trade that day of our life for something. When we try to follow Jesus' example by bringing love and healing, we have a clear answer when situations and decisions ask us who we are. If we walk into a day intending to listen consciously to Christ and to do what Christ asks, we increase the chances that the trades we make will have lasting value. That's what Lenten disciplines are—expressions of our intention to walk deliberately with Christ.

Looking back over the last few days of your life, what have you traded it for? When we allow Christ to direct our choices and shape our attitudes, we trade our lives for what truly matters.

Holy God, show me who you want me to be. By your grace help me to live into your dream for me, one day at a time. Amen.

There's no such thing as a free lunch. That mind-set permeates our culture. For example, here in the South, we are taught never to return a dish empty after someone gives us food. So in order to keep my neighbors from reciprocating every time I share a treat, I have resorted to delivering my cookies (or whatever) on a paper plate or in a plastic storage bag. Otherwise they give me something back, when I gave them the food to begin with because I've made too much. I don't need more. The recipients of my treats have trouble accepting other small acts of kindness as well. Recently one neighbor needed a ride home after she dropped off her car to be serviced; the next day she left half of an apricot-nectar cake on my steps. Last week I gave another neighbor a lift to exercise class; she met me with a biscotti and a chocolate. We seem to need to balance the scales.

Perhaps in a much larger and more serious way, this is the source of my discomfort with Lent. We're told that we don't have to earn God's favor, yet we take up Lenten disciplines that involve either denying ourselves (a negative act) or doing some act of charity or service (a positive act). Either way, I am *doing* something, not resting in God's grace. I measure my performance and feel better about myself when I remember my resolve and worse about myself when I don't. The point of Lenten exercises is to focus more fully on Christ—and I end up focusing on me. Obviously I fail Lent. There I go again—grading myself!

Paul reminds us that the initiative and power in our salvation are God's. Before the law, God reached out to us. Apart from any rules or performance measures, grace guarantees that God accepts us.

Holy God, encourage us to give up our spiritual scales. May we allow ourselves to rest in your grace and to focus on relationship, not rules. Amen.

Uncomfortable with Grace   75

SECOND SUNDAY IN LENT

When I read that Abraham "did not weaken in faith when he considered his own body," I wonder how he managed that. I'm not even close to one hundred, and my literal and metaphorical weakness is daunting. But "did not weaken in faith" cannot mean easy and automatic acceptance of what God said, since as a story from Genesis tells us, both Abraham and Sarah laughed at the possibility of becoming parents.

So Abraham's faith encompassed more than never questioning. Scripture depicts him as a man who obeys God. He laughs, but eventually he does what God asks. That kind of faith means I can wrestle and question on my way to obeying. That kind of faith I can do. You've probably heard courage described as acting in spite of being afraid; perhaps faith is acting in spite of questions and even resistance. Perhaps it's coming to what philosopher Paul Ricoeur called "second naivete," where we acknowledge that something is impossible and yet choose to believe anyway because God says it.

Abraham's faith—not his action—was "reckoned" to him, credited to his account, as righteousness. Since I usually have trouble keeping a Lenten discipline for six weeks, this is good news for me. The righteousness of having faith is credited not only to him but to all of us who believe in the one who raised Jesus from the dead. The passage doesn't list what we have to believe, only that we believe in God—relationship, not a theological checklist. So whether we feel sure of everything about our faith or still wrestle with questions and doubts, we have the promise that grace depends on God, not on us.

O God, thank you for the unfailing grace that guarantees your promise to see us as righteous. Amen.

God's Pedagogy for the Faithful

FEBRUARY 26–MARCH 4, 2018 • RICHARD OLIPHANT RANDOLPH

SCRIPTURE OVERVIEW: As we continue in the season of Lent, we remember another important chapter in salvation history. Just as God established covenants with Noah and Abraham and their descendants, so did God renew the relationship with the Israelites by giving them the law. Obedience to the law was not the means of earning God's love, but a response of love by the people to the love God had already shown them. The psalmist understands that God's law creates a cause for rejoicing, for it is more valuable than gold. Both Paul and John address situations in which some had distorted the worship of God. Either they considered themselves too good for the gospel (1 Corinthians), or they had violated the covenant by altering proper worship for the sake of profit (John).

QUESTIONS AND THOUGHTS FOR REFLECTION

- Read Exodus 20:1-17. How do you keep God central in your life? When do you relegate God to the margins?

- Read Psalm 19. What do the heavens tell you? How often do you spend time in nature? In what ways does that activity renew your spirit?

- Read 1 Corinthians 1:18-25. In what ways is the cross a stumbling block to you?

- Read John 2:13-22. What signs do you ask of God? In what ways might they be life-giving, a renewal of relationship with the Creator?

Senior pastor, Christ United Methodist Church, Lincoln, Nebraska.

Many Christians are ambivalent about the law—and perhaps with good reason. The apostle Paul depicts the law as a force that holds us captive. Paul claims that Christ replaces the law with a new covenant, which we access through faith: "Now we are discharged from the law, dead to that which held us captive, so that we are slaves not under the old written code but in the new life of the Spirit" (Rom. 7:6).

In contrast to Paul's understanding, the psalmist views the law as life-giving and a source of true joy. For him, the law is not some dusty list of obligations that humanity cannot possibly fulfill. Instead, the law provides structure for relationship with the Divine.

The psalmist recognizes that humans cannot keep the law perfectly. Indeed, we commit some errors to which we are blind, despite our best intentions. Yet, rather than seeing the law as an inflexible source of condemnation, he suggests that the law can be our teacher. Through the law, we learn about our shortcomings and seek reconciliation with God. Thus, the law teaches us and facilitates our relationship with God.

Pedagogy, as I am using the term, refers to the philosophy, principles, and methods of teaching students. This week, we will examine God's methods of teaching the faithful. The psalmist suggests one way of viewing the law. Although Christians obtain forgiveness and reconciliation through faith alone, the psalmist helps us see that the law can serve as our teacher, helping us learn about God and God's intentions for our living.

Thank you, O God, for the law. Open our minds to what it teaches us about you. Amen.

Many organizations develop "codes of ethical conduct." I find such ethical codes fascinating. They reveal a great deal about the identity, outlook, commitments, and values of the organization.

We may consider the Ten Commandments as a code of ethical conduct for the faithful. Our scripture covers the first four of the Ten Commandments, which describe humanity's relationship with the Divine. We usually think of these commandments as rules that God expects us to obey. Instead of focusing on our obligations under the rules, let's ask a different question: What do these four commandments reveal about the nature of God? Let us look at these commandments as God's self-disclosure.

God's self-disclosure begins with the proclamation that Yahweh is a God of liberation, freeing the people from Egyptian slavery. The first two commandments establish an exclusive relationship between Yahweh and the faithful. God expects them to place God at the center of their lives. No idol will come before God: no personal ambition, no private wealth, no pride in accomplishments—nothing takes the central place of God.

Similarly, the third commandment against misusing God's name refers to treating God as a means rather than an end. When we invoke God's name as a means for advancing our personal agenda, then we move God to the margins of our lives and place ourselves at the center. We become the center of our world, and we use God to serve us. This is self-idolatry.

The fourth commandment to keep the sabbath requires a vulnerability in which we suspend our work. We rest and trust in God's ultimate provision. God envisions this relationship as one in which we trust God's providence completely.

Spend a few minutes reflecting on what idols you are tempted to put in God's place. Pray for strength against these temptations.

God's Pedagogy for the Faithful   79

Rather than focusing on these commandments as obligations, we are exploring what they teach us about the nature of God. We acknowledge a God who loves us and desires a covenantal relationship with us. This relationship requires us to trust God and to keep God at the center of our lives. The commandments establish this covenantal relationship and God's expectations.

Today, we reflect on the remaining six commandments, which concern relationships with other people. Again, we will ponder what these commandments teach us about God and how God intends us to live. We immediately observe the interrelatedness of the two sets of commandments. The commandments that help us consider relationship with neighbor grow out of the four that focus on our relationship with God.

Just as God desires a loving, caring relationship with us, so God expects that we will enter into a loving, caring relationship with our neighbors. The individual commandments develop the contours of this covenant. The broad, generic fashion in which these commandments are stated suggests that we as individuals assume responsibility for developing the implications within our particular context.

Consider the last commandment against coveting. On the surface, it seems directed against a general covetousness of others' possessions. Reflecting more deeply from our present context, we may determine that a relentless consumerism stokes covetousness in our society. Left unchecked, this covetousness tempts us to see others as means to more stuff, rather than as ends in themselves. Further, covetousness encourages us to place stuff at the center of our lives, pushing God to the margins.

Choose a commandment and reflect on its implications for contemporary life and covenant relationships. Pray for the strength to uphold the commandment.

Our Gospel reading tells the story of Jesus cleansing the Temple during the Passover celebration. Although the merchants and money changers undoubtedly abused the system, they contributed in a useful way, especially during the three pilgrimage festivals of Passover, Shavuot, and Sukkot. Jews scattered all over the Mediterranean region returned to the Temple for worship. Those traveling long distances found it impractical to bring animals for the required sacrifices. Instead, they bought animals when they arrived at the Temple. Additionally, there were restrictions on the money used to pay the Temple tax. No foreign coins could be used because they had human images on them. So money changers helped the pilgrims procure an acceptable coinage for the tax.

When Jesus drives out the merchants and money changers, he disrupts a system designed to facilitate the spiritual life of Jewish pilgrims who traveled great distances to keep the law. Why would Jesus disrupt this religious system?

Jesus' actions challenge a rigid religious system. The law has ceased to be the life-giving source of joy and learning. Instead, the system has become a fossil that supports the religious institution—no longer open to fresh, new revelation.

We can draw significant parallels between the Temple authorities and the contemporary church. We live in a time when church participation has declined. Surveys of the unchurched suggest that many do not experience Christian worship as life-giving and joyful. Our faithfulness to God demands that we reexamine our practices and remain open to change. Then we will experience the fresh movement of the Spirit.

Empower us, O God, to release fossilized religious practices and to open ourselves to your fresh revelation. Amen.

How does God teach us about God's love for us and plan for our salvation? Paul argues that Christ's crucifixion is "a stumbling block to Jews and foolishness to Gentiles." Twenty-first-century people frequently wear the cross as a piece of jewelry, and we can easily forget how scandalous Christ's crucifixion was for the first century. The Roman government practiced crucifixion as a form of deterrence of crime and rebellion. It intentionally tortured and humiliated the accused. Thus, the cross symbolized rejection, shame, and weakness.

Conventional wisdom of any age would find human redemption through crucifixion incomprehensible. Yet, for Christians, Jesus' crucifixion is transformative and salvific. When Jesus prepares his disciples for his crucifixion, he says, "No one has greater love than this, to lay down one's life for one's friends" (John 15:13). Of course, this is exactly what Jesus does in the crucifixion. Jesus lays down his life for us by being raised up on the cross. By accepting torture, humiliation, shame, and the ultimate death of the crucifixion, Jesus demonstrated the awesome and incomprehensible nature of God's love for us. In God's profound wisdom, we see the depth of God's love for us through the crucifixion.

Paul links this wisdom with God's power. By submitting to crucifixion, Jesus voluntarily relinquished divine power and prerogative in order to fully experience the human suffering of crucifixion. Jesus willingly became weak so that humans could know God's deep love and experience God's redemptive power. This power of God's love can only be accessed through Christ's self-emptying. Thus, Paul concludes, "God's weakness is stronger than human strength."

Most loving God, we give you thanks for the knowledge and power of your awesome love. Amen.

The first six verses of the psalm celebrate a different form of God's pedagogy. For the psalmist, the heavens proclaim God's glory and handiwork. Perhaps gazing up into the heavens on a starry night, the psalmist sees the awesome glory of all creation. To translate his thoughts into the conceptual framework of contemporary scientific cosmology, our Earth, our sun, other planets and stars, galaxies, nebulae, black holes, and novae all praise God and tell of God's handiwork.

How have you experienced God's presence in nature? Walking in a forest of tall trees, I have been overcome by their majesty and felt God's presence. Watching the unmitigated joy of my dog, Mr. Snuggles, as he bounds around the backyard, I am overcome by his exuberance for life and I feel God's presence. Feeling my finger in the firm grasp of a newborn infant, I sense the sacredness of life and know that God is with me.

In its praise and proclamation, all of creation—from the tiniest raindrops to the immense galaxies—teaches us about God the Creator. Through creation, we witness God's rich creativity and ingenuity. Creation is constant in its praise and proclamation: from day to day and night to night. This communication does not take the form of human speech, however. Creation communicates on its own terms. Left implied is the psalmist's understanding that we humans must open ourselves to creation's unique forms of instruction about God. We learn from God through creation only if we experience God's presence in nature.

Take a leisurely walk today, or sit by a window and look outdoors; open your heart and mind to God's presence and what God seeks to teach you through the natural world.

THIRD SUNDAY IN LENT

Throughout this week, we have reflected on God's pedagogy for the faithful. Today, we will focus briefly on those who "don't get it." In his cleansing of the Temple, Jesus seeks to overturn religious rituals that are no longer instructive or life-giving. Unfortunately, some Jewish leaders "don't get" what Jesus is doing. They remain encased in a narrow vision of relationship with God. By contrast, Jesus brings fresh vision for a new, extravagantly rich relationship with the Divine.

The Jewish leaders ask for a "sign." They do not seek a revelatory sign; they seek a sign that establishes Jesus' authorization to drive out the merchants and money changers. Jesus replies, "Destroy this temple, and in three days I will raise it up." Only after his resurrection do the disciples realize that Jesus was referring to his own body as a temple. Whereas the Jerusalem temple had been the locus of God's presence, now in the Incarnation, Christ's own body becomes the locus for God's presence.

Throughout this week, we have seen that God employs many different methods for teaching the faithful: the law, the life and teachings of Christ, creation itself. Each of these pedagogies is unique. Yet, all of them share one common denominator: faith. Without faith, the law is just an onerous list of dos and don'ts. Without faith, we do not see the new relationship Jesus opens with the Divine. Without faith, the Crucifixion becomes a stumbling block and foolishness. Without faith, the forest becomes just so many cubic feet of lumber. Faith is fundamental to God's pedagogy.

O God, who loves us extravagantly, may we grow in faith through the many ways you teach us. Amen.

Behold God's Redeeming Love

MARCH 5–11, 2018 • WILLIE JAMES JENNINGS

SCRIPTURE OVERVIEW: Sometimes we get ourselves into trouble by our words and actions. It's okay to admit it. It happens to all of us. The Israelites experienced this when their constant grumbling provoked God's wrath in Numbers 21. Yet even in this story, God provides the means of salvation. The psalmist echoes the refrain that when we put ourselves in bad positions, we may cry out to the Lord for deliverance. We read in Ephesians that all of us were living in disobedience to God, but God has done all the work of reconciliation by grace given through Christ Jesus. John ties all this together, gesturing to the story in Numbers 21 to teach us that Christ is the means of restoration and salvation for all who believe in him.

QUESTIONS AND THOUGHTS FOR REFLECTION

- Read Numbers 21:4-9. When has your complaining distorted your sense of reality? How do you maintain a sense of God's presence?

- Read Psalm 107:1-3, 17-22. Consider implementing a practice of rising from sleep to give God thanks and to call to mind the many ways God works in your life.

- Read Ephesians 2:1-10. Does your sense of God's salvation engender a sense of grace within you and a desire to do good? Why or why not?

- Read John 3:14-21. Do you consider yourself a creature of light or darkness? Why?

Associate Professor of Systematic Theology and Africana Studies, Yale Divinity School, Hartford, Connecticut.

Difficult journeys sometimes bring out the worst in us. No one wants to be in the middle of taxing travel with no end in clear sight. At such times and in such places, our patience often crumbles into complaint. The children of Israel have reached just such a time and place in their journey. God has already delivered them from great harm; but now in this new part of the journey, they lose the sense of God's presence and guidance. When our anxieties meet our exhaustion, we often cannot see the God who has always been with us, upholding us on the journey. Like the children of Israel, we give in to complaint.

Complaining can distort our reality, blinding us to the truth. The children of Israel tell themselves that God has abandoned them to die in the wilderness. But in fact, God is with them, leading and guiding them. God wants them to have faith in the divine guidance of their lives. They say they will die of thirst and starvation when, in fact, God daily supplies them with food and water. Their complaining clouds the facts of their blessings and leads them to see God's gifts to them as a curse.

It is understandable that in harsh times we are tempted to complain. Yet when I complain, I declare that I no longer believe that God loves and cares for me. My complaint denies my experience and history with God. When we complain, we open ourselves to poisons that can harm us. Yet even when we allow our unbelief and complaining to poison us, God provides a way to deliver and heal. We, like the children of Israel, can confess our sin to God and confront the serpents of our complaint. Then we can look to the serpent of salvation and live.

Gracious God, keep me from the poison of complaint, and show me your merciful presence in my life today. Amen.

The most significant bit of information for us to remember each day is the goodness of the Lord. In troubling times we can easily close down our "saving" memories of God's presence when moments of pain and frustration confront us. We forget the wonderful things that God has done for us, like granting us the beauty of a new day and a chance to be in God's presence in this world. Forgetting God's goodness is understandable when we experience the shock of unanticipated troubles or while we endure what feels like an unending struggle.

So the psalmist offers us wise counsel in suggesting that we do two things daily. First, we rise to the day giving thanks to the Lord. Even if we imagine it will not be a good day, we live in the presence of a good God who goes with us in this day and every day. God's very presence makes the day good. Second, we speak to ourselves of what the Lord has done for us and for others. We live always in the testimonies to God's goodness, and we remember those testimonies of God's redeeming action. Like Israel, we too must speak to one another of the redemption that God has brought to us.

God redeems us from trouble, and through Jesus Christ we now live in the space and time of our redemption. A cloud of witnesses, past and present from all over the world, surrounds us and speaks of God's redeeming work in their lives. Open yourself to hear the echoing sounds from around the globe of people who speak to us about the goodness of a redeeming God.

Help me, faithful God, to remember today your goodness to me, and draw me ever closer to your life so that I may experience your love and your touch. Amen.

God redeems; God pulls us from the pits of despair, destruction, and death. We may find ourselves in dark places either through our own sin or the sins of others or simply because life has taken a difficult or tragic turn. This passage reminds us that our God takes pleasure in pulling us up and out of that darkness. These verses speak of God's nature. God takes no joy in our despair or in seeing us suffer because of our sinful action or inaction. We also learn that God hears us when we cry out in our troubled moments and in our pain.

God remains faithful; through God's faithfulness we learn of God's power. Many of us imagine God as an all-powerful deity who could help us if desired but has, for whatever reason, chosen to withhold help. Yet we witness God's power in our experiences of divine faithfulness. We recall God's response to our petitions and God's attempts to draw us from our places of misery and hopelessness. God's very presence sustains us, giving us a sense of God's holy hands that will never release us.

We can find ourselves in pits so deep and dark that we cannot even imagine our escape; at those times we can remember what God has done for us in the past. Sometimes others remind us of what God has done for them or we remind others. Those who have experienced God's redemption must speak of it often. We join the throng who tell of God's "deeds with songs of joy."

Today, great God, remind me of your redeeming power found in your faithfulness to me and others in moments of despair and trouble. Amen.

God gives life and light to us through the Son. Receiving this gift is more challenging than we often realize or admit to ourselves. These verses from John remind us that choosing life with the Son of God means *not* choosing a life of hiding from the truth. Hiding from the truth of who we are or what we have done harms us and those we love. Yet too many people choose a life of concealment because they carry shame, are burdened by fear, or believe that no one can actually help them. Jesus confronts us with the truth that God already sees and knows us completely and yet refuses to condemn us. Jesus himself offers healing for our deceit and our inability to see God's work in our lives. God invites us to look to the Son and believe in him.

The children of Israel reached the point where their desire for God's help overcame their willingness to hide. They confessed their sin of complaining against God and denying God's love and care for them. We move in a good direction when we speak the truth of what we feel or know to God and to ourselves. It is never a mistake to confess our sins to God because words spoken to God are always spoken to the One who knows us and loves us completely. To hide from ourselves or from God denies that love.

Darkness and light in this regard are not physical or visible. Darkness is the captivity of concealment that makes us susceptible to harm or to harming others. The light is the freedom of life with Jesus in the love of God who leads us into all truth without fear or shame. Hiding is not God's way, nor should it be ours.

Loving and saving God, show me all the ways I hide from you and from myself. Guide me into the truth for the sake of Jesus. Amen.

This well-known verse from the Bible has drawn praise and also has been held up to ridicule and mockery. Yet it captures the truth of the way God wishes to be seen and known through the love of the Son. We could call this verse a calling card for the divine life—a message sent to each of us. God wants to be known by the overwhelming reality of divine love. God gives—this is the deepest truth of God's life and our life. God gives us life, and God gives God's own life to redeem our lives.

The grievous error some have made when reading this verse is to imagine that God gave us someone other than God's own self in Jesus Christ—that God sat back and tossed the Son of God into our world and into our plight. Nothing could be further from the truth. God gave God's own life to us. God became human to take hold of our life. From the position of a deep and intimate embrace, God takes hold of us. This message is yet to be heard fully by people: a God who saves us by embrace, who heals us by word and touch, and whose love is so deep and intense that it overcomes the power of death.

To say that God loves us can seem trite and a slogan unless we understand the story of Jesus Christ, who has made God's love real. God's only Son is yet with us through the Holy Spirit, seeking to convince us of God's love. God's love draws us from death to life, but to know its full reality requires that we focus on the Son of God, who came to us and still comes to us when we believe on his name.

Loving God, reveal your love to me this day through your Son, Jesus Christ. Amen.

I find it interesting to look at before-and-after pictures and see positive transformation of homes, objects, or people. We are the recipients of the world's greatest before-and-after. We were once caught in sin and disobedience and enslaved to destructive forces both inwardly and outwardly that drove us toward living in harmful ways. But God changed us. God lifted us up in and with Jesus Christ, drawing us from slavery to freedom in Christ. This transformation is sometimes difficult to see in ourselves or others, especially when we experience behavior and attitudes that suggest destructive forces still enslave us.

The passage reminds us that the transformation wrought by God was not based on our efforts or merit. Only God's love and mercy brings this change. This change, which was not done by us, cannot be undone by us. Once we accept Jesus' life as the place from which we will live life and Jesus Christ as the one who will guide our lives, then we cannot escape God's faithfulness to us. Even if we try to cover over that change or deny it by retracing destructive paths, the Spirit of God will daily remind us of who we are and where we are. We are raised up with Christ!

Our transformation in Christ is the beginning of our journey, not its end. God will not abandon us to anything that seeks to claim or reclaim our lives. We move forward each day with the knowledge that we inhabit a royal position, freed from every oppression and poised to follow Jesus in doing God's work in the world. We have been transformed into signs of grace both to the world and to ourselves.

Thank you, gracious and loving God, for transforming me into a sign of grace. Amen.

FOURTH SUNDAY IN LENT

We meet our Creator in Jesus Christ. He is the source of life and the one who introduces us to God's love. Too often we forget that we are God's creation; simply to be alive is an immeasurable gift and a sign to us of God's love. The gift of our life finds its home in the gift of God's Son, Jesus. These two gifts merge into one through the journey of our life with God. God intends our life journey to be one in divine love, knowing and trusting a God who has given us all things in Jesus Christ. God's love, once we yield to it, will shape the way we live our lives.

Yet difficult times and dealing with difficult people can dull our senses to the greatness of life's gift in Jesus Christ. We easily squander moments, days, even years distracted by our troubles and closed off from the joy of seeing each new day with God. We cannot ignore our problems; they can feel like a deep inescapable pit into which we have fallen.

But God has raised us up with Jesus Christ, drawing us out of the pit and placing us with Christ high above our troubles. They yet exist, but we are not trapped in them or by them. We are with Christ. Our problems don't define our lives; Christ does. Those who acknowledge life as a gift found in relationship with Jesus Christ ready themselves to do good work.

We find ourselves destined to bear witness to God's victory over death and despair and to declare by our lives that God's love surrounds us from our beginning into eternity, drawing us toward our destiny in this life and beyond.

I give you thanks, glorious God, that your love for me is greater than anything I will face on this day or any day. Amen.

Losing Life to Gain It

MARCH 12–18, 2018 • AMY ODEN

SCRIPTURE OVERVIEW: We can maintain outward appearances for only so long. At some point what is in our hearts will come to the surface. God understands this, of course, which is the reason for the promise in Jeremiah. God promises a day when God's law will no longer be an external standard that we are trying to follow, but will be written on our hearts. In the aftermath of his sin with Bathsheba, David cries out in Psalm 51 for God's forgiveness and a new heart. The New Testament readings begin to focus our minds toward the end of Jesus' life. God's transformative work comes at a cost to God through the death of his Son, who suffered in obedience but through his death was glorified.

QUESTIONS AND THOUGHTS FOR REFLECTION

- Read Jeremiah 31:31-34. In what areas of your life do you find yourself keeping score? How can you release that tendency?

- Read Psalm 51:1-12. What clutters your heart, making it unavailable for love?

- Read Hebrews 5:5-10. When have you fallen into the *habit* of faith rather than exhibiting *authentic* faith? What distinction do you draw between the two?

- Read John 12:20-33. How does the author's illustration of the seed and flower help you understand Jesus' crucifixion and death?

Professor of Early Church History and Spirituality, Saint Paul School of Theology; born and raised on the Oklahoma prairie, Amy's spiritual home is under the wide-open sky.

Have you ever compared a flower in bloom with the seed that produced it? The flower is tall, colorful, and moving with layers and textures. The seed is a tiny, hard kernel, motionless and plain. When comparing them, it's hard to believe they are related, much less the same plant. It's such a marvel! The tiny seed transforms into a luscious flower—the mysterious work of God!

If we protect the seed and keep it exactly as it exists, it will never become a flower. That is the temptation of "the way we've always done it." We want to keep our lives, our churches, our world exactly the way they've always been. This impulse to preserve what we cherish, however, often does not lead to life or fruitfulness.

The seed must "die," that is, break open, transform so completely into a flower that it is no longer recognizable as a seed. The seed relinquishes its current form in order to bear fruit in the world. This dying is an obedience to the mysterious work of God.

Jesus invites us to learn from the seed. We too can let ways of being in the world, ways of thinking, ways of being church die so they break open and are completely transformed by God to bear fruit in the world. Here's the rub: the fruit the Spirit produces may look nothing like the seed we let die. It is beyond our imagining! It takes trust and courage. Yet the hard and amazing truth is that to bear fruit, we first have to let things die. Jesus calls us to follow his way of life and death—and Life.

God of big things and small, give us courage to let some of our current ways of being die. May we trust in your mysterious transforming power. Give us eyes to see the amazing fruit you produce. Amen.

An anthropologist once wrote an article on the cleansing rituals of the Nacirema tribes. They have elaborate holy places where they perform daily purification rituals, sometimes more than once a day! They are obsessed with sacred liquids and ointments for ablutions and often submit themselves to thorough inspection using instruments of refracted light.

Of course, this article was a tongue-in-cheek description of American (*nacirema* spelled backward) bathing and grooming practices. In Psalm 51, the psalmist equates unclean to sin and clean to salvation. Cleanliness is important. God's people focused on being clean to be acceptable to God.

Many people today wash even more often than in ancient times and buy antibacterial soap to ensure cleanliness. Washing our bodies is one thing, but what about our hearts? Our hearts get unclean in lots of ways. Sometimes shame coats our hearts so thoroughly that no light can enter. Sometimes our hearts are soiled by life circumstances or feel trashed by our own mistakes.

To make matters worse, we sometimes prefer to keep our hearts that way. We cling to grudges and resentments like badges of honor, yet these sully our hearts. We keep our hearts unclean by living in a constant state of fear or worry that clutters every corner. Anything that keeps us from God's presence makes our hearts unclean. What clutters your heart making it unavailable for love?

In today's world, constant busyness can distract us. We are too preoccupied to examine our hearts or to listen deeply to God. Perhaps the first step is simply to stop. Stop right now and explore your heart. What do you discover?

Holy One, as close as each heartbeat, show me the contents of my heart. Amen.

Losing Life to Gain It   95

What constitutes a "clean" heart? It's more than a heart free of dirt and debris. A clean heart exhibits openness and spaciousness, making room to love God and neighbor—a heart resting in God's presence and living in joy.

The psalmist's cry here involves not only what our hearts are clean *from* but what our hearts are clean *for*. A clean heart has cleared out the clutter, dissolved the resentments, swept away worries; but it does not remain empty. Our clean hearts make room for "a new and right spirit." A clean heart offers "a willing spirit," an openness to what God is up to. The clear, wide-open spaces of our hearts create room for courage and freedom to follow God's lead.

How does this happen? Not by our own willpower. We cannot wash and declutter our hearts on our own. We do not need to scrub harder or get more soap. Only God can create a clean heart. We lay down our self-help efforts in order to surrender our hearts to God, who alone can cleanse, free, and open up spacious hearts.

Turning to God is a first intentional step. Rather than rush headlong into the day, we pause and reach out to the One who knows us better than we know ourselves. You already know this because you read this daily devotion. Take a moment now to stop and breathe deeply. Feel your heart open as your lungs expand with life-giving breath. Let God's Spirit clean out every chamber of your heart and open you for love in the day ahead.

Help me surrender my heart to you, O God, so you can make my heart clean, open, and free for love. Amen.

The score-keeping life is the way that leads to death. God's generosity leads to life. God says here, "I will forgive their iniquity and remember their sin no more." No more keeping a record of sin, a list of wrongdoings. No more keeping score. No big scoreboard in the sky displays God: 10 and Me: 0.

Yet, as humans, we tend to keep score. We keep track of good and bad deeds, of what we think we and others deserve. I have a running joke with my husband. On occasions when he does something especially thoughtful, I accuse him of trying to get more points than me "on the big scoreboard in the sky." It's my way of reminding myself that no such thing exists; there is no secret competition going on where I'm always behind. I want to receive kindness without feeling an obligation to stay "even" or to suspect that the other person is racking up merit points for the win.

This scoreboard mentality can subtly accompany our loving acts toward others. When I reach out to a friend in distress or remember someone's birthday, I'm tempted to expect them to do the same in return—keeping score. No wonder we project the same behavior onto God, expecting God to keep score too—like Santa Claus with a list of who is naughty and who is nice.

God's overflowing heart offers a new covenant, built upon God's faithfulness and written on our hearts. We can stop trying to figure out what we or others deserve. God's love doesn't keep score. Thanks be to God!

Free us from the bondage of score keeping in our lives, with others and with you, O Lord. Hold us in the wideness of your mercy and love. Amen.

Losing Life to Gain It

The Israelites are desperate by the time God offers this new covenant. They are in exile in Babylon, in bondage, and far from home. They have no king, no temple for holy offerings, no priests. Their previous way of life no longer exists, and they lament in a foreign land.

Have you ever felt this way? As though you woke up one morning and found yourself in a different life? An unfamiliar landscape of emotions or relationships? A place you felt stuck and captive? Maybe you filed for bankruptcy or were laid off from your job or ended a marriage. Sometimes entire congregations feel this way because "the way we've always done it" doesn't work anymore in the new, unfamiliar landscape.

Notice what God does not suggest in the midst of this pain: "Work harder!" or "get busy!" or "reclaim the original covenant!" God does not prescribe a program of self-improvement or a doubling down on rule-following. Instead, God makes a new covenant to restore relationship. The new covenant does not involve taking a pledge or writing on stone tablets. Instead, God, the Creator of the universe, establishes it and writes it on our hearts. God forgives, wipes the slate clean, and offers a new relationship! And this new covenant is not based on people's ability to keep it. It's based on God's forgiveness and love.

God writes this covenant on our hearts today too. When we find ourselves in an unfamiliar landscape where the old ways don't work and we feel lost, our first step is to look and listen for what God is up to. We will miss it if we try harder or get busier. Our God is always doing "a new thing"; the law within us written on our hearts requires our attentiveness.

Open our eyes and ears to what you are up to, Lord, in the midst of our stuck places and unfamiliar landscapes. Amen.

Many of us expect to feel good all the time. In fact, if we don't feel good, we think something is wrong or that God has abandoned us. When we experience disappointment or frustration, we assume there's a problem and want to blame someone. Or, we turn to whatever brings relief, like gossiping or alcohol or busyness. We want to escape our troubled feeling, believing that trouble can't be from God.

Jesus offers us another option: the way of a troubled soul. "My soul is troubled," says Jesus. Let that sink in. Jesus, God incarnate, experiences a troubling in his soul. But he doesn't try to suppress it or escape it. In fact, Jesus says that the very thing troubling him is the "reason that I have come to this hour." The path that lies ahead disturbs Jesus. Even so, he embraces it as purposeful to reveal God's love.

What if instead of trying to run *away* from the troubling in our souls, we moved *toward* it? What if we got curious about what that troubling might signify, what God might be up to within us? Such disruptive moments wake us and get our attention so we can recognize God's calling us to a new path, however uncomfortable it may be. When we move *toward* rather than *away* from the troubling in our souls, we open ourselves to God's holy wisdom inviting us to take a closer look.

The path of self-giving that lies ahead troubles Jesus. At the same time, he understands it as the way to reveal God's love for the whole world. We too can walk the way of the troubled soul, pouring out our lives to reveal God's love for the world.

Lord, give me a troubling in my soul that will reveal your love for the whole world. Amen.

FIFTH SUNDAY IN LENT

Have you ever arrived home at the end of the day and been unable to recall how you got there? You knew your route so well you didn't have to pay attention. You had no awareness of the turns and stops as you went through the motions by rote—yet there you are.

This rote behavior can affect our spiritual lives too. We fall into routines, going through the motions of church or prayer or worship. Throughout the ages, people of faith have fallen into this trap, the trap of confusing the habits of faith with authentic faith itself.

Jesus' ministry bore witness to authentic faith. He had authority, but not because he took the credential of "high priest" or held a fancy title. Jesus had authority because he poured out his life through his melted heart of "loud cries and tears." He became the "source of eternal salvation" not through donning priestly robes or conducting elaborate rituals but through an authentic faith lived from the inside out. He was "made perfect" not by being born into a dynasty of priests or fulfilling a formal requirement but through God's gift.

When we are tempted to put our hope in doing things the right way, saying the right words, or doing the proper rituals, we may fall into the age-old trap of rote patterns of spiritual life. We get home in one piece but miss everything God was doing along the way. Authentic faith pays attention with melted hearts and poured-out lives. How can you pay attention to what God is up to today?

O God, keep our eyes open and alert for you on the way home. Amen.

Who Is This King of Glory?

MARCH 19–25, 2018 • FLORA SLOSSON WUELLNER

SCRIPTURE OVERVIEW: This week's readings prepare us for Palm Sunday, a joyous event. Jesus rides into Jerusalem on a donkey, a symbol of kingship in ancient Israel. The people greet him with loud acclamations. He is coming in the name of the Lord! Standing along the road leading into Jerusalem, how could anyone imagine what would happen that following week? Wasn't Jesus finally going to manifest the fullness of God's power, take his place on the throne of David, and overthrow the Romans? No, because that was not his mission. He came not to build an earthly kingdom but to lay aside his rights. He came to be glorified by being humiliated . . . for us. He came to suffer and die . . . for us.

QUESTIONS AND THOUGHTS FOR REFLECTION

- Read Isaiah 50:4-9a. What situations have called you to move forward in vulnerability, "knowing that God promises not safety but limitless strength"?

- Read Psalm 118:1-2, 19-29. When have you claimed God's strength to see you through "the gates of righteousness"?

- Read Mark 11:1-11, 15-18. In a trying time in your life, when have you turned to the love and care of friends? How have you experienced God's entering your life calmly and gently?

- Read Philippians 2:5-11. How does this early Christian hymn of the church speak to you as you enter Holy Week?

United Church of Christ minister with a specialized ministry in spiritual renewal that includes authorship, teaching, retreat leading; living in Fair Oaks, California.

Through this hymn of the early Christian church, we enter into what has been traditionally known as Passion Week. For centuries this week was set apart, along with Holy Week, as the culmination of Lenten devotions.

During these two final weeks of Jesus' life, he emphasized prayer and works of compassion for the poor. Many early Christian leaders even released some slaves and prisoners during these days in the spirit of Jesus who sets all free.

Scripture indicates that Jesus' teachings and healings intensify as he approaches Jerusalem for the last time: blessing the children, healing the blind and those with leprosy, casting out unclean spirits, raising Lazarus from death, experiencing union with God on the Mount of Transfiguration.

Through these culminating experiences as he turns his face toward Jerusalem, as indeed throughout his whole life, Jesus longs to reveal to us the heart of God, which had so deeply enfolded and shone within his own heart. What do our weekly scripture readings show us this week about the heart of God that was one with Jesus' heart?

"Who is this King of glory?" (v. 10) asks Psalm 24. The psalm gives one answer. Our scripture reading from Philippians seems to show another aspect. What answer do we begin to see and feel as we draw closer to God?

God of mercy, God of healing, help me in my reflections and experiences of this day to see into your heart more fully and to respond to the mystery of your love more deeply. In the name and light of Jesus. Amen.

As we approach Passion/Palm Sunday, we traditionally reflect not only on Jesus' healings and teachings but also on the suffering and death that await him. Psalm 118 is one of the most significant lections for this period. If we read the whole psalm, we see intertwined with the exultant praise and confidence in God the definite signs of the hostility and conflict that will confront the bold children of God.

Jesus, of course, would have known this psalm well. Perhaps he found it often on his lips and in his heart as he moved toward Jerusalem, knowing that rejection and danger awaited him there along with the triumph and welcome. But while realistic, the psalm is clearly not the lament of a victim moving toward doom. It is a song of strength empowered by God's hand, God's heart.

As Christians we are often called to encounter conflict along with joy, but our loving and suffering were never meant to be a victim stance. God, who rides to the gates of our hearts and who rides with us through "the gates of righteousness," does not force or compel us as slaves. God sets us free to choose our risks of love.

Jesus is never a victim; he makes every choice in freedom. His eyes are open. He sees clearly, even as did the psalmist, that the choice of love is costly. But when we choose to enter our gates of righteousness, we enter them enfolded by God. The vulnerability to which we are invited is an empowered vulnerability.

"The Lord is God, and he has given us light."

God of our strength, God of our peace, as I enter into whatever gates of righteousness open to me today; as I make my choices, help me face the risks of love, knowing that your heart holds me forever. Amen.

This scripture opens with Isaiah's wonder and gratitude over the rich gifts God has given him: the depth and eloquence of a true teacher, the healing power to renew those who are weary, and the openness that hears what God says to the heart. But then he speaks of the underlying empowerment without which these gifts would be useless.

"I was not rebellious, I did not turn backward." With each gift, the risks and cost of love intensify. Without God's strength to keep moving forward, our gifts atrophy. Anyone who loves, anyone who serves, knows that as we use our gifts we will experience times of antagonism and hostility as well as times of love and appreciation. Our scripture reading refers to insults, blows, and spitting in scorn. There are many ways of being struck or spat upon, and often they are not bodily attacks. Verbal, emotional, or competitive attacks can inflict deeper wounds than bodily ones.

But we are asked to keep moving forward. Our first reading of this scripture seems to imply that we are urged to submit passively to abuse. A more careful reading gives a totally different picture. As I read the passage, I remember the poignant, powerful television pictures from our not-too-distant past of school children surrounded, embraced, supported by parents and neighbors as they walked forward steadily to their school each morning for many weeks through the shouts and insults of angry crowds hostile to their race.

This picture is not one of passivity to abuse but of a forward motion of immense power, going through one's chosen gates with both face and back vulnerable, knowing that God does not promise safety but limitless strength.

God of peace and empowerment, may I walk forward as Jesus did, not as a victim but as a child within your light. Amen.

Jesus made no further reply, so that Pilate was amazed." We too are amazed. Why didn't Jesus give Pilate, the priests, the crowds, a final deathless discourse comparable to the Sermon on the Mount or the Last Supper discourses in John's Gospel? As I reflect on Jesus' silence, I see something far deeper than the silence of one who just wants to get it over without more words. I see a divine act of release, a choice to release all those around him to their own free choices.

Jesus has already told them who he is. Far beyond words he has also shown them throughout his whole life who he is and the nature of his reign. Who he is has been there all along for them to see through his healings, his stories, his compassionate mercy, his clear and decisive discernments, his empowered stance of love. More words will add nothing. He never forces or indoctrinates anyone. When people turn away, he does not run after them with pleas or threats, for his is a love that sets others free. Now as he faces death, he makes this supreme act of silent release of his disciples, Pilate, the priests, the crowd. They see him. Now they must choose.

This silence is a great mystery of God's heart. We are confused and angry when God seems silent. We batter God with our perplexities, demands, and accusations. Even the psalms—those great love songs to God—are full of lament about God's silences. Why doesn't God answer, explain, and tell us step-by-step what to do?

But God has already answered us. God has already told us who we are and what God longs for. God's silences in the midst of our furious demands are not God's absence or indifference but acts of love and release. We are released, set free to choose.

God, your love sets me free. May I embrace my freedom and hear your answer within your unfailing love. Amen.

We want to turn away. We haven't yet reached Palm Sunday! Why are we asked to preview all the terrible anguish to come? We will have to face it, read it again next Friday, Good Friday, which comes all too soon.

Mark's account of the crucifixion is almost unbearably stark compared with other Gospel accounts. Its brief, blinding intensity hurts. Nevertheless, the scripture invites us to see the full dimension of the story, to see the triumph of Palm Sunday through the eyes of the crucifixion to come. But lest we despair, let us remember that the story of the Crucifixion was written by those who had also witnessed the Resurrection.

It is the same in our personal lives. We understand our suffering more deeply when we see it and share it through the eyes of our healing. In the midst of suffering, we value all the more poignantly the precious love given to us. We see love through the eyes of pain; we see pain through the eyes of love.

On the day of Jesus' crucifixion, as he faces the hostile crowds, I do not believe that his thoughts are bitter as he recalls the triumphal entry just days earlier. Perhaps he remembers the eyes of those who genuinely loved him in the welcoming crowd and find that memory precious. Seeing those same eyes now weeping for him, perhaps he gains strength through their love.

We are invited to this blended vision that is not the same as the vertigo of double vision. God's watchful heart breaks through to us as we read the Crucifixion story through the eyes both of Palm Sunday and the Easter to come. The loving gaze of God's heart holds this blended vision together.

Open the eyes of my heart this day, O God, that I may see both your pain for us and your strong joy in us. Help me to hold both pain and joy in my heart as I relate to others. Surround me with your heart. Amen.

Today's passages again invite us to a blended vision: the struggle and agony of Psalm 31 and the exultation of Philippians. How can both be true? The God we see through scripture is a God of polarities but not of polarization. The apparent opposites are held together in God's heart.

Jesus also holds the opposites together in his heart. During his desperate praying in Gethsemane, he feels the anguish Psalm 31 describes: the brokenness, the lash of scorn, the desolation of desertion, "the whispering of many—terror all around." At the same time Jesus feels, as did the psalmist, the face of God shining steadily on him and the strength of God forever upholding him. Certainly he is thinking of that psalm as he prays one of its early verses at the moment of his death: "Into your hand I commit my spirit."

Out of this union of suffering and trust in Jesus' heart rise such Christian hymns as that of Philippians. I do not sense a scenario of a manipulative God first smiting and crushing Jesus and then raising and exalting him. Rather I see the exaltation of Jesus in the very moment of his humility. He can be humbled because he is already exalted.

Humility involves being open to full humanness. The most truly great and gifted persons I have known are the most human and approachable; they are not ashamed of laughing, crying, grieving, being angry, loving—all expressions of the human condition. Likewise Jesus, with his immense God-given powers, is not ashamed of "being born in human likeness" or of "being found in human form" (Phil. 2:7). In this mingling of giftedness and humanness, we see the mystery of Emmanuel, God with us. We see deeper into God's heart.

O God, show me more fully the mystery of your love that enters our pain and transforms us in your power. Amen.

Who Is This King of Glory?

107

PALM/PASSION SUNDAY

As Jesus enters Jerusalem with friends and followers waving palms, not swords, we see again into the heart of God. A significant detail (often overlooked) noted by Matthew, Mark, and Luke is that Jesus rides into the city on a colt that has never been ridden. An unbroken colt! As student pastor in the Rocky Mountains many years ago, I attended many riding and roping shows and saw what usually happened to people who sat on untamed colts, especially in the midst of shouting crowds! I sense an underlying smile here as the writer of Mark's Gospel contemplates this little miracle, less spectacular than stilling a storm or raising the dead but no less significant in its depiction of gentle power. Jesus does not need a warrior's stallion. The untamed young horse makes the point just as well. The power that enters the gates of our hearts does not force or violate but calms, transforms, and guides us.

We read another often overlooked detail in the clamor of Palm Sunday in the last verse of today's reading. At the end of this incredible day, Jesus does not set up a command center in Jerusalem. He leaves the city and goes to the suburb of Bethany, we assume to spend the night with his beloved friends Mary, Martha, and Lazarus. At the height of his triumph, all he wants is to rest in that quiet, loving circle of friendship. We know that extraordinary days of intensity, confrontation, and challenge lie ahead of him. But on that first night perhaps what he most needs is the hearts of his friends.

"Who is this King of glory?" All week we have reflected on glimpses of God's heart through scripture. How do we feel more prepared to respond to that ancient question?

God of supreme yet gentle power, I open my heart to you, so that you may enter and be at home with your friend. Amen.

In the Leaving, Love

MARCH 26—APRIL 1, 2018 • JAN RICHARDSON

SCRIPTURE OVERVIEW: This week's readings take us through the depths but then into the eternal light. We walk each step with Jesus, who suffers betrayal, abandonment, and death in our place. But it is more than that. He also enters into the brokenness of our human condition and feels our pain, such that on the cross he even feels abandonment by God. He walks through the valley of the shadow of death because of God's amazing, reckless love for us. This is the power of Holy Week. But that is not the end of the story. Jesus' steps do not end at the cross, for he walks out of the tomb! Now we can follow in his steps and participate in his new life. He is risen indeed! Alleluia!

QUESTIONS AND THOUGHTS FOR REFLECTION

- Read Psalm 70. What help do you need from God? from others?

- Read Isaiah 42:1-9. Where do you see signs of God's work in the arena of justice? Where does Creation provide signs of restoration?

- Read John 12:20-36. As you ponder the reign of God in your midst, what images call to your mind God's presence?

- Read John 20:1-18. When have you, in love, released the life expected in order to take up the life God intends for you?

Artist, author, and ordained United Methodist minister; director of The Wellspring Studio, LLC; janrichardson.com, Orlando, Florida.

The season of Lent strongly resembles the season of Advent. Waiting, preparation, anticipation; living in the now and the not yet; the call to recognize God in the present even as we yearn for a time when God will appear in fullness and redeem all creation. The themes that draw us into the story of Christ's birth also draw us into the story of his death and resurrection.

These themes are at full play in today's passage from Isaiah. The God who fashioned all things—"who created the heavens . . . , who spread out the earth and what comes from it, who gives breath to the people upon it"—promises a time when creation will be restored and justice will come upon the earth.

For now, we wait. This waiting, however, is not a passive waiting. It is active. It is hopeful. It is a waiting that asks us to consider where God is calling us to work for the healing of the world now.

Today's Gospel reading provides a powerful image of this waiting. When Mary of Bethany anoints Jesus, it is as if her whole life has been distilled into this gesture, this pouring out of this most extravagant gift. She offers no spoken words, yet with her entire being Mary proclaims a message both prophetic and priestly as she ministers to Jesus just days before his death.

Mary both anticipates and mirrors what we will see Jesus do this week: even in pain, she pours herself out in a remarkable act of grace and love. As we enter this Holy Week, she invites us to do what she did: recognize Christ; minister to him as he appears in our lives; and give ourselves to him in love, here and now.

In love, in hope, in grace, may we seek the face of Christ who waits with us.

Even as he prepares to leave this world, Jesus retains a passionate interest in it. He does not consider this life a mere prelude to heaven. He wants us to perceive the reign of God in our very midst.

To describe the things of heaven, Jesus turns to the things of earth: yeast, seeds, dirt, water, fish, flowers, birds. He continually employs the ephemeral to explain the eternal. This both comforts and unsettles; taking what is familiar, he turns it on its head—and us as well.

In today's reading, Jesus uses familiar images once again to talk about strange things: grain and earth and fruit to talk about loving life and hating it, losing it and gaining it.

Jesus clearly loved this life and this world, so his words here may perplex us. On this day, this is part of his point. In this week of all weeks, Jesus asks us not to shrink from what bewilders us but instead to look deeper into those very places.

Jesus tells his hearers to go into the questions, the mysteries, the paradoxes. He tells them to go into the dying that is not dying after all. We sometimes make letting go such a hard thing. We resist giving up. But what if it is not about giving up but giving in? Falling into dirt, as Jesus says here. Going where grain is supposed to go; following the spiral within the seed that takes us deeper into the dark but also—finally, fruitfully—out of it.

After Jesus finishes speaking, he hides. Perhaps he means for us to do the same at this point: to allow ourselves to withdraw for a time. To stop wrestling with the mysteries and simply rest with them. To secret our souls like a seed in the earth and see what grows.

This moment, may we let ourselves rest in the mystery and in the love that meets us in the dark.

Letting go, giving in, falling into the mystery. This is not easy, especially when the mystery becomes painful.

Several years ago, my husband, Gary, died after developing complications during what we had anticipated would be routine surgery. After his death, people wanted to help. In the early, most raw time of grief, I could not imagine what would possibly help.

The psalmist recognizes our need for help. He understands too that sometimes we scarcely know what help we need or where to turn to find it. He does not hesitate to give voice to his concern and to open his heart to the One who is the source of all help. "Be pleased, O God, to deliver me," he pleads as the psalm begins. "O LORD, make haste to help me!"

The psalmist's words assure us that knowing our need and asking for help are part of what it means to belong to God—and to one another. We need not navigate our lives on our own or wrestle with the mysteries all by ourselves.

When we are at our most vulnerable, asking for help can feel like weakness. Usually the opposite is true. Seeking help is a way of recognizing we belong to one another and to the God who meets us in our deepest pain.

In verse 4, the psalmist reminds us that seeking God's help provides a pathway to gladness; drawing near to the God who takes delight in delivering us becomes a road to rejoicing. With this verse, the psalmist counsels joy in the presence of panic. "Let all who seek you rejoice and be glad in you," he sings. "Let those who love your salvation say evermore, 'God is great!'"

What help do you need this day? Are you willing to ask for it and to offer thanks when it arrives?

Help me, God. Help me. Help.

MAUNDY THURSDAY

We press deeper into Holy Week, and the momentum grows. There is no stopping the events that will unfold from here. But lest we rush toward what lies ahead, a table calls to us.

Here at the table, Jesus stops. He will not be hurried. He will not be rushed, even as events draw him closer to his death. The table provides time to linger and to speak of what matters most. "I give you a new commandment, that you love one another," Jesus tells them at the table. "Just as I have loved you, you also should love one another. By this everyone will know that you are my disciples, if you have love for one another."

Again and again at this table, Jesus speaks of love. By the time he comes to the end of what is called his "Farewell Discourse" (John 14–17), he will have spoken the word *love* thirty-one times. He wants to be sure the disciples get it. He wants to be certain they understand why he came in the first place and what he needs them to do after he leaves.

In the washing of feet, in the breaking of bread, in each breath, in every word down to the final sentence of his final prayer for them: love. Of all that he says and does at the table, love is what he most wants them to know.

On this day, Jesus gathers us into the circle of his beloveds. What he tells his companions, he tells us. What he wants them to know, he wants us to know.

As we linger with Jesus at the table, how will we receive this love? Where will we let it lead us?

On this day, in this circle, may we open our hearts toward the One who meets us in love.

GOOD FRIDAY

Waiting. Keeping watch. In the hours and minutes and moments of his dying, breathing with him, breathing for him, every breath catching in your throat and rattling through your breaking heart, wondering if it is the last.

The final intake, the final release. You hold your own breath in an agony of waiting, watching to see if another will follow. But nothing comes, and you know. Not relief but recognition of the release that has taken place. If the door to life and healing cannot be opened, then at least his struggle has ended; he has moved beyond the possibility of pain.

Today we stand in the place of dying, the place of devastation. We stand with those who have come to bear witness, who have not turned away, who watch and wait with Jesus. Today we stand where life is coming to a horrendous end. We stand where breath—the *pneuma*, the living Spirit—is leaving.

On this day, can we believe there is anything beyond this? Can we believe there is anything good ahead of us, that life still waits for us?

Perhaps this is not a day for belief. Perhaps we are not meant to rush toward what we hope and pray lies ahead. Perhaps the invitation now is simply to let ourselves feel the loss. To grieve what has gone. To lift our voices in lament.

In this place, I ask you, is there some space of desolation within or beyond you that is present today—a place where something has come to a heartrending end? How would it be for you to be present to this loss, to offer lament, to let yourself breathe, to know in your bones you do not breathe alone?

In this place, in this parting, in this pain, may we know the love of Christ. Still.

HOLY SATURDAY

Y*ou wake, and the awful wave of remembering washes over you. It is as if it has happened all over again: the dying, the loss, the utter and unfathomable goneness of the beloved.*

You want to be in motion. You want to flee, to hide, to fling yourself into anything that will distract you from the pain. You want to do anything but sit with your thoughts that overtake and overwhelm you. But there is nowhere you can go that this grief will not accompany you, clutching at you, propelling you into the labyrinth of loss that twists and turns you down its convoluted path.

How can it be that it has all come to this? How is it possible that the road has ended here, when until so recently it was about walking together, accompanying one another as you leaned into the dreams, the visions, the calling that had been given you?

What now?

Throughout his ministry, Jesus had been in nearly perpetual motion, always searching for the ones he came to serve. So how is it that we stand with Mary Magdalene and the other Mary in stunned stillness outside his tomb? How is it that the earth that quaked yesterday in rock-splitting outrage and grief can now so readily hold his body? After his astounding presence with us, how will we abide his absence?

Can it be that stillness is a journey too? Does waiting offer its own road, one that, instead of propelling us outward, spirals us inward? Is it possible that waiting is part of how a new way is made for us?

This Holy Saturday, I wonder how it might be for us to wait together, to breathe together. I wonder how it might be for us, in all the places we are, to enter into a shared stillness this day.

In the silence, in the stillness, in the sorrow, may we breathe the presence of peace.

In the Leaving, Love   115

EASTER SUNDAY

You would give anything to hear his voice again: the way his words resonated in your chest, your heart; the timbre of his laughter; how he would, in the most ordinary moments, suddenly break into song.

So when, in your weeping, you hear him speaking your name, you are stunned, then elated. You want to reach out, to gather into your arms the one you had thought forever gone.

What you do not know is that resurrection is not quite the same as return. You will learn, and soon, that it comes with a cost, that new life really means this: means new, means it will not be the same as before, means you cannot hold on to him, means you will have to let go of everything in order to love him as he is now. As you are now, yourself altered beyond imagining.

You will learn that the cost of resurrection is also the gift: that letting go will propel you into a life you could hardly have dreamed. Into the empty, aching space of your outstretched arms, a whole new world will enter. And this awful hollowing inside your chest: this is your heart becoming larger. This is the space you will need in order to hold him now.

At the beginning of this week, a woman named Mary drew close to Jesus. As this week ends, another Mary is sent away from him. Now love asks for letting go.

Mary Magdalene's leaving, like Mary of Bethany's anointing, is a gesture of astounding love. This love releases the life we expected and instead chooses the life meant for us. This is love that, even as we let it send us, will draw us closer to the risen Christ.

In the rising, in the rejoicing, in the releasing, may we fall deep into the love that will not leave us alone.

An Easter People

APRIL 2–8, 2018 • HANNAH DREITCER WITH ANDREW DREITCER

SCRIPTURE OVERVIEW: Easter promises us the possibility of new life in Christ, but what should that life look like? Scripture makes clear that one sign of union with God is unity with each other. How wonderful it is, the psalmist says, when there is peace among brothers and sisters. Unity and peace do not mean simply the lack of conflict but proactive care for one another. The Christians in Acts lived out this care in a practical way by giving of their material means to help one another. John in his epistle tells us that this fellowship with one another is ultimately modeled on the fellowship we share with God and Christ, while in his Gospel, John teaches that belief in Jesus the Messiah is what binds us all together in this new life.

QUESTIONS AND THOUGHTS FOR REFLECTION

• Read Acts 4:32-35. In what ways have you experienced the generosity of community?

• Read Psalm 133. How and where do you experience the wild, extravagant love of God?

• Read 1 John 1:1–2:2. How do you keep ever before you the urgency and joy of Easter?

• Read John 20:19-31. What fears keep you locked away from the world?

Hannah, associate pastor, Webster Groves Presbyterian Church, Webster Groves, Missouri; Andrew, Professor of Spirituality and Co-Director of the Center for Engaged Compassion, Claremont School of Theology, Claremont, California.

On this second day of the Easter season, we read the opening verses of First John, a letter sent to a congregation of the early church. For this early community, the Easter news is actually new. The Resurrection is a fairly recent event. They are still giddy with surprise and joy. The intensity of the writing conveys the newness of the Resurrection; the knowledge of so many senses—eyes and ears and hands—is named, for life's revelation is complete! The tomb is empty! Christ is risen!

This joy of the early church echoes our own. The good news has not yet grown old for the author of First John; the good news remains fresh in our hearts and minds today. We too are giddy with the surprise and joy of the Resurrection, which comes new to us each year. We still breathe in the heady aroma of Easter lilies, still hear the glorious harmonies of the *Hallelujah* chorus, still feel the joy of family and friends who assemble for worship and good food. All our senses are alight with the knowledge of Easter, for "God is light and in him there is no darkness at all."

Today Easter is still urgent for us, but as society and the world around us change out the chocolates for the trappings of the next holiday, we can easily lose that urgency and knowledge of the Easter news. Yet the good news is always good, and the good news is always new. Christ is risen! Our every sense declares this with complete and abundant joy.

What urgent good news calls out to you in the present moments of your life? Where and how has Christ risen in your life this day, this week, this month?

Loving God, help me hear the good news through all the clamor. May I see even the smallest way that Christ rises to greet me. Amen.

Have you ever been anointed with oil? What smell do you associate with that experience? Do you remember the feel of it? In my experience, which has always been in mainline Protestant settings, those doing the anointing tend to be fairly stingy with the oil. Their hands barely skim the tip of a single finger along the surface of the oil before marking my forehead with a cross.

And, having anointed others, I know this stinginess comes with good reason. Oil is abundant and overwhelming. Its aroma lingers far longer than I would expect. The skin stays heavy with it, fingers and face carrying the feel and look of the oil for hours after.

Yet here the psalmist proclaims a true abundance of oil, anointing oil poured out over the head of Aaron, running down his beard and over the collar of his robes. The psalmist describes a wildly indulgent and overwhelming richness of oil that spills out in excess, far beyond what could possibly be needed, even to the point of waste.

God promises this abundance of goodness in the midst of community: a wild, indulgent, excessive goodness that lingers; that remains far longer than expected; that changes all it touches, leaving behind a lingering aroma seen and felt for hours and days after—far longer than we have any right to imagine or expect.

In the union of community, God pours out blessing, changing the fabric of being for all who participate. When have you been met with abundance in community? How have you offered abundance to those in your community?

Abundant God, pour out your unity and peace like oil upon my head. Open my every sense to your blessing, so that I may bless others, unafraid of scarcity and trusting in abundance. Amen.

An Easter People   **119**

How very good and pleasant indeed is this vision of the early church. All is shared. All are known. All are cared for. No one allows fear of scarcity or need into their hearts. Instead, each member of the community commits to their unity with no hesitation or discord.

Imagine participating in this new community—listening to the apostles. What powerful testimony offered by those who not only walked with Jesus and heard his words but who also had broken bread with the risen Christ!

Consider the energy in a gathering led by those whose tongues the Holy Spirit had unleashed on Pentecost. Ponder what it was like to be among those whose voices the Spirit unleashed and those who came to understanding in that chaos and cacophony, who heard the good news preached in their own languages.

Envision the excitement, the restlessness, the urgency of this group of believers. Picture their eagerness for the future, the anticipation of further miracles and wonders, the continued new thing done by God. So much had already been done! So much was coming to fruition before their very eyes!

In this excitement, in this energy, in this eagerness and enthusiasm, how easy to live in unity! How joyful to bring resources—large, mediocre, or meager—to foster the good of this group that believes Christ has risen. How very good and pleasant to live generously and graciously with kindred of faith, wholeheartedly sharing gifts.

What gifts have been shared with you? To what generosity might God be calling you?

Giving God, you know my every need, and you reach out with your grace before I ask. Help me see the needs of the world and reach out to help. Amen.

Christ is risen, but fear remains. The first day of the Resurrection, the first day of the world made new, is marked not by joy but by fear. The disciples hide away—not overcome with celebration but with terror. The particular fear John names has a direct tie to the Gospel writer's time and place. It has no bearing on our own time except for its having inspired generations of horrific anti-Semitism, which makes many more fearful.

We know too well from our own lives what it feels like to be too afraid to move. Christ is risen, but there is still doubt. We know what it is to be uncertain and full of worry.

So into this fear, this doubt, and this worry, Christ shows the disciples his hands and his side. He speaks to them, breathes on them, and brings the whole group joy. *Except* the one who wasn't there.

And not being there, Thomas didn't see, feel, or receive. He just wants the same experience as the rest. He doesn't want extra proof or special proof. He simply wants what has already been given to his community. And Jesus appears again to offer Thomas his hands, his side—and his peace. And once again the group is united in experience and belief and joy.

Yet discord has been part of their community even after Christ has gifted them with the Holy Spirit. Division has entered and fractured their unity. They struggle to understand their different experiences of the world.

What fears keep you locked away from the world? What doubts and differences sow discord in your community?

Living God, breathe your peace upon me and all who surround me. Make me an instrument of your peace in the world; strengthen my heart in the face of anxiety and fear. Amen.

We are an Easter people. Your faith community is an Easter people. Together we make up the body of Christ, and we sense the Holy Spirit's presence among us. We are members of the body—incomplete without one another and our gifts.

Consider the global church or the national church or simply your congregation. Is the whole group of those who believe of one heart and soul? Does anyone claim private ownership, keeping goods and resources and gifts from those in need? Are there any needy among you? Do any members lord their power, their wealth, their privilege, their position over others?

This vision of the early church feels far removed from church as we know it today. We experience discord, division, pettiness and politics, and any number of conflicts big and small. Yet Acts still speaks great truth to us.

This vision is not impossible. It is not a myth or a daydream or a wishful thought. It was the church. And we can see this early church in our churches, for we are still the church. We still hear powerful testimonies to the resurrection of Jesus, both from the apostles of ages past and from those disciples next to us in the pews. We still share our gifts and our resources. We still bring our whole hearts and selves to meet the needs of others. We are still an Easter people, and we have received a great grace.

How do you see this vision of the earliest church embodied today in your congregation? in the greater world? How can you help your community live into this vision?

Gracious God, grant me empathy for those who are not like me, and grant me patience with those whose experiences have not been like mine. Bring our hearts closer together through your Spirit. Amen.

Sometimes I suspect this psalmist had no siblings. I have a wonderful relationship with my younger sister, and we have a wonderful relationship with our parents. And it is, indeed, very good and pleasant when the family lives together in unity and peace.

Yet sometimes, maybe even most times, that unity feels impossible to maintain. The busyness and brokenness of life gets in the way. Our work in the course of each day makes the work of relationship feel too overwhelming. So relationships break down. Days stretch out without true communication, with no real goodness or pleasantness. The shape of the connection becomes one of discord and frustration.

But perhaps the psalmist speaks these words into that very situation. Maybe the seeming impossibility of unity is why this psalm speaks of community's abundant blessing.

So even though I sometimes suspect this psalmist had no siblings, maybe I'm wrong. Maybe this psalmist had an abundance of siblings and so knew firsthand the chaos, frustration, and hard work of relationship. Therefore he can sing profoundly of the beauty and nurture of peace and concord.

Maybe the psalmist knew intimately that unity and communion are like heavy dew falling upon parched mountains. And the wonderful thing about dew? It arrives overnight, in the darkness, when no one watches for its arrival. And dew arrives fresh each morning, no matter what argument or division the previous day has wrought. What an abundant, forgiving blessing of life! Where in your life, community, or world does unity feel most impossible? What morning dew might refresh and restore relationships and communities?

Triune God, grant me patience and compassion for those with whom I live, work, serve, and worship. Amen.

On this second Sunday of Easter, much of the world has moved on. The stores promote another holiday. Society's attention turns elsewhere. Even within the church we may witness some surprised side-glances as we sing more Easter hymns and continue to wish one another a happy Easter. It's only been a week; but in the fast-paced secular world, Easter is already a distant memory. The urgency of the good news has lost its edge. We know this already, after all.

In my church, we often use words from First John to call us to confession and also to declare God's pardon. We are an Easter people, and yet we are broken. We have sinned, and yet we have received abundant and overwhelming grace.

Our church knows discord too well. Our congregations know division and disagreement. Need exists among us, as well as greed and selfishness. Few of us find ourselves united in experience as were the first disciples.

God forms the basis of our communion with one another. In Christ we are one body, despite our discord. We are sinners, but we are a people, a community. And we are a forgiven people.

We are an Easter people with all our faults and our goodness. In our unity and discord, in our belief and doubt, we are an Easter people—loved, forgiven, and freed.

This good news is always good, and this good news is always new. Christ is risen!

Through the rest of the Easter season, how can you find ways to remember the urgency and joy of the good news?

Risen Christ, keep my senses alive to the newness and joy of your good news. Teach me attentiveness, that I may seek love everywhere and live the gospel in each moment. Amen.

Questions of Identity: Who Am I?

APRIL 9–15, 2018 • ANNE BROYLES

SCRIPTURE OVERVIEW: A repeating theme in scripture is our failure to recognize God's work among us. In Acts, Peter declares that the death of Jesus happened because his fellow Israelites acted in ignorance. The psalmist decries the fact that so many people follow lies, yet God's blessings for the faithful continue unhindered. John tells his audience to expect that the world will not recognize them as God's children because the world did not recognize God to begin with. In Luke, Jesus appears to his doubting disciples. He proves the reality of his resurrection by allowing them to touch his body and by eating food in their presence. Only then do they feel certain that they recognize him. In what places in our lives do we not recognize God's work?

QUESTIONS AND THOUGHTS FOR REFLECTION

- Read Acts 3:12-19. When have you initially bristled at someone's remarks only to discover some truth about yourself as you reflected on your strong reaction? What did you learn about yourself?

- Read Psalm 4. How do you daily reinforce the idea that you are "more" rather than "less"?

- Read 1 John 3:1-7. When have you been an "upstander" for love on behalf of another? In what ways did that empower you to take more initiative to love?

- Read Luke 24:36b-48. To what do you look as a revelation of Christ's presence?

Author and retired United Methodist minister living in Portland, Oregon; www.annebroyles.com.

Years ago, my identity was stolen. I cried when I heard the tape-recorded voice of the man who impersonated me to access my credit card and pensions funds. This stranger claiming to be me stumbled in answering basic questions like date of birth, address, phone number. Yet he was convincing enough to "prove" he was me. For a time, the burden of proof lay with me to prove that I was the *real* Anne Broyles in order to get my money back.

I was not to talk about the case. I felt vulnerable and alone, let down by the institutions I had assumed would protect me. Eventually, I received remuneration and life returned to normal. However, I could never go back to the time of an uncompromised social security number.

In spite of all the things I felt I could NOT count on, God remained faithful. God didn't need my social security number, a copy of my signature, or a tape recording of my voice to know who I was.

I once participated in a large-group exercise where members moved around a room, stopping briefly to take another person's hands and say, "I am _____." The only rule: We could not repeat any word. I am . . . *creative, female, mother, friend, strong, Christian.* The first twenty words came easily, adjectives and nouns I had used countless times to describe myself. But as I met person after person, I had to dig deeper, discovering more about myself. All the words seemed secondary to my core identity: child of God.

The author of First John reminds us, "What marvelous love [God] has extended to us! Just look at it—we're called children of God! That's who we really are" (3:1, THE MESSAGE).

Who am I? A child of God.

Gracious God, help me remember that no matter what happens, I am your beloved child. Amen.

I wear a silver necklace made by a Hopi artist. It's a simple design of a stalk of corn that reminds me of meaningful weeks spent working on the Hopi reservation with Sierra Service Project. The Hopi have lived for centuries in northern Arizona on and around three majestic mesas that rise out of the desert. For centuries, Hopi farmers have farmed the arid lands. They grow sixteen kinds of corn, in addition to beans, melons, sunflowers, and squash. Some people might consider the Hopi landscape stark; their traditional foods and menu, plain. But to the Hopi, corn is life. Blue corn piki bread, white corn stew, baked sweet corn are appreciated delicacies.

I wear the corn necklace to remind me to look for plenitude in life. As we read in Psalm 4:6-8:

> There are many who say, "O that we might see some good!
>   Let the light of your face shine on us, O LORD!"
> You have put gladness in my heart
>   more than when their grain and wine abound.

There will be always be others whose "grain and wine abound," but when God's love surrounds us, we experience gladness of heart. Peace. Joy. No need to compare ourselves to others who seem to have more money, things, opportunities. My necklace prompts me to give thanks for what I have instead of dwelling on what I don't have.

List at least ten things for which you are thankful. You may want to make a gratitude list part of your daily routine. And if, like me, you occasionally find yourself feeling "less," remember the many ways God has blessed and continues to bless you.

Who am I? A person with plenty.

God, I want to experience the joy that comes in relationship with you. May I remember that you give me more than enough. Amen.

Questions of Identity: Who Am I?   **127**

The disciples' world has been turned upside down. In the past days they celebrated a memorable meal with their beloved Jesus, then saw him dragged before Pilate, crucified, and buried. Deep sadness, confusion, and fear fill them. Three days after his death, some of the women discover Jesus' empty tomb and are told he has risen. Other followers actually break bread with Jesus in the town of Emmaus.

And now, as the disciples discuss these recent events, Jesus himself joins them. They cannot believe who stands right in front of them: Jesus, very much alive. Can you imagine the looks on their faces? Can you identify with the fear in their hearts?

Jesus asks, "Why are you frightened, and why do doubts arise in your hearts? Look at my hands and my feet; see that it is I myself." Despite Jesus' numerous attempts to prepare them for this day and his standing in their midst, the disciples cannot set aside their doubts. This man looks like Jesus, sounds like Jesus. He seems to know them—but they are sure he is dead.

How are the disciples to understand a risen Christ? One whose presence is known in the breaking of bread? in affirmation of scripture? How do they bear witness to the witness?

When have you experienced something so wonderful that it seemed too good to be true? Did you doubt its possibility or discount God's power because what appeared to be a miracle could be explained by coincidence or human action? This week, expect miracles. Keep your senses at the ready. Enter the week with eyes open and ears ready to experience what God might be doing in your life and in the world.

Who am I? A believer in miracles.

God, may I be open to the miracles you have in store for me and the world. Amen.

Jesus comes to us in the midst of our ordinary lives. We know him from scripture, in worship, as we pray and sing songs of faith. In this passage, Jesus attempts to establish his identity and dispel his followers' disbelief and wonder by eating a meal.

Jesus has been absent from his followers for a few days; already their fear has caused much of his teaching to leave their minds. From offering hands and feet and eating fish, he moves to recall what he has told them about his connection to the scriptures. "Everything I told you while I was with you comes to this: All the things written about me in the Law of Moses, in the Prophets, and in the Psalms have to be fulfilled. . . . You're the first to hear and see it. You're the witnesses" (THE MESSAGE). The miracle of the Resurrection does not hinge on Jesus' physical reappearance after death; the miracle is that God's plans and purpose as laid out in scripture have come to fruition.

We contemporary Christians have centuries of faithful believers sharing the story of Jesus. We have numerous translations of the Bible, thousands of books written about the Christian faith, opportunities for small-group spiritual growth. Yet even those of us who regularly attend worship and hear the story of Jesus told again and again may have ho-hum moments. Sure, Jesus lived among humanity as an example of how to conduct our lives. Oh, yeah, he died and by the way, rose from the dead. Our familiarity with the story causes us to overlook its power. Like the disciples, we need to be shaken up, to hear Jesus tell us, "You're the witnesses."

Who am I? A witness to God's power.

Jesus, help me know what it means to be your witness to the world. Amen.

People express astonishment when Peter heals a "man lame from birth." Rather than bask in the limelight as a miracle healer, Peter speaks plainly to the crowd. He walks them through the story of Jesus and reflects on the many ways God has worked throughout history. Peter's words to the crowd remind us that we are called to be faithful followers of Jesus. In this passage, he encourages us to

- believe in God's power to change lives and work miracles,

- be witnesses to Christ's resurrection,

- have faith in Jesus' name,

- repent "so that times of refreshing may come from the presence of the Lord, and that he may send the Messiah appointed for you, that is, Jesus," and

- be open to other ways that God may speak to us.

Peter says nothing earthshakingly new, but I imagine he employed a gruff tone as he admonished those who were stunned at the miracle they had just observed. Don't we sometimes need someone to speak to us in a way that gets our attention? When I find myself bristling at a remark that hits home from someone who knows me well, I try to step back to see why I reacted so strongly. Often I realize they spoke a truth about me and to me!

Who am I? A faithful follower.

Reread Acts 3:12-23 and reflect on ways you can grow as a faithful follower of Jesus Christ. Do you consider yourself a witness to Jesus' power? How can you manifest your faith? How is God speaking to you today? Choose a way you would like to increase in faithfulness, and record your commitment.

In seventh grade, I felt torn between the popular crowd and a longtime friend the other kids considered dorky. The popular girls were cute, well-dressed, bragged about fabulous parties, and felt free to pick on anyone they didn't like. My friend proved an easy mark: frizzy hair, thick glasses, low self-esteem. I navigated between the group and my friend until one day the popular girls' leader told me I had to choose. Them or her.

From where I stood, I could see my friend standing alone with no one to protect her from mean girls. With longing, I considered all the parties I would not be invited to—and then chose my friend.

The overarching theme of First John is love, particularly love of "brothers and sisters." The children of God do not pursue the way of lawlessness; they choose to do what is right.

There have always been people who pick on others. Bullies use emotional or physical intimidation, act in person or on the Internet. Hate crimes are on the rise. The anti-bullying movement encourages kids and adults to be "upstanders," reaching out to anyone who seems bullied, offering support, speaking up when necessary. The children of God are upstanders, those who do what is right.

"My dear children, don't let anyone divert you from the truth. It's the person who *acts* right who *is* right, just as we see it lived out in our righteous Messiah" (THE MESSAGE). We are called to be upstanders even when no one else sees our good works or when it takes courage to speak truth to situations that demean others.

Who am I? A person who seeks to do right.

Strong God of love, give me strength always to do the right thing, to protect those who need protecting, and to show the love of Jesus in everything I do. Amen.

People lose jobs, accidents happen, loved ones die. The wicked seem to prosper, and sometimes life is downright scary. Many psalms give the psalmist voice as he tells God his problems.

> When I call, give me answers. God, take my side!
> Once, in a tight place, you gave me room;
> Now I'm in trouble again: grace me! hear me! (THE MESSAGE)

During the seven weeks between my mother's cancer diagnosis and her death, I found it hard to know what to pray for. She was seventy-two, had just returned from a camping trip, and lived a healthy lifestyle. "God has been with me through all the hard times in my life," she told us in the moments after her doctor gave the dire prognosis, "and I trust God to be with me through this too." Her positive attitude set the tone for how we as a family spent those precious days.

"Don't you want a miracle?" people asked me. Though I wanted my mother to live, she helped me see that a miracle of a different sort was happening: She was enjoying her final days, and our family was brought even closer in her illness. She did not perceive her impending death as a failure of God's power but as a sign of God's work even in difficult times. She chose "God, shepherd me home" as her breath prayer, and the psalmist's words made sense to her:

> I will both lie down and sleep in peace;
> for you alone, O LORD, make me lie down in safety.

Who am I? A person who rests safely in God's arms.

What have been the hardest obstacles you have faced in your life? Give thanks for how God worked and is working in your life, on good days and bad.

Living the Resurrection

APRIL 16–22, 2018 • MAGREY R. DEVEGA

SCRIPTURE OVERVIEW: This week's readings open with a confrontation in Acts between Peter and John and some of the religious leaders. Peter speaks in harsh terms to the leaders, stating that they had killed Jesus; yet by the power of Jesus' name, a man who could not walk has been healed. By that same name spiritual healing happens as well. The other three passages employ the metaphor of the Good Shepherd. "The Lord is my shepherd," the psalmist declares, and the shepherd cares for all our needs. In John's Gospel, Jesus declares that he is the Good Shepherd who lays down his life for his sheep. First John repeats this imagery. Jesus proved his love when he lay down his life for us. If we truly love one another, we also ought to sacrifice in tangible ways.

QUESTIONS AND THOUGHTS FOR REFLECTION

- Read Psalm 23. How comfortable do you feel about God's provision for your life? Do you believe you have enough?

- Read Acts 4:5-12. When have you gotten into difficulty for exercising your Christian faith and values? If never, why not?

- Read 1 John 3:16-24. The writer notes that we may find being called sheep unbecoming. He goes on to mention that the epistle of John addresses followers of Christ as "little children." Would you prefer to be a sheep or a child? Why?

- Read John 10:11-18. Which of your assumptions about God have been turned upside down? How did this come about?

Senior pastor, Hyde Park United Methodist Church, Tampa, Florida; author of numerous books.

It's hard enough to be scrutinized when you've done something wrong. It's even more difficult when you've done something right. Peter and John do a good and right thing: They heal a man born lame. When healed, the man jumps up and makes a spectacular show of himself in the Temple. That act of healing and the ensuing celebration attract a crowd of amazed people. That's when Peter begins preaching the truth about Jesus, the possibility of forgiveness, and the reality of the Resurrection.

None of these actions merit trouble. But before long, Peter and John are hauled before the religious legal experts to answer for themselves. Nothing tests our moral compass quite like being questioned for doing the right thing. Like confronting a friend for self-destructive behavior. Or challenging a politician with immoral policy positions. Or pressing for reforms within our faith community.

Peter and John bring a powerful Exhibit A to the trial: the testimony of the healed man himself. When the interrogators see the well-being of a man who can now walk, "they had nothing to say in opposition."

This is what the truth does. This is what belief in the Resurrection does. It demonstrates even to the most ardent skeptics the possibility that God works in surprising ways. Despite pressing Peter and John to cease their actions and stop preaching the gospel, the religious leaders release them. They escape punishment, and public support now favors them.

It may be hard—seemingly impossible—to stand up for God's truth and goodness when you are persecuted for doing so. But there's a reason that Jesus in the Beatitudes calls us blessed when we do.

God, grant me the courage to stand up for you when it is difficult to do so. Amen.

Psalm 23 is a cherished scripture because it expresses a lot about life in the real world. It does not paint a picture of a perfect life in which days are always sunny and simple, when our relationships with others are friendly and uncomplicated. This psalm understands a life with shadows and valleys, especially in the face of death. It gives us permission to acknowledge our enemies, neither denying their existence nor being consumed by their threats. Whether those enemies are human beings or other imposing forces, the psalmist knows we face them.

And that's why it is odd that its opening words seem so unfamiliar to us: "The LORD is my shepherd, I shall not want." The psalmist may not have wants, but we sure feel like we do. In fact, we allow our wants to drive us. We tend to assess our lives not based on what we have but on what we haven't yet acquired. We compare our lives with those around us and listen to the messages of material desire from our culture. We want to be more admired, more respected, and more appreciated. We want to have the best house and the best car. We want to wear clothes that won't embarrass us and sport bodies that others envy. We want to have the brightest children, the most accomplished career, and the most adorned trophy case.

But this psalm offers a contrary message: God has already given us everything we need. And the future tense of the verb suggests that we "shall not want," no matter what happens next.

So while this psalm brings comfort, it challenges us in a significant way: to find contentment in the present day, to locate God's blessings in our lives, and to give thanks for them.

God, thank you for supplying all my needs. May I be grateful for your sustenance daily. Amen.

We may find it insulting to be called a sheep. That's what this psalm seems to do. We often have disparaging images of sheep as dim-witted, bumbling, and prone to wandering. And as accurate as that may be in describing us at times, it doesn't seem like a very endearing self-image.

Both the psalmist and the Gospel speaker know what sheep are really like. The attributed author of the psalm is David, whom we first meet when he is tending sheep in the field, watching them, caring for them, and protecting them. And when Jesus describes the life of a shepherd in this reading from John, we get some insight into a sheep's life.

"My sheep hear my voice," Jesus says in John 10:27. "I know them, and they follow me." Jesus says not only is it acceptable for us to be like sheep, but it is compulsory for sheep to know the voice of their shepherd. The relationship between shepherd and sheep is one of familiarity, which means that Jesus knows us fully and deeply. We are not a random combination of protein and water, taking up space on the planet with no meaning in life. We are people with a purpose, known intimately by the God who created us and by Jesus who offered his own life for us. And our only task is to allow that shepherd to lead us to green pastures, to still waters, and in paths of righteousness.

We may feel dim-witted, bumbling, and prone to wandering. But Jesus knows us intimately, and Psalm 23 reminds us of the command he gave his disciples and gives us all: "Follow me."

God, thank you for knowing me fully. In you I find my truest purpose and meaning. Teach me to follow you. Amen.

The epistle writer appears to assume that the Christians of his day are *not* following the way of love. He offers an epistle whose central theme is the call to love. To be Christian means to love. We cannot separate the two; the definition of one is intricately tied to the other. A doctor cannot intend to inflict harm; a carpenter must know how to handle a hammer. The number one job description of the follower of Jesus is to love— not seek revenge, not harbor resentment, not fail to forgive.

The kind of love the writer talks about is not a squishy sentimentalism. He knows little about candy hearts and chocolate valentines. When this letter was written, Christians were persecuted for their allegiance to Jesus; a profession of faith in Christ could sign their death sentence. Where the human instinct in these situations might be to flee in fear or sit in passive acquiescence, John calls them to a tough kind of love born of strength and stamina, based on principle and bent toward justice.

This kind of love does not amass riches and privilege for personal benefit but helps those who cannot help themselves. This kind of love is not self-seeking but self-sacrificial, laying down lives for others. This kind of love does not simply *say* the right things but *embodies* love with action. This kind of love, as exemplified in the story of Peter and John in Acts 4:5-12, stands up for justice against the oppressed despite persecution from the powerful and privileged. This love is truthful and tender.

And the author reminds us: It is precisely the kind of love that God has for us.

Dear God, help me to love others, even when it is costly to do so. May I remember that through Jesus, this is the way you love me. Amen.

You can tell a lot about the speaker and the speech by the opening line. If you hear the words, "Ladies and gentlemen, children of all ages," you are probably listening to a circus ringmaster introducing the big show. If you hear, "Dearly beloved, we are gathered here," it is probably a minister welcoming people to a religious observance. But if you read the words, "Little children," then you may be reading First John. Eight times throughout the epistle, John addresses early Christians in this way and therein underscores his central message of love.

But it's more than that. First John was written during the time of the Roman Empire, which was built on a strict hierarchy of power. At the top was Caesar, followed by the government leaders, the militia, and so on, all the way down the ladder. And at the bottom of this hierarchy—even below women—were children. They were often bought and sold as slaves, moved from family to family as mediums of exchange. They had no rights of their own and were the least of all Roman life.

Then along came Jesus, who told the disciples that the kingdom belongs to them. That alone was a defiant message against systems of oppression and abuse. But it was also a theological game changer. God favors not the powerful—but the powerless. God sides with the marginalized and the disenfranchised.

When the author calls followers of Jesus "little children," it is not just a term of endearment. It is a reminder that during hardship, they have not been forgotten by God. They may be devalued and dehumanized by others, but God loves them and favors them. And guess what? You are a little child of God too.

Dear God, I am grateful to be your child. Thank you for loving me, even when it is hard for me to love myself. Amen.

Shepherd appears to be a favored occupation in the Bible. Abraham, Jacob, Esau, and Amos were all shepherds. Moses became one while on the run. David was a singing shepherd before he became king. And then we recall the Bethlehem shepherds, the first to hear the news about Jesus' birth.

The Bible probably values shepherds more than biblical people did. Society despised and often marginalized shepherds. Being a shepherd warranted no fame or glory; the vocation largely garnered public ridicule and humiliation.

So, for Jesus to name himself the "good shepherd" would shock John's audience. Jesus, in effect, says that he will become the object of ridicule and scorn much as the common shepherds were. As he often does throughout his ministry, Jesus takes conventional wisdom and flips it on its ear.

But here's another reversal. Shepherds eventually sacrificed their sheep, providing the means through which people could make blood offerings in the Temple and restore their relationship with God. Without the shepherds, there would be no sheep, no means to sacrifice and, ultimately, no restoration of divine relationship.

Jesus, in identifying himself as the good shepherd, says this: "I know my own and my own know me. . . . And I lay down my life for the sheep." This shepherd is not in the business of leading his sheep *to* slaughter but saving his sheep *from* slaughter. He does not allow them to die but dies in their place. This is the most radical reversal of all: The shepherd is sacrificed, not the sheep.

God, thank you for Jesus' sacrifice, that I may be in relationship with you. Amen.

The theme running throughout both the Gospel of John and the epistles of John is this: Just as God has loved us, so must we love one another. This reverses our culture's conventional wisdom. Our culture pushes us to think of ourselves first and to climb ladders of success and fame.

Jesus flips that assumption upside down. He says the first will be last, and the last will be first. He states that he came into the world not to be served but to serve. He tells us if people gain their life, they will lose it; but those who lose their life for his sake will find it. And he says that the greatest kind of love we can demonstrate is laying down our lives for our friends.

So, the questions that confront us are these: What is God calling us to surrender for the sake of others?

What prideful notion must die in order for us to practice the healing act of forgiveness?

What material possessions must we release in order to give sacrificially to someone in need?

What ambition must we surrender so someone can achieve his or her dreams?

What act of self-sacrifice do we have to perform in order to see justice in a world of injustice?

What is God calling us to give up so someone else can experience the gift of life, love, peace, and joy?

Jesus gave up his life. Only the God we serve would do something as radically unexpected as dying so that others could live. If we follow this Jesus and if we have the image of this God within us, we are called to do the same. What is God calling you to do?

God, thank you for the new life you have given me through the resurrection of Jesus. Help me embody resurrection and new life for others. Amen.

A Braided Love

APRIL 23–29, 2018 • ANN FREEMAN PRICE

SCRIPTURE OVERVIEW: Two primary themes emerge from our readings for this week. In Psalm 22, we find the promise that even faraway nations will turn and worship the Lord. The book of Acts provides partial fulfillment of this promise. Through the action of the Holy Spirit, a court official from distant Ethiopia hears the gospel and can take it home to his native land. The Johannine readings focus on the theme of abiding (remaining) in God. "God is love," the epistle states, so all who claim to abide in God manifest love to the world. The author pushes the point: If we maintain animosity toward others, we cannot claim to remain in the love of God. In John, Jesus states that we must remain in him if we want to bear good fruit for God.

QUESTIONS AND THOUGHTS FOR REFLECTION

- Read Acts 8:26-40. What boundaries do you draw? How would God view such boundaries given what you know of God?

- Read Psalm 22:25-31. How will you create a daily remembering of God? How will you tell the story?

- Read 1 John 4:7-21. How do you comb out the tangles in your life—in relationships, in your work setting?

- Read John 15:1-8. How secure do you feel about being attached to the vine? What has God done in your life to make it more productive?

Active laywoman, Sparta United Methodist Church, Sparta, New Jersey; author and freelance writer.

She was three years old and loved swimming with her family at the pool but hated having her tangled hair combed out at the end of the swim. The grandmother spoke quietly, talking in a soothing tone as she combed the messed-up hair, "It was fun swimming today. You were so brave to jump in; the water didn't seem cold at all." The tangles slipped out as the voice continued, "I love coming with you to swim, and actually I love getting your tangles out too." As the comb tugged and slipped and slid through the hair, it became time to braid it—separate the hair into three parts, start near the top, one over, one under, the other over, the other under, and the voice continuing.

Though the task at the pool involved getting tangles out of the hair, the overarching theme was love—the love of the grandmother for the little girl, the love of the three-year-old for the grandmother. The quiet voice, the gentle hands. Love pervaded all—just as it does in these verses from First John. Love each other—period. Love God—period. Feel God love you—period.

The *New Interpreter's Bible Commentary* talks about this passage as being braided, like the little girl's hair above. As you read the words of these verses, you hear the words tumble around one another, a strand going over, then one going under, over and under, and woven together.

Take time to read these verses aloud. Use a soft and loving voice like the grandmother in the story. Then commit the seventeen words in the last half of verse 16 to memory and carry them through your day: *God is love, and those who abide in love abide in God, and God abides in them.*

Remind me, O God, to abide in love throughout this day. Amen.

A Braided Love

Remember the elements of three: First, God is love. Second, those who abide in love abide in God. Third, God abides in them. *Abide*—we don't say the word much anymore. Someone once painted a word-picture for me of abiding being like leaning against a large tree and letting yourself sink into that tree. That's abiding.

Abiding means staying in touch with God. Jesus did that in his life. He sometimes separated himself from other people, even from his disciples, so that he could reconnect with God. That time away, that time set aside, also provided an opportunity for God to be in touch with Jesus—time for Jesus to listen. Listening deeply supports the being in touch. And you may have to rearrange your life to achieve that time apart.

A woman drove to physical therapy twice a week. It was only twenty-five minutes away, and she sometimes stopped in the town to go to a store or to check the used-book shelves at the library. But most of the time she drove there and came back home. At home she always had a list of tasks to accomplish.

One day as the woman drove home from therapy, she realized that halfway home she passed a small, peaceful-looking lake. On this particular day she pulled into the fairly vacant parking lot. It was cold and she stayed in her car, but she took some time to see the lake. In those set-aside moments, she also took time to connect—to be in touch with God—to abide.

At the close of the passage, the author issues the challenge to love. Verse 19 declares that we love because God first loved us. And verse 21 puts a *must* into the words: "Those who love God *must* love their brothers and sisters also" (emphasis added).

God, help me know you are always available to me. Help me notice where I can pull over and be in touch with you. Amen.

A Braided Love

Jesus says, "I am the vine, you are the branches." The Bible makes numerous other references to vines. "Now, inhabitants of Jerusalem and people of Judah, judge between me and my vineyard" (Isa. 5:3). "Yet I planted you as a choice vine, from the purest stock" (Jer. 2:21). "You brought a vine out of Egypt; you drove out the nations and planted it" (Ps. 80:8). Now Jesus says, "I am the vine, you are the branches."

Dave, a man in my Bible study class, looked thoughtful as the group discussed this passage. He then said, "You know, I have a wonderful picture in my mind of the vine and the branches, and I think of that being Jesus and me. And God is the gardener who prunes when it's necessary." Dave laughed and confessed, "And with me, sometimes it really *is* necessary." He then continued, "I also love the idea that other branches are woven around my branch. That's all of you and also people I don't even know. We are connected and need to bear fruit."

We are the branches—now, today. God ensures our productivity. Jesus' instruction to his disciples involves connectedness and responsibility. We pray and bear fruit. Jesus in his ministry gave many clues as to what bearing fruit could look like: forgiving, loving, caring for orphans and widows, feeding the hungry, visiting those in prison, releasing captives, welcoming the stranger, and so on.

Vines sometimes chaotically intermingle but retain a sense of being braided together. Again a braid has three parts: the vine, the branches, the fruit; Jesus, us, acts of love.

God of vines who prunes carefully, hold me in your love and encourage me to look at the fruit I am bearing. Amen.

I watch the vine outside my window—the green leaves in spring look soft and gentle—and yet the vine is tenacious. It has been there all winter, readying itself for a new season.

Often we desire to express our independence, but the truth is we cannot produce fruit away from the vine. Jesus even reminds us, "Apart from me, you can do nothing." A life spirit flows through the vine. There is a connectedness between abiding in Christ and bearing fruit. There is a connectedness between our becoming disciples and bearing fruit and glorifying God. Our interwovenness and interconnectedness make us one: vine, fruit, Christ, us.

But we can miss the connection and the fruit born of that connection. Two friends were talking about an event that took place five or six years before. One said to the other, "You know, I've always remembered that on that particular day you took the time to listen to me—not just politely but really listened to me. Your listening saw me through a number of rough years. I always meant to say thank you and never did."

When we act in love, we bear fruit and sometimes do not know it. The passage closes with these words: "My Father is glorified by this, that you bear much fruit and become my disciples." Once again time interweaves: now, then, today, tomorrow, first, last. It's not a matter of *first* bearing fruit and *then* being a disciple. It takes time and many acts of love to "become." And always it glorifies the Father.

God of love, help me stay connected to you and bear fruit daily. Amen.

An Ethiopian eunuch has charge of the money for the queen of Ethiopia. He rides in a chariot, holding and reading the scroll of Isaiah. He is returning from Jerusalem where he had gone "to worship." He had probably been denied entrance to worship there, however, since he was both a foreigner and a eunuch. Throughout history, power or tradition draws boundaries to exclude people.

Exclusion may relate to people of different races, the inclusion of women, sexual orientation, differing native languages. Many aspects can cause people to draw boundaries.

Exclusion and boundary-drawing can start when we're still very young. A kindergarten teacher named Vivian Gussin Paley wrote a book titled *You Can't Say You Can't Play*. She worked successfully with children ages four and five to teach them about including other children rather than shutting them out.

It is interesting that the verses the eunuch is attempting to understand are the very verses Christians believe Jesus fulfilled as messiah. The verses speak of injustice done to an individual. Does the eunuch take these verses personally? Humiliation, justice denied. He asks Philip to whom these verses apply. Philip then shares the good news and the eunuch chooses to be baptized. A foreigner, a eunuch, baptized and ushering in a new age. Clearly exclusion is not a God-drawn boundary. The Spirit directs Philip throughout the account. Philip listens and follows through, acting in the name of justice and love.

Look closely at your own life. Whom do you exclude? Where do you draw the boundaries around your community or the church you attend?

God, help me pay attention to acts of exclusion, and guide me to listen to you carefully. Amen.

This scripture deals with more than exclusion, more than boundaries, more than power. Three in the story are active in their own way: the Spirit, Philip, and the Ethiopian. And each of these three illustrates a significant theme.

The Spirit (angel) talks to Philip at the beginning of these verses and directs him and continues to direct him throughout.

Philip pays attention, hears the Spirit, and follows directions.

The Ethiopian searches, asks questions, even becoming creative toward the end of the story by saying, "Here is water! What is to prevent me from being baptized?"

Today's passage continues our braid of three, and all three weave themselves through our lives too.

Are you listening, tuned in to know when the Spirit prompts you to take action? Are you ready to release your plans for God's plans? Are you prepared to tell the story, to interpret as the Ethiopian asked Philip to do when he said, "How can I [understand what I am reading] unless someone guides me?"

Are you searching also, just as the Ethiopian was doing? Do you ask questions in order to grow?

And when the stranger has an idea, are you ready to move and do what you never before dreamed you would be doing?

Are you ready to go down into the water?

God, may I listen, follow, and go into the water. Amen.

Notice these three phrases from Psalm 22: "All the ends of the earth shall remember and turn to the LORD; and all the families of the nations shall worship before [God]. . . . Future generations will be told about the LORD."

"All the ends of the earth shall remember and turn to the LORD." Make this a daily remembering—a daily turning to God, finding some time to pause and turn.

"And all the families of the nations shall worship before [God]." Within each day, find a space and a time to worship. You may gather with a community you are part of and worship together. You may take some gratitude time when you are alone and give thanks for God's gifts. You may choose to avail yourself of some meditation time where you are quiet and listen. You might take some "lake" time and simply consider creation.

"Future generations will be told about the LORD." All of us take responsibility to tell the story. Speak the parables, memorize a psalm, study the scriptures—so future generations will know how to abide. This abiding leads to an abundant life rich in love, busy in doing, and verbal in telling.

Take the braids from each passage, and weave them together. Sometimes I create a spoken chant, learn it, and then walk with it—around the yard, around the house, or lie in bed at night and say it. Create a beat and fit the words into that rhythm: Abide in love. Bear fruit. Worship—and tell the story. Listen, and do justice. And abide in love.

Keep watching the braid. Make sure it has balance; make sure God is part of it. Comb out the tangles and whisper words of love.

God, help me create a braid in my life, a weaving together of abiding in you, bearing fruit, doing justice, and telling the story to others. Amen.

A Wonderful World

APRIL 30—MAY 6, 2018 • J. MICHAEL RIPSKI

SCRIPTURE OVERVIEW: The Acts passage continues to tell the story of the advance of the gospel. The Holy Spirit falls on a group of Gentiles. They believe and are baptized, thus showing God's inclusion of all peoples in the plan of salvation. Psalm 98 is a simple declaration of praise. All creation will sing to and rejoice in the Lord. The two passages from John are linked by their emphasis on the relationship between love and obedience. We do not follow God's commandments in order to make God love us. On the contrary, because God has first loved us and we love God in return, we follow God's teachings. Jesus provides the model for us, being obedient to his Father out of love.

QUESTIONS AND THOUGHTS FOR REFLECTION

- Read Acts 10:44-48. When has the Spirit of God brought you to a new understanding?

- Read Psalm 98. Does the guest of honor's coming to judge the earth make you feel easy or uneasy? Why?

- Read 1 John 5:1-6. Is your life one of "oughts," "musts," and "shoulds"? Do you impose them on yourself, or do they come from others? How do you move toward loving obedience?

- Read John 15:9-17. How do you experience yourself as a manifestation of the Logos?

Assistant professor and university chaplain, Cumberland University, Lebanon, Tennessee.

In his book, *The Sacred Canopy: Elements of a Sociological Theory of Religion*, sociologist of religion Peter L. Berger describes how we humans create worlds of meaning to combat the anxiety that accompanies the fear that life is absurd. These created worlds have our human fingerprints on them. Our worlds are as impermanent as we are. The human response is self-deceit, which Berger calls "false faith." We cast a "sacred canopy" over our worlds and, "Ta dah!" we assert they are God's creations—not ours. And, since they are God's, they are permanent. Who are we to think we can change them?

In Peter's world a separation existed between the clean and the unclean, between the acceptable and the unacceptable. Then one night in a dream, a voice speaks eternal truth: In God's wonderful world all is "clean."

God removes the sacred canopy of Peter's belief system, and Peter sees life differently. Now his life has new meaning and purpose. His mission will take him precisely where he had assumed he should not go—to the unclean whom he'd believed would make him unclean too.

Peter shares the gospel with them, and something happens that turns his world upside down—again. Before Peter has finished his sermon and given the altar call, "the gift of the Holy Spirit had been poured out even on the Gentiles."

"The circumcised believers who had come with Peter were astounded." They believed in a divinely ordained order: 1) be circumcised; 2) believe Jesus is the Christ; 3) be baptized; 4) then receive the Holy Spirit. This Holy Spirit has a mind of its own. The Spirit blows where and how it will and creates a new world with a new law and order.

Holy Spirit, inspire in us your vision of your wonderful world. Amen.

"Can anyone withhold the water for baptizing these people who have received the Holy Spirit just as we have?" Peter realizes if the answer is no, all heaven will break loose among those who, like himself, have believed what religion has taught: God chose Us; God did not choose Them. Us and Them. Won't any religion worth its salt give true believers reason to view themselves as special?

The same Holy Spirit that brought to Peter's mind on Pentecost the prophet Joel's vision is doing it again: "In the last days it will be, God declares, that I will pour out my Spirit upon all flesh" (Acts 2:17). *All flesh.* Even Them?

I grew up in a time of separate water fountains, restrooms, classrooms, and restaurants. White people were considered superior, African Americans inferior. Or so the culture, including some churches, taught.

I know a church whose leaders had strategized with its pastor about how the church would respond if an African American were to show up at a Sunday service. The decision was made to allow Them in and to seat Them. But the pastor would not issue an invitation to church membership. Today an African American pastor serves that church.

Some of Us encountered Them and experienced in Them the image of God that is in Us. That realization, like Peter's, confronted Us with a crisis: How can we not include Them?

The same Holy Spirit breathes life into all humanity. It opens our eyes to see one another as the sisters and brothers we didn't think we had. The mighty wind will blow until everything false disappears. When that happens, what a wonderful world it will be.

Recall times when the Holy Spirit used your experience of Them to make it impossible not to view Them as Us.

The psalmist invites us to join the choir for the Lord's victory celebration. There will be instrumental accompaniment, strings, and brass. Even Creation's children will be there: the seas roaring, the floods clapping their hands, and the hills alive with the sound of music. What a victory party it's going to be!

But wait. It's a party with a kicker. The guest of honor will judge the earth. Come to the victory party and then be told you're a loser? When the church's new-member dinner is over, you're told about self-sacrifice and handed a pledge card. Or does the psalmist trust that the victory celebration results precisely *because* the guest of honor will "judge the world with righteousness, and the peoples with equity"?

It all depends on your perspective. If you've spent your life winning by taking advantage of the weak, then the weak will likely enjoy this party more than you will. If your victories have come through intimidation, manipulation, and deceit, this won't be like the champagne and caviar parties you're used to. If you're used to attending black-tie galas with the rich and famous, you may feel uncomfortable with these come-as-you-are attendees in their thrift-store attire. If you're complaining about how tired you are of going to dinner parties, be prepared to overhear conversations about this being the first party some have ever attended. And, if you're Creation and you've been ravaged, this day of victory has been delayed way too long. In fact, you've doubted that it would ever come.

Then again, maybe in the judgment of the guest of honor you and others will discover grace. You'll find that by losing, you and the whole world win. Now that's a victory worth celebrating.

Eternal Guest of Honor, teach me that in losing I win a wonderful life and a wonderful world. Amen.

Some in the early Christian communities asserted that Jesus was fully divine but not fully human. The writer calls them liars and antichrists (2:22). It's easy to appreciate his passion. If Jesus Christ is only divine, then we who are "only human" can't expect to love and live as he did.

Lest we assign such heresy to the dustbin of church history, an honest reading of our history reveals that the doctrine is alive and well. Whenever Christians focus exclusively on the satisfaction and substitutionary doctrines of the Atonement, what "Jesus did for me on the cross," the focus shifts from our obeying God's commandments as Jesus did to our believing that only Jesus did.

Scholars suspect the distortion may have risen from the Docetists or the Gnostics. Both camps value Jesus' spirituality to the exclusion of his humanity. The Word that became flesh and lived among us, it is claimed, did so to free us from the flesh the Word became.

For this reason the writer of First John affirms that believing Jesus is the Christ entails our being born of God as he is. When we are born of God, we become conquerors with Jesus of the world of dehumanizing belief and social systems. Our faith is not an intellectual assent to an esoteric doctrine but a transformation into being the transformers of the world that Jesus shows us we really are.

It makes all the difference in the world whether we limit Jesus by thinking of him as an abstract idea to be believed or as a voluntary enlisting into an group of people that seeks to love the world as God so loved it through his only Son. When such love conquers the world as we know it, what a wonderful world it will be.

O God, make us your children as revealed in Jesus. Amen.

Today's epistle lesson and tomorrow's Gospel lesson describe the radical difference faith in Jesus Christ makes in who we become through him. Both offer antidotes to a religion of "oughts," "musts," and "shoulds."

The epistle writer's familial language of parent and child depicts the conversion from the self-centered motivation of legalistic obedience with its preoccupation with reward and punishment to self-denying yet self-fulfilling love. We become, by the truth the Spirit conceives in us, a "love child." As such, we love all that the Parent loves. When we love what and whom the Parent loves, we trust and obey not because we are forcing ourselves to do something contrary to who we are but rather because not doing so would be contrary to who we are. God's commandments, Jesus shows us, are not burdensome because they give expression to our soul's deepest desires. However, "not burdensome" isn't the same as "easy."

With this faith we join Jesus in conquering the world as we know it so it may become the world he reveals to us through his own obedience to the divine commandments.

Most teenagers view their parents' commandments as burdensome. *Obedience* is another word for doing what they don't want to do. They can't wait to leave home and be free of the rules. Wise, loving parents accept that parenting is not an exact science. They try to release the tether of parental control in manageable increments. This way the discipline that has been authoritatively enforced slowly becomes inward self-control.

And, sometimes, by the grace of God, when we observe the child, we see a resemblance to the parent.

Spirit of Truth, help us conquer the world with love by living as though the victory is already won. Because when we do, it is. And what a wonderful world it will be. Amen.

While yesterday's epistle metaphor of parent and child is susceptible to a hierarchical power dynamic, today's Gospel lesson portrays a mutuality of the divine-human relationship that is so nonhierarchical it's mind-blowingly incredible and disconcerting. As Marianne Williamson observes, "Our deepest fear is that we are powerful beyond measure. It is our light not our darkness that most frightens us" (*A Return to Love: A Reflection on the Principles of "A Course in Miracles"*).

Here Jesus continues the good news that seems too good to be true. Earlier he told his followers that they will do what he's done and "greater works than these" (John 14:12). They will not be ignorant, for the Helper, the Holy Spirit, will call to memory the wisdom he's taught and demonstrated. Now he calls them his friends and promises the Father will give them whatever they ask in his name.

As long as the relationship is that of master-servant, Jesus knows he spares his followers the vulnerability that friendship entails. But their naïve bliss of ignorance is dispelled when Jesus makes known everything that the Father has made known to him.

Living in this holy friendship is what Jesus means by "abiding" in the love that entails laying down one's life. In the laying down of one's life, fruit is born that will last. We enjoy eternal life by living life the way Jesus shows us is eternal.

The fourth-century church father, Athanasius of Alexandria, professed of Jesus Christ: "He became what we are that we might become what he is." It's not our idea. Jesus chose us. When we become his friends, the relationship turns us into manifestations of the Word, the Logos, as Jesus was.

Hear Jesus say, "Let us be friends and see what a wonderful world it will be."

A Wonderful World   155

Sometimes I don't understand Jesus. This is one of those times. I've wondered what his joy is that he not only wants in me but also desires to complete in me. How does keeping God's commandments and abiding in love contribute to this joy? I guess I am joy-challenged. Could the following experiences qualify as the joy Jesus desires for us?

The voice said, "You may not remember me." I did, despite the decades since I'd taught him in a college religion course. He went on, "At the time I was struggling with the belief system of my childhood. I was outgrowing it and was confused. You told me I wasn't crazy. Struggling with my questions and doubts was necessary for making my faith my own. I just wanted to thank you and let you know that today I'm an ordained minister and a prison chaplain." When I hung up the phone, I felt what I believe is joy.

Early in my ministry I invited the former president of Rust College to preach at the church I served. He was an ordained United Methodist pastor. He would be the first African American preacher to fill that church's pulpit. In that day such an event was still out of the ordinary and risked controversy. As the date neared for his visit, I learned that a family would leave the church if he preached. I informed the administrative board that if the invitation was not rescinded, the church would lose a family. When the floor opened for discussion, only one person spoke. He said, "I don't see how we can withdraw our invitation to someone due to skin color and still call ourselves 'Christians.'" The vote was unanimous. And I felt what I believe is joy.

By the way, the family left but returned. And I felt what I believe is joy.

Let us sing: "Joy to the world, the Lord is come!" And what a wonderful world it will be!

Sent into the World

MAY 7–13, 2018 • ANNE DELOACH NELSON

SCRIPTURE OVERVIEW: Scripture tells us that in our lives in general, and especially in our spiritual lives, we need to distinguish what is true from what is false. The psalmist admonishes us to follow the truth of God and flee wicked ideas. This week we read about Judas, who did not follow the psalmist's advice—with disastrous results. In Acts the apostles seek to replace Judas among their number with a witness to Jesus who has not been led astray. In John's Gospel, Jesus bemoans the loss of Judas and prays that his followers will cling to his words. The author of First John testifies that God's words are trustworthy above all others. They bear witness to the life that comes through Christ, whose legitimacy was confirmed by his ascension into heaven.

QUESTIONS AND THOUGHTS FOR REFLECTION
- Read Acts 1:15-17, 21-26. When have you experienced the disruption of a meaningful relationship through death? How did you eventually recover?
- Read Psalm 1. When have you allowed the world to define you? How do you avoid that?
- Read 1 John 5:9-13. How have you come to know the testimony of God in your heart?
- Read John 17:6-19. What helps you sense God's presence and protection?

Member, Hickory Flat United Methodist Church, Canton, Georgia.

Every night my daughter, Sarah, asks me to tuck her into bed and pray with her. She's comforted to know that as the night comes, she's safe and secure because I'm nearby, loving her and praying for her. We all gain a sense of security in having someone we love close by.

John 17:6-19 reminds me a bit of Sarah's bedtime ritual. In the passage Jesus offers his disciples an understanding of his abiding presence with them. The disciples anticipate a figurative dark night coming when Jesus returns to the Father. So Jesus prays for his disciples: "Holy Father, watch over them, . . . keep them safe from the evil one. . . . Make them holy" (CEB).

Jesus has been sharing daily life with his disciples for several years. He's their teacher and mission-giver, beloved rabbi and friend. He sends them out and lovingly receives them at the completion of their mission. So he prays for them specifically—that when he is gone, they will continue to go out in mission to the world and be protected, safe, and holy.

We teach, guide, and show our children the way to live and send them out into the world. Then we lovingly receive them when they return home to us, helping them feel safe from the darkness. When they grow up and eventually leave home, we pray that God goes with them.

The time nears for Jesus' disciples to go into the world without him. He will no longer send them off and receive them. The same is true for disciples today. When we go out in mission to the world, Jesus' prayer encompasses us. God goes with us, protects us, keeps us safe, and makes us holy.

Jesus, thank you for your loving prayer for us—protecting us, keeping us safe, and making us holy. Amen.

For many Christians the word *evangelism* evokes a sense of fear and dread. The word often conjures up visions of preachers on street corners with bullhorns or stacks of spiritual tracts to be passed out door to door.

What does the word *evangelism* actually mean, and what does it actually call us to do? The original Greek word for evangelism translates as "gospel" or "good news" and as a verb, "to announce" or "bring good news." Evangelism is what God calls us to do: announce God's good news to the world.

In this passage, Jesus prepares his disciples to go into the world to share this gospel message. In so doing, he prays that the disciples "will be one just as [God and I] are one" (CEB). Before sending them out, Jesus calls them into relationship with God, with himself, and with other believers. What a blessing that we aren't asked to do this evangelism thing alone!

This good news is "eternal life: to know you, the only true God, and Jesus Christ whom you sent" (John 17:3, CEB). The gospel message isn't simply eternal life eventually; it's relationship now—with God and with others. Richard Rohr, in his book *The Divine Dance: The Trinity and Your Transformation*, says the Way of Jesus is "an invitation to a Trinitarian way of living, loving, and relating—on earth as it is in the Godhead" (46). Living, loving, and relating with God and living, loving, and relating with people is how we can evangelize, sharing this gospel in our everyday lives.

Jesus prays this hope-full prayer before crossing the Kidron Valley on his way to the Garden. Jesus, knowing his death approaches, still speaks of the good news of love, relationship, and eternal life.

Holy Father, no matter what we face, may we continue to speak your good news of relationship, love, and life. Amen.

Sent into the World 159

The author writes his epistle to believers who are trying to understand what eternal life means and how to live a holy life in the context of the Christian faith. These believers would benefit from a faith manual; instead, the author speaks to them in metaphor: Jesus is light; Jesus is love; Jesus is life. The conclusion of the book, our text for today, speaks of God's testimony about Jesus as truth.

But this "testimony" surely doesn't sound like one that would hold up in a courtroom, where just the facts and the whole truth are demanded. Light, love, and life aren't compelling testimony when proving points in court. So, why does the author use this type of language "to testify"?

Because we're not speaking of courtrooms. We're speaking of human hearts, our inmost spiritual place. Facts and figures speak to the mind; those who saw Jesus raised from the dead can speak to eternal life out of fact. But what about those who came after? God witnesses to the human heart through the Son. Our testimony comes secondhand from God the Father to the Son. "Those who believe in the Son of God have the testimony in their hearts."

I can explain in factual, scientific terms how my children were formed and born. But I'd need poetic words (like *light* and *love* and *life*) to describe how holding them for the first time felt.

Love and light and life testify to our human hearts of the hope of eternal life, which has already begun. We know this because we live in the joy and fellowship of God today and every day.

Gracious God, may we testify to your love, light, and life. Thank you for the gift of eternal life. Amen.

ASCENSION DAY

Christians in the early church stressed the importance of Jesus' ascension by including it in both the Apostles' and Nicene Creeds. But churches today tend to gloss over Ascension Sunday. Sandwiched between Easter and Pentecost (after having already endured the long days of Lent), we're too tired to work up special music and decor. Not to mention that the story is rather strange—Jesus goes up into a cloud. What?

But the early church viewed Jesus' ascension as its call to action. After the Resurrection, Jesus spends forty days with his followers, proving he has indeed overcome death and "speaking about the kingdom of God." Jesus encourages his followers to "wait . . . for the promise of the Father." More power is on the way—the power of the Holy Spirit!

And as different as the day's political kingdom is from the kingdom of God, so too will be the work of the Holy Spirit when the mission kicks into high gear. The Spirit will guide the disciples whether they are in Jerusalem, Judea, Samaria, or the ends of the earth.

This passage closes with Jesus' ascension. Again, the disciples seem confused, staring up into the clouds. Two men in white robes inquire, "Why do you stand looking up toward heaven?" It's a good question and one we must ask ourselves. Are we looking toward heaven, or are we looking for mission opportunities? Will we be ready to act when the Spirit nudges us? Let us pray so, as we move from promise to fulfillment.

Holy Spirit, help us to wait, to see, and to act. Amen.

In Luke 22:28-30, Jesus notes that the Twelve will rule over the "twelve tribes of Israel." With the death of Judas, the "wholeness" of the Twelve is incomplete—eleven is one too few. So the disciple community prepares to select Judas's replacement. Peter emphasizes the need for a personal relationship with Jesus. The two candidates put forward, Matthias and Joseph called Barsabbas, have been with Jesus and his followers from the time of John's baptism through Jesus' ascension, living together in community, witnessing to the Resurrection, and experiencing a change in heart and life.

The two candidates understand the call to share, to serve, and to live in faithful community, loving God and loving neighbor. I expect that's why they are the top two candidates for the spot of disciple number twelve. They aren't seeking the limelight; they are faithfully serving, as they have been all along.

The community casts lots, and Matthias becomes the new number twelve. Oddly enough, the New Testament doesn't mention either man again. Does one go off to pout? Does one flaunt his new position? We can only assume, given their background, that both men go on to serve in love, bearing witness to the kingdom of God among them.

We are all allotted a share in Jesus' ministry. Sometimes we feel unfit or unready. We may not feel that we have the personal history with Jesus. Maybe the call to mission seems too difficult. The Lord knows our heart; we simply love God and love neighbor.

Loving God, help us to serve faithfully—loving you and loving our neighbors—in our ordinary, everyday lives. Amen.

Psalm 1 calls us to love Torah, to love and live in "the law of the LORD." Torah moves far beyond a mere book of rules. Only when we understand its scope can we fully embrace its meaning. In essence, the law is the sum of all God's good gifts to Israel. We joyfully ponder the goodness of each day, throughout the day. We often find that hard to do in our crazy-busy lives.

Lauren Winner, raised Jewish, converted to Orthodox Judaism in college and converted to Christianity during graduate school. In her book *Mudhouse Sabbath*, Winner speaks to the fact that as a Christian she misses the Jewish practices that helped ground and sustain her belief. She writes, "Jews do [spiritual practices] with more attention and wisdom [than Christians] not because they are more righteous nor because God likes them better, but rather because doing, because action, sits at the center of Judaism. Practice is to Judaism what belief is to Christianity" (ix). She argues that by practicing our faith, we will come to understand and believe more fully.

We follow Jesus, our living Torah, in a way that is itself a God-centered practice and belief. Jesus sums up this living in his own words: *"You must love the Lord your God with all your heart, with all your being,* and with all your mind. This is the first and greatest commandment. And the second is like it: *You must love your neighbor as you love yourself.* All the Law and the Prophets depend on these two commands" (Matt. 22:37-40, CEB).

When we delightfully ponder and live into God's word, we can faithfully serve the world.

Father, help us love your word and ponder your goodness daily, so that our practice, our belief, and our action can lead to righteousness. Amen.

One of my favorite stories is Max Lucado's *You Are Special*. It tells of the Wemmicks, uniquely created wooden people carved by Eli the woodworker. Every day the Wemmicks give one another stickers: golden stars for good looks and fine talents; gray dots for things that seem "less than." One Wemmick in particular, named Punchinello, accumulates only dots—a lot of them, which makes him very sad.

One day Punchinello meets a Wemmick to whom no stickers stick, neither the golden stars nor gray dots. He asks her how that can be, and she explains that she visits her creator, Eli, every day. Eli helps her know who she truly is. He affirms her as special and because of that affirmation, the stickers don't stick. As Eli states, "The stickers only stick if they matter to you."

This story reminds me of how often I allow the way of the world to define me, rather than God's way. I often wonder what our world would be like if we all visited our Creator before heading out in the world each day. What if we pondered God's word, experiencing the quiet endurance of a steadfast faith, fully and firmly planted, drinking from the streams of living water? If we did, wouldn't we value our personal Jerusalems, Judeas, Samarias, and ends of the earth more? Wouldn't we then walk in the way of the righteous, producing good fruit? And wouldn't we better resist the way of the wicked?

True blessedness, true happiness, is the gift of a firm foundation. The true reward of God's word comes in allowing it to transform us.

O God, may we walk in the way of righteousness, delighting in your law. Amen.

Praying Our Way to Pentecost

MAY 14–20, 2018 • SAFIYAH FOSUA

SCRIPTURE OVERVIEW: This week's readings remind us of the powerful role of God's Spirit. For many Christians, the Holy Spirit is the person of the Trinity we understand the least. In the book of Acts, the Spirit empowers the apostles on Pentecost to speak in other languages and, in so doing, initiates the establishment and missional reach of the church to the wider world. The psalmist uses a wordplay on *ruach*, the Hebrew word for breath or spirit, to teach us that God's Spirit was present at Creation and is necessary for the ongoing survival of all life. Paul writes that God's Spirit confirms that we are children of God and can approach God with confidence, not fear. Even the disciples feel uncertain about what will happen when Jesus leaves, so John provides Jesus' assurance that God will remain with them and with us through the teaching of the Holy Spirit.

QUESTIONS AND THOUGHTS FOR REFLECTION

- Read Acts 2:1-21. How often do you take solace in praying in private without moving to take action in the public square? Which site is the more comfortable for you?

- Read Psalm 104:24-34, 35b. Where have you seen evidence of nature's resources being spent? How can you help?

- Read Romans 8:22-27. How consequential is it to you to acknowledge that God prays for us and the world? Why?

- Read John 15:26-27; 16:4b-15. What instructions do you wish Jesus had left for you?

Elder, Greater New Jersey Annual Conference of the United Methodist Church; currently serving as Associate Professor of Spiritual Formation at Wesley Seminary at Indiana Wesleyan University.

Here stands Pentecost, tall, proud, and long-legged. Originally a celebration for the children of Israel, now the "birthday" of the Christian movement—repurposed by the faithful who have seen Jesus! More than a holiday or a holy day, Pentecost is a movement born of prayer: not prayers judiciously measured or metered by a three-minute kitchen timer but protracted prayer. Those who prayed their way to Pentecost prayed with no ability to predict or dictate the answer. They followed instructions and waited to be clothed with power from heavenly places. (See Luke 24:49.) But, how does one prepare for a baptism with the Holy Spirit that no one has known or understood?

Early on the day of Pentecost, the transformation begins with wind and fire. Holy Spirit! Empowering God's people to move from the safety and seclusion of an out-of-the-way prayer room into the scrutiny and vulnerability of the public square.

Just as the Spirit of God drove Jesus into the wilderness to be tempted, so the Spirit drives these Pentecost people into a wilderness after their baptism. They do not go silently; they go speaking the message of God in ways their neighbors have never seen before. For them, temptation takes the form of a label: Drunks! Drunks! These praying Pentecost people do not succumb to the temptation of embarrassment or allow negative comments to draw them back into lockstep behavior. Peter, standing boldly with the eleven, calls upon the prophets to help the crowds make sense of their actions. "God's Spirit has been poured out on your sons and your daughters. We are simply fulfilling God's word."

When we are tempted to retreat to the comfort and safety of the fold, remind us, O God, that we also have a message for the public square. Amen.

Jesus still has much to say in this last conversation before his arrest and execution, but the disciples cannot bear what he needs to tell them. The rest will have to come later. Why? Probable reasons range from their preoccupation with grief over the prospect of losing Jesus, to spiritual inexperience, to spiritual immaturity. Perhaps the weight of the happenings of that Thursday evening keeps them from hearing the rest of the conversation. It may be more likely that they are unprepared for the conversation because they cannot imagine the coming days.

Some days I wonder how my departed grandparents would have coped with the present digital era. As a child, I watched them move from wash pot to wringer washer to electric washer and dryer! I cannot imagine how I would have advised them about computers or smartphones.

Thirty years ago, we could not conceptualize the global terrorism we face today or a Christian response to the resulting mass displacement of peoples. One hundred years ago, who could have imagined the collateral damage of twenty-first-century warfare and the moral issues it has raised? Or the surprising impact of Christianity's global expansion upon Western Christianity? Like the disciples, we also need God's continued guidance.

Jesus understood that the disciples would face new challenges—just as we do. Thank God that we have received the Spirit of truth to guide us through "the things that are to come." The Spirit of truth, the Advocate, reminds us of Jesus' message and the spirit of his ministry. We are not alone. God is with us.

God, we give thanks for your Spirit, who will lead us through the living of these days and remind us of Jesus' ways. Amen.

It is small wonder that we hesitate to pray about some things. Our culture has wired us to believe that we can dictate the results as we pray our prayers. On days when we do not know if we will face a speed bump or a derailment, we are tempted to retreat from prayer for fear that we might somehow initiate the wrong outcomes. Then, we find ourselves alone at the very time we most need God's presence. But take heart! Paul reminds us that the Spirit intercedes for us according to God's will.

In my family, everyone around the table recited Bible verses for table prayers. My grandmother often smiled as she remembered a three-year-old who sat at such a table. He was too young for long memory verses but old enough to know that we were thanking God for daily food. One day, when his turn came, he refused the verses usually reserved for small children like "Jesus wept" or "God is love" in favor of something much more ambitious. He had heard his older brother say, "The Lord is my shepherd, I shall not want," so he clasped his hands, closed his eyes, opened his mouth, and shouted, "Sheppity, sheppity, SHALL NOT WANT!" Surprisingly, no one in the family laughed or rushed to correct him.

Perhaps it is okay that we do not always know how to pray. As self-sufficient as humankind thinks itself, we more closely resemble the three-year-old. We see through a glass darkly and find ourselves on a journey that often makes no sense to the finite mind. Only the One who sits on the circle of the earth and views the end and the beginning at the same time knows if we are truly on course, and, thankfully, that One is also praying.

Lord, in your mercy . . . pray for us. Amen.

Some days even the most silver-tongued find it difficult to pray. Stupefying days, like 9/11, when life's harshness has slapped the words of prayer out of our mouths. Prayerless days because we are in a lightless season. Days when even the usual flood of insipid prayer "suggestions" to God is dammed up and replaced by mute silence because we have come to realize we do not know how to pray—not about this.

Surely Paul knew those days intimately. Romans 8:22 notes a world (both creation and creature) groaning in anticipation of complete redemption. Throughout Acts, we read that Paul himself had a reason to groan. Though he overcame his past, others never did. He was held in suspicion by Jewish Christians and often beaten or persecuted by those whose cause he once championed. Ironically, both Paul and those who persecuted him believed theirs was a faithful response to God. Paul understands what it is like not to know quite how to pray. But he quickly reminds us that the Spirit will pray alongside us. "We do not know how to pray as we ought, but that very Spirit intercedes with sighs too deep for words."

We mirror the groaning of Paul's time: groaning polluted waters, groaning endangered species, groaning polluted and endangered peoples. We live in a polarized world that needs Pentecost. Nations are fragmented and distant from one another, and even the church is engaged in varying forms of civil war! How can we possibly discern the need or how to pray? But we are not alone; the Spirit of God is praying with us.

Spirit of God, pray with us in our weakness. We are confused and cannot find our way. Lead us to Pentecost again. Amen.

If you knew you were about to leave your family abruptly, what would you say to them? John 14–17 essentially records Jesus' leave-taking conversation with his disciples. We learn so much in this long discourse on the Holy Spirit that we almost miss an important point: The church serves as a testimony. Collectively, we are the body of Christ, arms spread across the seven continents.

We are Pentecost people, gathered from every nation, tribe, and tongue. The engine that propels us is the Spirit of God. Together, we testify to the way of Jesus: The way God wants us to live. Jesus Christ has been among us and we are his people, his kin, having sworn our allegiance to continue his mission.

Individually, we also testify. Jesus is the living Lord; we have seen him and been transformed by the experience. Watch him and see.

We cannot help but wonder if the Holy Spirit weeps today over the many missed opportunities and false testimonies offered in the name of God over the last two thousand years. We can do little about the past failures of the Christian family, but we can commit to testify on this day.

Holy Spirit, empower me to testify to Jesus. I covenant with my eyes to look for God's goodness in people. I covenant with my hands to do good and with my tongue to do no harm. I covenant with my arms to reach lovingly toward those who have been cast aside and with my feet to walk in places where Jesus would walk. Holy Spirit, Holy God, today I make a covenant with you to look for opportunities to testify. Amen.

The grandeur of creation reminds us of God's glory. Trees older than countries, canyons deeper than rivers speak of the power and majesty of the God who created them. Birds tiny enough to perch upon a blade of grass and the God who knows each time they touch the ground remind us that God has intimate acquaintance with our footfalls. The prehistoric-looking sturgeon and the brightly colored tree frog received life from a God who values diversity.

How can we, the ones created in God's image and likeness, also be the ones guilty of diminishing the spectacular beauty of creation? Have we become so preoccupied with the sight of our own faces in the reflecting pool that we missed the face of beauty around us? Or, worse, did we become preoccupied with taming that which God created to testify?

The glorious words of the psalmist bring to mind the stark realism of nineteenth-century poet, Gerard Manley Hopkins:

> Generations have trod, have trod, have trod;
> And all is seared with trade; bleared, smeared with toil;
> And wears [humanity's] smudge and shares [humanity's] smell: the soil is bare now, nor can foot feel, being shod.
> And for all this, nature is never spent.

Despite our misuse, the earth continues to be a beautiful and glorious place. Professional photographers still vie with one another to offer testimony through one breathtaking photo after another, while amateurs strive for one clear picture of a hummingbird in flight! How glorious is God's creation! "May the glory of the Lord endure forever."

God, we confess that humankind has diluted the beauty of creation through the pursuit of its own agenda. Forgive us, and teach us your ways. Amen.

PENTECOST

While some come only out of a sense of duty or obligation, others have saved up to make the pilgrimage. It is Pentecost Day in Jerusalem, a fixed holy day for God's people. From far and near the people come, acknowledging that those other people would also be there—Jews and proselytes from outlying areas with the smell of distance on their clothing and the sound of strangeness in their speech: Parthians, Medes, Elamites, Mesopotamians, Cappadocians. Where did you say they came from? Libyans, Egyptians, Arabs. Is this really in the Bible? Were they really there too? Yes.

Our story begins on Pentecost Day in Jerusalem when familiar ones and strange ones gather for a typical religious holiday. They have gathered for years, though they do not always understand one another or the songs and ritual speech of the gathering. Acts 2:1 states they were all together in one place, which brings the theater to mind. Once we are all together in the theater, the lights dim and the story begins. The lights do not dim in Jerusalem that Pentecost Day, but the wind blows and there is sighting of fire on the heads of some. Imagine the sigh of relief when Peter rises to make sense of the scene.

Our story began on Pentecost Day in Jerusalem. It began with the messiness and confusion that happens when wildly diverse people try to do anything together. It began with a commitment to gather as God's people, even when we feel a bit ambivalent about the goings-on of the gathering. More significantly, our story began with the God of wind and flame.

God of wind and flame, thank you for breaking into the ordinariness of our existence with a fresh demonstration of what it means to be one people. Amen.

Born Anew

MAY 21–27, 2018 • ARIANNE BRAITHWAITE LEHN

SCRIPTURE OVERVIEW: This Sunday we will celebrate the Trinity, the Christian belief that God is one being and exists in three persons: Father, Son, and Holy Spirit. Christian theologians point out that there are many references to this doctrine throughout the Bible. In Isaiah, the voice of the Lord asks, "Who will go for us?" not, "Who will go for me?" In the passage in Romans, Paul speaks of all three persons of the Trinity: We pray to the Father through the Spirit because of the work of the Son. Jesus also speaks to Nicodemus about the role of all three persons of the Trinity. This may not be the simplest of Christian doctrines, but it is foundational because it explains the nature of God and God's work throughout human history.

QUESTIONS AND THOUGHTS FOR REFLECTION

- Read Isaiah 6:1-8. When have you experienced a cleansing by God, resulting in a greater willingness to serve?

- Read Psalm 29. As you read about the power of the Lord's voice, do you find yourself frightened or drawn in? How approachable is God to you?

- Read Romans 8:12-17. What have you released to God? What bitterness has taken its toll on your soul? Are you ready to let it go?

- Read John 3:1-17. How has your life been reshaped by the Spirit? How did sins and failings manifest in the new creation?

Mother and ordained minister, Presbyterian Church (USA); living in Wilmette, Illinois; blogs at www.ariannebraithwaitelehn.com.

God offers Isaiah a fresh invitation to serve. Isaiah finds himself entangled in regret and shame as he witnesses God's glory and holiness firsthand. He doesn't feel "clean" enough to be God's messenger.

Yet God meets Isaiah with grace. God loves and accepts Isaiah, but Isaiah doesn't perceive this. He needs a tangible act of love and coal-cleansing to transform his heart and perspective.

This outward action causes an inner rebirth. When God asks for a messenger, Isaiah feels ready to respond. With love and eagerness, he feels emboldened to say immediately, "I'm here; send me" (CEB).

Like Isaiah, we gain courage and confidence when we recognize God's love for and belief in us. God meets us in our shame, guilt, or disappointment, doing whatever it takes to cleanse us and make us whole.

God offers you a tender cleansing of the way you've understood your identity and your place in God's work. What risks might you take today in your relationships, conversations, priorities, and even seemingly small choices that grow from how God knows you? What hang-ups and beliefs hold you back from bravely embracing God's call on your life?

Patient God, you come to my fearfulness and boundaries with mercy and compassion. You come to my small vision with an eye, a word, a touch that swallows the universe in love. You come sharing forgiveness as an unlocked door, always giving me a chance to change. Please work within me today to bring my soul to new life and courageous trust. Amen.

The focus of Isaiah's objection and God's subsequent healing is the lips. The mouth holds much power. As Rabbi Abraham Joshua Heschel says, "Words create worlds."

God links the mouth with creative power. Creation originated with God's speech. God spoke and everything we see, touch, and love came into being. And when Christ came to live with us, side by side, we came to know him as the "Word made flesh."

We've all experienced times when words someone spoke destroyed us inside. Or times when a word of encouragement changed everything.

Like Isaiah, God births anew our mouths today, asking us to use our lips to create a world of blessing. The words you pray over your children, partners, friends, those you love, even those you can't stand, all enliven the world with light.

Each night as my husband and I put our two-year-old daughter to bed, we say over her a prayer I wrote based on the fruit of the Spirit: words that remind us what a life after God's own heart looks like and how God produces this in and through us even when we struggle to see it. I encourage you to pray this prayer on behalf of someone you love. Insert her or his name. Maybe write it down on a scrap of paper, in a journal, or an e-mail. Let your heart rest there, giving thanks for this person and knowing God prays this over you every day.

Loving God, I pray for your love in _____'s life. I pray for your joy in _____'s heart. I pray for your peace in _____'s soul. I pray for your patience in _____'s words. I pray for your kindness in _____'s actions. I pray for your goodness in _____'s sharing. I pray for your faithfulness in _____'s relationships. I pray for your gentleness in _____'s spirit. And I pray for your self-control in _____'s choices. May this fruit blossom in and through _____. Amen.

Psalm 29 invites us into a realm resembling that of Isaiah 6—a place bursting with God's glory, power, and rule. This psalm takes its place in the "enthronement psalms," or songs of praise describing God as king.

Another connection with the Isaiah text is the central role of words and voice. "The LORD's voice" occurs seven times in the Common English Bible. The psalmist praises the powerful effects of the Lord's voice on the world. With seven as the number of wholeness, this symbolizes the way God holds power over the entire world.

People witness with awe the authority of God's voice, then use their voices to worship ("everyone shouts 'Glory!'" CEB). The description of God's voice feels violent and intimidating—it "unleashes," "shakes," "convulses." It can make us uncomfortable. However, notice that while the psalm depicts God as completely unapproachable, it closes with the psalmist calling on God for strength and peace.

The psalmist acknowledges the ruler's responsibility to provide for the people. His faith and soul are reborn as he takes hope in the awesome Ruler upon whom he can call! Worship is exactly that: an invitation to be born anew as we focus on praising God and entrusting God with the desires of our heart. How does this understanding change the way you live? How can you more deeply invest in your own faith community to help worship become a vital, life-changing experience for all?

Powerful and providing God, I also shout, "Glory!"
"Glory!" with my words today.
"Glory!" with my decisions today.
"Glory!" with the prayers I place in your hands.
Amen.

Running is a passion of mine. A year ago, I found myself on a muddy trail run, praying over and struggling with some areas of life where I yearned for freedom. For a long time, I thought freedom—being born anew—would come through one glorious breakthrough. I'd burst through the bramble into a fresh clearing, never to turn back or tread the old path, ready to leave the darkness of the forest behind me.

But as I kept living and kept running, I saw a trail that ran parallel to my life: a path where I would weave and wind—not always moving forward—but still make progress. The dirt sticking to the crevices of my shoes, the roots kneaded by the soles of my feet, the pine needles collecting in my hair, all taught me that what I wanted to leave behind actually became my story. And that with Christ there are no dead ends or pointless loops. They are part of the journey, the story; I need them.

Romans 8 encourages us to embrace new life through the Spirit and the freedom of confident living in Christ. We can see our past as stepping-stones to where we are now. We are always on the path to becoming, and we can choose at any time, through God's grace, to take a fresh path.

Perhaps your past sins and struggles can be your best teachers. Can you embrace them as midwives in your rebirth? Let the Spirit lead you onto this new stretch of the path.

Loving God, as I take in what dim light I find within the trees and keep making each step on the uneven trail, help me trust. To trust I am not lost but burrowed in a womb of life-giving mystery. To trust I am reborn and already free. To trust in the mercy and beauty of daily rebirths. Amen.

Born Anew

Many circumstances can become invitations to rebirth: a move to a new community, a new role or relationship, a major loss, or an offer to try something fresh vocationally. It's often scary to encounter and embrace the invitation in any of these situations.

Romans 8 invites us to a freedom amid fear. Fear need not control us because we are "children of God" and "joint heirs with Christ." If our root identity is as God's children, then we share in the trinitarian family of Creator, Christ, and Spirit. We are like part four of the loving circle! If we live from our identity as God's children, then we can call on God as parent and find a divine nearness that settles our spirits.

Because of this promise in Romans 8, we experience rebirth both through releasing and receiving. We release the anxiety that's gnawed a tender spot in the bottom of our souls. We release our fear of the future's uncertainty (because it is uncertain, and that's okay. God will be with us). We release the simmering bitterness that's bubbled on the back burner for way too long. We release the unfair expectations, the frustrations and secrets we've carried for years. We release the stories we no longer want to live. And instead, we receive new life. We are freed to make courageous decisions, live generously, extend grace to all (including ourselves), and find peace amid ambiguity. Trust and an abundance mentality steer this new life.

Abba God, today I receive your love that promises I am your child. I receive your peace that reminds me all will be well. I receive your voice as the wise whisper I follow. I receive a new story. Thank you, God, that you enfold me in a giant embrace, releasing me to freedom and receiving me to love. Amen.

When my husband and I returned home from the hospital after I gave birth to our daughter, I remember thinking, *This precious child depends on me in every way. What do I do now?*

Children, while vulnerable and dependent, are also trusting and joyful in their sense of security. My daughter, now a toddler, completely trusts that all she needs is right here in the present moment and that I will be faithful in my promise to care for her.

This is how I understand Jesus' words to Nicodemus when he invites him to be born anew. The fresh life to which Christ calls us is one of vulnerability—the vulnerability of a child. When we are "born of the Spirit," we find our lives in the Holy Spirit's care, and we trust God to be the guiding and providing parent God promises to be.

It can feel threatening to become vulnerable and dependent. Nicodemus struggles to embrace this option, and I do as well. It is hard to live vulnerably in an image-driven, independence-idolizing culture, and it is all the more challenging to depend on the "unseen."

Jesus asks us to live from the seemingly invisible—the Spirit's work in us. But such dependence produces very visible results. When we hold life and all that's in it with open hands, we do not find security in our surrounding circumstances or ourselves. We pray deeply and listen intently. We become open to change, set free in our vulnerability.

Lord Jesus, because of your love and mercy, it is never too late to be what you call me to be. May I be open to what I never expected before, never experienced before, and never thought was possible. May I live in delightful dependence on you. Amen.

TRINITY SUNDAY

Jesus came not so God would see or love us differently but so we could see and love God in a fresh way. Jesus offers Nicodemus and us the renewal of our eyes and hearts, our mouths and minds, where we experience wholeness simply because God holds all the pieces together.

Our new birth in God doesn't require that we leave behind who we used to be. God uses that, integrating it into the fresh creation we are now. Like the potter who takes the same clay and refashions a new creation (Jeremiah 18), God made our essence good. We simply need to relax into a formless shape in God's hands, trusting the Spirit to mold us.

Franciscan priest Richard Rohr states in his book *Falling Upward: Spirituality for the Two Halves of Life*, "Salvation is sin turned on its head and used in our favor" (60). God doesn't judge or jettison who we've been. God's redeeming hands take those parts, transforming what once held us back into something with which we can bless others.

I painted a picture for my niece with a heart in the canvas's center. Within the heart, the viewer sees both light and dark colors. In my note to my niece that accompanied the painting, I told her that each one of us holds light and shadow within us, and we need both. All we experience, all we are, coalesce in shaping us. It's challenging to embrace a wholehearted life; but when we do, we experience rebirth and wholeness.

Perfection is not being flawless but being whole.

Loving God, I know the power a broken heart can generate. The world changed because of your broken heart, and we discover beauty in the pieces. I embrace all I've been and all I am in you. Make me whole today. Amen.

Serving God on the Ground

MAY 28–JUNE 3, 2018 • JAMES MELCHIORRE

SCRIPTURE OVERVIEW: The call of Samuel and the intimate language of the psalmist this week reflect God's knowledge of and care for each individual. God sees each one of us, no matter where we are in life and no matter how far we might feel from God. Paul seeks to encourage the Corinthians with this same truth. Believers may be afflicted, perplexed, persecuted, beaten down, even killed; but they are never defeated. The power of a personal God flows through them, even if this is not evident to the eyes of the world. We likewise should be personally caring toward those around us. Jesus models this in Mark, demonstrating that showing mercy is more important than following even religious regulations, for mercy is the heart of God.

QUESTIONS AND THOUGHTS FOR REFLECTION

- Read 1 Samuel 3:1-20. When has a young person in your life or that of someone you know had to face the devastating consequences of a single bad decision? How did that affect your actions and behaviors?

- Read Psalm 139:1-6, 13-18. When have you experienced that life has no guarantees? How did you sense God's presence in that time?

- Read 2 Corinthians 4:5-12. How do you attempt to be open to seeing Christ in everyone you meet?

- Read Mark 2:23–3:6. When do you, like Jesus, try to be proximate to persons in need? How has that changed your life?

Reporter, video producer, and documentarian, New York City; serves in leadership for a volunteer-supported interfaith shelter for women who are temporarily homeless.

So about those disciples who walk through the fields "to pluck heads of grain" on the sabbath, leaving Jesus to endure the rebuke of the religious authorities. We can infer from scripture that Jesus was an observant Jew, educated and versed in the traditions and customs of the faith. And while the core group of apostles was coming together, I suspect that other excited, curious, and hopeful people who didn't know all the rules also followed Jesus.

My church in New York City does a lot of "urban ministry," which means people show up at Sunday worship who first connected through the food pantry, tutoring program, our theater, or even our homeless shelter. This phenomenon is common with congregations in larger cities in the United States and even more prevalent at most churches in the Global South, the "majority" world. Holy Communion is not the first meal folks eat at church; they've already dined in the soup kitchen. Suppose a man walked into your church on Sunday morning wearing ragged clothing and pushing a shopping cart of belongings up the aisle. Something motivated that person, something drew him to your sanctuary. Maybe the same thing that motivated those grain-plucking field walkers; maybe the same guy, Jesus of Nazareth. If that happens, here's your to-do list: goodwill, kindness, and, above all, patience.

Years ago, I produced a video about the then-new Common Cathedral movement. The street minister, a priest, told me many of her congregants on the Boston Common preferred outdoor worship and only reluctantly went inside because "buildings have assumptions." Let's not be like those buildings.

Creator God, inspire us with a spirit of welcome to the new thing you're always doing, even when—especially when—it may feel uncomfortable to us. Amen.

Paul writes that God has shone in our hearts to display God's glory in the face of Jesus Christ. So, in Jesus, we get a glimpse, a hint of what God is and who God is. We believe Jesus is fully divine and fully human, the latter quality more difficult because we can't imagine Jesus sharing our frailties. Even harder is seeing Jesus in the humanity around us. Dorothy Day wrote of a custom among early Christians to keep a room ready for any stranger needing shelter "not because the man or woman to whom they gave shelter reminded them of Christ, but because — plain and simple and stupendous fact—he [or she] was Christ."

Let's admit, the people in whom we see the face of Christ are greatly determined by how we identify our faith and our politics. Whether we lean left or right politically in the United States, we will not so easily see the face of Christ in people whose values and opinions differ greatly from our own.

Most difficult to see the face of Christ, for both sides, is on social media where we inhabit echo chambers filled with people who think like us and become enraged at those on the other side because we cannot understand how they believe as they do, so opposite from ourselves. We're looking at the world through different lenses, for sure. Yet the task, the instruction, the requirement really, for both sides, comes back to that idea of seeing the face of Christ. Difficult, unless we trust in God's assistance. And we can trust, because God has this long-established tradition of always showing up in our midst. So let's expand the meaning of that word *Emmanuel* we use in Advent to: The God Who Shows Up. Let's watch for those sightings.

Redeemer God, grant us the vision to see the face of Christ in everybody we meet. Amen.

A pastor of ours often would say "God is God—and we're not." The psalmist may have that idea in mind while musing on God's eternal nature, creative powers, and skills at surveillance. The psalm also offers a complementary viewpoint: God considers all of us very important. We often say, "We're all God's children," giving little thought to the implication of that statement. In this scripture, the idea of God functioning as a parent—an involved, detail-oriented parent—is inescapable.

When I was growing up, a child of parents who had been formed by a Roman Catholic, urban, blue-collar, immigrant-influenced culture, we didn't discuss *self-esteem*. I never heard the term until college, and I was skeptical for a long time. Why do people need this ego-massage? Over the years, I have been humbled by my hard-hearted, judgmental attitude. Though the Italian peasant immigrants who were my grandparents and with whom I grew up had little privilege, I now have a lot. I grew up in a stable home with two parents, three grandparents, and a sister. I am a straight, white male. I had to try very intentionally to put myself in the shoes of a person who was bullied or struggling with a psychological or emotional challenge or who grew up surrounded by domestic violence or substance abuse. I am still working on getting better at practicing empathy, not only offering it but also receiving it. Psalm 139 reminds us that we are beautifully made, that the smallest aspect of our lives is known and considered important to the Creator of the universe—the God who's always paying attention to what we're doing, what we're thinking, how we're hurting. And the God with the power to be the ultimate "helicopter" parent.

Eternal parent, keep us mindful of the needs of our neighbors shaken by fear and anxiety, and direct us in ways we can offer your shielding love and care. Amen.

If "visions were not widespread," then those days are like our days, perhaps like all days. Some folks find that thought disappointing, longing for a miraculous manifestation of God's power, an instantaneous healing on television. Let's not be patronizing toward our neighbors who feel this way. In scripture, people constantly ask Jesus to legitimize himself with a "sign."

We don't always need drama. Once on a Volunteers in Mission trip, a fellow pilgrim talked about how faith, or being "born again," can come differently to each of us. Maybe a sudden blinding light—Saul outside Damascus. Or more frequently, a shade opening, light gradually filling the room. The sacred in the ordinary. Verse 7 tells us Samuel lacks direct experience. Nothing has changed. Young people learn from behavior we model; they need to make mistakes without devastating consequences. Once on jury duty, we were brought into a courtroom where the nineteen-year-old defendant was on trial for burglary, with a twenty-seven-year-old prosecutor and a twenty-six-year-old public defender. I asked to be excused—the defendant reminded me of my youngest son and his friends. I couldn't judge the kid. He should be allowed one mistake. I keep thinking about this ear-tingling news Samuel must bear: Eli's sons will be killed; Philistines will seize the ark; and Eli himself will die. It's a lot to lay on a young boy. Children never choose such burdens but still receive them today: family illness, food insecurity, a father's incarceration, fleeing from war. Maybe this scripture is a call to action, to recognize our obligation not only to our own children and grandchildren but to *all* God's children. A call to ease their burdens and provide a worthy model for behavior—in whatever community we live.

Sustainer God, grant us illumination and strength to live up to your call to build up the beloved community. Amen.

Serving God on the Ground

When we read of Jesus' face-offs with religious authorities, our attitude toward the Pharisees can easily move from indignation to righteous indignation to self-righteous indignation. Let's take a breath. Veneration of the sabbath was not some crazy, corrupt idea of the Temple elite. I mean, it's in the Ten Commandments. I live in New York City and our United Methodist congregation runs a shelter for homeless women in partnership with a neighboring synagogue. When we have fellowship activities, I attend Friday evening services. I never cease to be impressed by Jewish observance of Shabbat, which doesn't even begin to address its value in bringing holy balance to our lives. And since Jesus and his fellow Jews lived under occupation by a foreign, pagan empire, maintaining customs became even more important. We can stipulate that sabbath observance is and was good.

So let's consider the man who, other than Jesus, is the primary character in this story. His hand is withered, useless. He's caught up with this itinerant rabbi who's famous as a healer. He believes Jesus can cure him. Sure, Jesus could delay until Havdalah (the end of Shabbat). But this man is afraid to wait. There's no guarantee he'll cross paths with Jesus again. He can't miss his chance. If one of the Pharisees had spoken with this man, he might come to a different conclusion. I suspect Jesus' anger stems more from their ignoring the man—their hardness of heart—than from their religious legalism.

When we meet each other one-on-one and swap our personal stories, our insights evolve, as many in the United States learned in the journey toward marriage equality. Institutional thinking wields power, except when compared with human relationship.

Lord of all people, may our eyes always be open to the need for human dignity and the ways we can work to ensure it. Amen.

That the life of Jesus may be made visible in our mortal flesh." That's very aspirational and not easy. Tougher than seeing the face of Christ in everyone we meet. Jesus is such a worthy model—the best example, many of us would say—so it makes sense to emulate him. But how?

One answer: Imitate a practice we witness in Jesus throughout the Gospels—being proximate. He's proximate to events, to people, to the context of life in his society. When a terrified woman faces an early morning stoning by what sounds like a lynch mob, Jesus is there. Likewise with a man crippled for thirty-eight years who's lying by the pool of Bethesda. Jesus gives special attention to the poor and marginalized, and he's also proximate with the privileged in society. He has a sycamore-tree conversation followed by dinner with Zacchaeus, two encounters that change the previously dishonest tax collector's life. He agrees to see the sick daughter of Jairus, the synagogue leader but interrupts the trip to heal an unnamed hemorrhaging woman. So for the life of Jesus to be more visible in our mortal flesh, how then are we to live? Volunteer at a shelter for temporarily homeless women. Share a meal with someone whose circumstances differ from yours, and discover the similarities of your lives. Tutor a bilingual child, whose undocumented parents speak only Spanish at home, and learn the challenging nature of the child's life. Join a prison support group and get to know the parents of a son caught in the web of mass incarceration. The news photographer Robert Capa is quoted as saying, "If your photographs aren't good enough, you're not close enough." We can say the same for Christian discipleship. Let's get proximate.

Jesus, keep us near the Cross and near to our neighbors with all the small crosses they must bear. Amen.

Psalm 139 can trigger contradictory feelings depending on mood, atmosphere, and circumstances. A God of constant surveillance can be unnerving, especially since we all have moments when we're not proud of how we look or what we're doing. I can think of such episodes in my own life. The older I get, though, the more comfortable I am with the idea of accompaniment, that we have a "companion" God. The passing of time helps, because life teaches us rather emphatically that there are no guarantees; no bulletproof vests to protect us from illness, job loss, romantic heartbreak, poverty, political oppression or, ultimately, death. Yet, the reality that God doesn't "protect" us doesn't mean God abandons us.

Two years ago, I had an extremely eventful medical year for the first time in my life: a cancer diagnosis despite no symptoms, three surgeries, a blood clot, and a toxic reaction to chemotherapy that hospitalized me twice for a total of seven days and included more than two dozen units of intravenous potassium. As much as I might have wanted to rewrite history and remove my new status of "cancer survivor," God did not intervene to prevent any of that. However, I never doubted that God accompanied me through it. Did I see God? Not in any dramatic beatific vision, no. I did see nurses and doctors practicing their medicine on me; neighbors offering to take walks with me; colleagues bringing hard candy on days I couldn't eat; family, friends, and congregation members sending e-mails, paying visits, preparing meals, and sending cards. The God of the psalmist who is "acquainted with all my ways" is not a God of bulletproof vests but rather the God who walks beside us in shoes that we and our neighbors wear each day. The God who assures me and you that when we "come to the end—I am still with you."

God, thank you for accompanying us, now and forever. Amen.

Who Are We Really?

JUNE 4–10, 2018 • MELISSA EARLEY

SCRIPTURE OVERVIEW: We sometimes struggle to believe in the power of a God we cannot see. The psalmist declares that God is greater than any earthly king and will preserve us in the face of our enemies. However, in the time of Samuel, the Israelites demanded a human king to lead them into battle, as other nations had. God was not enough for them. Paul admonishes the Corinthians not to repeat this mistake. We should not think that what we can see is the ultimate reality. What we see is temporary; what cannot be seen is eternal. Perhaps Jesus is teaching a similar idea in this somewhat troubling passage in Mark. Jesus is not against family, but he is emphasizing that human families are temporary; spiritual family is eternal.

QUESTIONS AND THOUGHTS FOR REFLECTION
- Read 1 Samuel 8:4-20. How influenced by culture and neighbors are you? How do you attempt to keep your priorities aligned with God's reign?
- Read Psalm 138. How do you evaluate the "gods" in your life? How do you recognize when those gods have gained control of your life?
- Read 2 Corinthians 4:13–5:1. When life's circumstances overwhelm you, how do you avoid losing heart?
- Read Mark 3:20-35. Who is your spiritual family? Whom do you identify as your brothers, sisters, mother and father?

Lead Pastor, First United Methodist Church of Arlington Heights, Arlington Heights, Illinois; read her blog "Waking up Earley" at www. melissa-earley.com.

A friend of mine and I are going skydiving to celebrate our birthdays—his fiftieth and my forty-ninth. We will put on parachutes, be strapped to an experienced diver, get on an airplane, fly up to fourteen thousand feet, and then launch ourselves out into thin air. We will free-fall for sixty seconds and then pull the rip cord and glide down to the earth for a hopefully uneventful landing. Some of my friends and neighbors will think this makes more sense than being a disciple of Jesus.

Today's scripture reminds us that it's countercultural to follow Jesus. Jesus' family has come in an act of intervention, "to restrain him." Do they worry what the neighbors think or do they themselves believe Jesus is not quite right? Obviously, following the crazy man from Nazareth won't help our respectability. We won't receive heaps of praise from our neighbors. In fact, they may snicker at us behind their hands.

Following Jesus means daring to include the people our neighbors would leave out, serving those who can't pay us back. It means loving our enemy and forgiving those who hurt us. It means not caving in to the pessimism of our age or the false optimism based on nationalism or nostalgia. It means knowing deep in our bones that our value comes from our creation in God's image. Following Jesus means not fearing death because we know that we trust God with everything. We know the source of Jesus' power and continue in the sphere of its influence.

God, whose voice was heard through prophets we today would call crazy; whose love was made visible in Jesus of Nazareth, a man whose own family suspected he was not right in the head, set us free from the need to conform to our community, to our context, and to our generation so that we may go a little crazy in love with those you love. Amen.

Who Are We Really?

When I was in my midthirties, I took a sabbatical year and volunteered for an organization called International Child Care in Santiago, Dominican Republic. My coworkers and neighbors there expressed surprise that I wasn't married and had no children. The lay leader at the church I attended couldn't figure out in which small group I would participate. The small groups included a group for married couples, a group for widows, and a group for young people. I didn't have a spouse. I was too young for the widows group. I was advised to attend the group for young people. Though I liked being considered a "young adult," these young people were college age. I still attended church, but I didn't attend the small group.

"Do you have a family?" continues to be one of the first questions raised when someone meets me. I watch as a cloud of disappointment crosses their faces when I tell them I'm divorced and don't have children. They don't know how to place me or where I fit.

I have found belonging through Christian community. My best friends include a married straight couple in their early sixties, a single woman in her fifties, a gay man in his late forties, and a mother raising two boys under five.

When Jesus states, "Whoever does the will of God is my brother and sister and mother," he invites us to rethink our identity and our primary place of belonging. We may be a son or daughter, a brother or sister, a mother or father—but according to Jesus our primary identity is child of God, disciple of Jesus. In Christian community we receive the gift of family that transcends categories people might assign.

Loving God, help us live out our identity as your children. May we create communities of love, support, and forgiveness—true family. Amen.

Who Are We Really?

The fight over keeping the United States flag in the church's sanctuary had been bitter. It was bitter enough that it came up in conversation several years later when I first started my ministry with the congregation. The feud ended with an agreement that the flag would reside in the fellowship hall every Sunday except those that fell on national holidays. If I forget to move the flag into the sanctuary on the weekends of July 4, Memorial Day, and Labor Day, a member moves it for me.

When the Israelites ask for a king like other nations, they complicate their lives by creating a world of two realms: subjects of God and citizens of nations. As followers of Jesus we strive to be good citizens. We vote, run for office, write and call our elected leaders, and try to be informed on national and local issues. We hold our leaders accountable and insist that the government include the most vulnerable in its plans.

As followers of Jesus we can easily mistake national pride for discipleship. We live in an era when many of us quickly identify the prosperity of our nation with a sign of divine providence and think the victory of our political party is God's will. Therefore, it is jarring to read this story from First Samuel, which reminds us that a theocracy was God's first choice. Good kings will follow bad kings; bad kings will follow good kings, but all human governments will fall short. Good governments care about what is best for the people, but all governments are ultimately concerned about their own self-interest and maintaining their power. God proves over and over again that God's interest lies in giving God's self to us. That is what is best for us and deserves our primary allegiance.

God, our sovereign ruler, give us courage to live as your subjects while citizens of our nation. Amen.

Living is vulnerable business. We want to know if we are doing it right. Is that why "fitting in" has such a powerful pull on us? We steal glances to see how others are living their lives. It starts young and continues through adulthood—what kind of car, what brand of clothes? The questions become more serious: Should I get married if everyone else is? What's wrong with me if I don't want kids?

It makes sense to learn from our neighbors and to mine their experiences for lessons that might apply to us. How did you get your baby to sleep through the night? When did you know it was the right time to ask for a raise? The problem in this story of Samuel and the people of God is that the people forget what God has done for them. They forget that God led them out of slavery in Egypt and brought them to the Promised Land. They forget that God fed them manna in the desert and provided quail in the wilderness. Instead of trusting God, they choose to be like the other nations.

We fall prey to the same temptation when we let our neighbors' choices become our plumb line. When the fear-mongers convince us that the stranger is our enemy and that persons different from us are potential threats, we reject God. When we believe that we come first and allow the poor to fend for themselves, we reject God. When we believe that forgiveness is naïve and mercy is for fools, we reject God. We reject God because we forget what God has done for us. We reject God because we forget that our very existence is divine gift.

Remind us of your love, O God. Give us courage to rely only on you. Amen.

Who Are We Really?

I was tired. Tired of the apathy an affluent community felt for religion. Tired of cajoling people with packed schedules to make room for worship. Tired of begging people to give a little more money to the church instead of a coffee shop. The joy had gone out of ministry, and I was spiritually dead.

With news reports of refugees spilling out of Syria and Nigeria, children fleeing gang recruitment in Guatemala, and a people wanting to build a wall, it just didn't seem that anything we did in church really mattered. Preparing good sermons and meaningful Bible studies felt pointless. No one would show up anyway. I wanted out of local church ministry. I knew I wasn't doing the church any good in my current state, but I couldn't see other options for income. I told God to either make me love ministry again or get me out of it.

And I gave up. I quit trying to get people to come to events; no amount of catchy titles and compelling series had worked. I eased my furrowed brow and didn't sweat the church budget. I couldn't make people give more money. I accepted that worship would take a backseat to sports and the desperation of families for a quiet morning.

I surrendered to the power of God. The Common English Bible translates Psalm 138:7 as, "Whenever I am in deep trouble, you make me live again." That was my experience. When our church worried how we'd make ends meet, I took a staff member's suggestion for a noisy coin offering but designated it for missions. Sermon writing became a process of spiritual discovery, not marketing. Most surprisingly, Monday night Bible study became a place where my own spirit showed up. I gave up needing to be in charge, and the conversation about scripture's intersections with our lives deepened. I found life.

Merciful God, thank you for saving us in so many ways. Amen.

Who Are We Really?

I sing your praises before all other gods" sounds quaint to the modern reader, like something a tunic-wearing, harp-strumming psalmist sitting on a mountain gazing down at the temple in Jerusalem might sing. It sounds quaint until we remember all the other gods before whom we so often bow. The words get stuck in our throats when we begin to recognize the gods we turn to when we find ourselves in trouble.

A god is anything that we give primary place in our lives. What gets our best attention, priority use of our money, and our deepest devotion? What do we thank when things go well and on what do we rely when we are in trouble? That is our god. In my community, status through career and income is our god. Participation in sports, clubs, and the arts paves the way to entry to excellent universities so that children can land great jobs. Often that participation takes precedence over church participation and involvement, which doesn't hold the same promise of upward mobility.

Education is valuable, and a good job is an asset. But they are not eternal; God's love lasts forever. The downward spirals of the US stock market, the raiding of pension funds by corporate executives, and the collapse of the real estate market remind us that even the most upwardly mobile fall prey to the vagaries of the global economy.

This psalm is a song of defiance. It's a song of defiance against all that promises us what only God can give. We need to sing this song of praise more than God needs to hear it. We need to sing this song to ground ourselves once again in God's love for us.

God who is above all, we confess that the shining promises of wealth and status often distract us. Draw our attention back to you. Amen.

Who Are We Really?   195

I've never cared that much about heaven. I don't follow Jesus in order to guarantee my reservation for the hereafter. I'm not faithful so that when I die I'll go to Paradise by and by. Heaven is not the carrot on the stick or the reward for running the race or the moment of great vindication against my enemies. "The Statement of Faith of the United Church of Canada" says, "In life, in death, in life beyond death, God is with us. We are not alone." That is enough for me. In fact, it is more than enough.

Paul calls to mind the strong connection of our present reality with the past. He links himself with the psalmist when he states the following: "I believed, and so I spoke," a direct pickup from the Psalms. We have the strong foundation of faith with an added promise: "The one who raised the Lord Jesus will raise us also." We will be brought into God's presence.

We can live in this promise now. We don't have to wait until death. I have experienced sustenance in the midst of great loss. I have received courage to start again after an experience of shaming failure. I have been freed of old hurts through the gift of forgiving others.

God's grace isn't a bridge across troubled water. We don't get to avoid painful plunges. Yet God's grace is with us in the depths of suffering. God's grace is our breath when life crushes breath out of us. God's grace encourages us to surface from our "momentary afflictions[s]" and place our trust in what is not visible to the eye, that which is eternal. Therefore, "we do not lose heart."

Thank you, God, for giving us a light that cannot be extinguished and a hope that cannot be vanquished. Amen.

Who Are We Really?

Trusting in the Lord

JUNE 11–17, 2018 • DOUGLAS L. CARVER

SCRIPTURE OVERVIEW: From a human perspective, we tend to judge people by appearances: how attractive they are, how wealthy they seem to be. God's standard, however, is not outward appearance but the attitude of the heart. David was the youngest brother in his family, yet God knew his mighty heart and chose him as the next king of Israel. The psalmist declares that God gives victory to those who put their trust in God, not in the outward appearance of might. Jesus reinforces this truth with the parable of the mustard seed. Though the seed appears small, it grows into a robust plant. Paul tells the Corinthians that we should no longer judge people by what we see on the outside, for God changes what really matters—what is on the inside.

QUESTIONS AND SUGGESTIONS FOR REFLECTION

- Read 1 Samuel 15:34–16:13. What clear guidance has the Lord given you regarding an area of obedience in your life?

- Read Psalm 20. How has the Lord answered you when you called out during a critical moment in time?

- Read Mark 4:26-34. What prevents you from trusting God to use your testimony to lead others to Jesus Christ?

- Read 2 Corinthians 5:6-17. How does your trust in and obedience to God affect your personal conduct and your attitude toward others?

Chaplain (Major General), United States Army, Retired; living in Waxhaw, North Carolina.

A key military leadership principle is the commander's intent, whose primary purpose is to focus subordinate units on actions that must be accomplished to ensure mission success. The commander's intent is nonnegotiable, requiring unwavering trust from subordinate units in the commander's strategy, even when faced with unexpected events or temporary setbacks.

The Holy Bible is God's "intent" for all who trust and follow in obedience. The word of God directs our life journey and keeps us on the path of righteousness.

In 1 Samuel 15:3, God instructs King Saul to annihilate the Amalekites. Surprisingly, King Saul disobeys God's intent, sparing the Amalekite king and keeping any of the enemy's property worthy of salvage. In this costly decision, King Saul exercises utter disdain for the Lord's clear guidance to him. Saul's life quickly spirals out of control as he sets up a victory monument to himself, lies to the prophet Samuel, blames the people of Israel for his own willful disobedience, denies any wrongdoing, and insists that his intentions were honorable. When confronted by the prophet Samuel, King Saul confesses that he had chosen to listen to the voice of his people instead of the Lord. As a result, God removes Saul as king of Israel.

The Lord calls each of us daily to hear and obey divine intent for our lives as revealed in the inspired word of God. God desires obedience. We are to love God with all our heart, soul, and mind. This love allows us to live righteous, loving, and humble lives. Jesus Christ commanded us to carry the gospel to the ends of the earth. What is God's intent for your life? What clear guidance has God given you?

Loving God, lead us daily into your glorious presence. May we trust and follow your plan for our lives. Amen.

Employers have unique sets of criteria when selecting the right persons for leadership positions. They often ask for a variety of personal information to ensure they have a comprehensive picture of the potential employee—resume, financial stability, family information, references—the list is endless. Candidates who seek church planter positions are assessed for many leadership competencies such as visioning, compassion for the lost and the unchurched, spousal support, and personal giftedness.

A formidable task lies before the prophet Samuel. God has rejected Saul as Israel's king. Samuel is to find his successor in Bethlehem at the house of Jesse, a farmer and sheep owner. In Samuel's mind, the choice is obvious: Eliab, Jesse's firstborn. He seemingly has all the qualities people look for in a charismatic leader. To Samuel's surprise, God offers him a valuable lesson in selecting leadership: "[Mortals] look on the outward appearance, but the LORD looks on the heart." God views matters differently with ways and thoughts that go beyond surface talk and personal observation. God examines the heart.

The Creator God has tirelessly searched for people who hunger and thirst for an intimate relationship. God finds that person in Jesse's youngest son, David, a shepherd boy whose heart longed for and trusted God. How often do you judge people based on outward appearances? How hungry is your heart for God?

Almighty and loving God, give us the hunger and desire to pursue you with all our heart. Amen.

This psalm opens with a reminder to place trust in God "in the day of trouble." Days or seasons of trouble certainly come in this earthly life. Those who trust in the Lord boldly call out to God during difficult times.

The psalmist petitions God's help on the king's behalf, perhaps as the king considers a military move. The psalmist calls on the worshiping community and brings to mind the king's offerings and sacrifices. What a great affirmation for the power of corporate worship! The psalmist closes this petition section by asking God to answer his prayers for salvation and success, knowing this dangerous situation is in the hands of God. Christians have the daily privilege of boldly praying to God in times of need.

The psalmist testifies to his experience of God's faithfulness and deliverance. He is so certain of God's help that he anticipates a joyful celebration of God's triumph over all his enemies.

Psalm 20 spoke to me in January 2003 as my military unit finalized its preparations for the invasion of Iraq. As I listened to the various battle briefings describing the powerful arsenal we had at our disposal to engage the enemy, this scripture came to my mind, "Some trust in chariots, and some in horses, but we trust in the name of the LORD our God" (Ps. 20:7, ESV).

What is your source of trust when faced with life's frequent challenges? Do you recall a time when your trust in the Lord proved to be your only source of salvation?

Gracious God, in whom we place our trust, may we look to you alone in our day of trouble as our only source of salvation, strength, and victory. In the name of our Savior, Jesus Christ, we pray. Amen.

We live in an age of instant gratification, same-day delivery service, and high-speed Internet. The insatiable demand for quick results fills our lives, and we have no patience . . . for anything. This attitude has seeped into every area of society, including the church. We expect immediate responses to the gospel, instant church growth, and split-second discipleship. Jesus offers another perspective: trust the Lord's timing for results once we have sown the seed of the gospel. We cannot expect immediate responses from our best evangelistic efforts.

The gospel comes to fruition in a hidden, mysterious process that yields results according to God's timing. In 1992 I participated in an "unofficial" military visit to the former Soviet Union shortly after its collapse. My role was to speak with Russian military officers and religious leaders about the organization of the US military chaplaincy and how the free exercise of religion strengthened the combat readiness of our troops and their families. The Russians had disbanded their military chaplaincy seventy-five years earlier during the Bolshevik Revolution.

My efforts seemed futile at the time, and I saw no immediate possibility of Russia restoring its military chaplaincy. Four years later my wife participated in a mission trip to Omsk, Siberia. While there, a Russian Orthodox priest met and presented her with a beautiful leather Bible marker, saying, "Please give this to your husband and tell him that I am one of Russia's first military chaplains in seventy-five years!" What a great reminder to trust in the immeasurable power of God even when we evidence no change from our best ministry efforts.

God of the impossible, keep us from measuring our gospel efforts through human means. Remind us that your ways are higher than ours. Amen.

I preached my first sermon over fifty years ago as a young teenager. The text and subject of the message escapes my memory, and I'm quite sure the congregation would say the same. Little did I know at the time that God was preparing me for a lifetime of ministry.

In the parable of the mustard seed, Jesus urges his disciples to trust the potential of the gospel, despite the seeming insignificance of their best efforts. He uses a mustard seed to illustrate his point. The mustard seed is a small vegetable seed that grows into the largest plant in the garden, large enough for birds of any size to build a nest in its strong, expansive branches. Once sown, it has the potential to spread rapidly. Simon Peter has no idea that God will use his frequent failures to grow him into an anointed messenger whose first sermon on the Day of Pentecost would bring three thousand souls to faith in Jesus Christ.

God has commissioned each of us to carry the gospel to the ends of the earth. Our efforts seem small and insignificant when compared to the countless global challenges and cultural obstacles that oppose the gospel message. Yet, through the gospel of Jesus Christ, God is growing something far beyond our comprehension. Jesus taught his disciples that faith as small as a mustard seed could move mountains. God used the efforts of twelve ordinary men to spread the good news. How deeply do we trust the powerful potential of the gospel to accomplish its intended work?

God, forgive us for despising small beginnings in our efforts to share the gospel of Jesus Christ. Give us your perspective on the world-changing message of Jesus Christ. Amen.

Individuals applying for employment in the federal government are often required to complete an administrative background investigation called the National Agency Check. This security check is a validation of public trust to federal employees who potentially have access to classified information.

Trust is vital in our relationship with God, as is confidence. Paul in these verses begins his discussion of being at home/away and being in the body/away from the Lord. He notes a preference for being with the Lord; but while in the body, we continue confidently because we walk by faith, not by sight. Paul's close calls with death only increased his trust in the Lord, allowing him to learn what God was teaching him through life's temporary afflictions.

The resolution comes in choosing always to do what pleases God. While in the body and away from the Lord, our day-to day living and how we do it matters. Paul calls us to be prepared and accountable for the way we live. The judgment does not come based on faith or right ideas; it is based on "what has been done in the body, whether good or evil." Each will receive recompense, or payback, for what is done in the body.

Paul exhorted the Corinthian church to trust the Lord, not their intellect, culture, or fleshly desires. Paul remains confident in his living and pleasing God. We all desire to live with such confidence. Do you trust God completely? As a result of that trust, are you experiencing greater boldness and confidence?

Merciful God, whether we are in the body or with the Lord, give us confidence in your ability to hold and keep us. May our lives bear witness to that confidence. Amen.

Trusting in the Lord   203

In today's reading, the apostle Paul outlines some tenets of trust for all who believe in Jesus Christ.

• Am I confident in the Lord, no longer clinging to this earthly life (v. 6)? At some point in the Christian life, we long for heaven.

• Do I choose to live by faith and not by sight (v. 7)? The Holy Spirit gives the believer an inward certainty, conviction, and assurance of God's trustworthiness.

• Is my primary aim in life to please God (v. 9)? Those who trust in God make it their life goal and passion to be holy and pleasing to God.

• Am I preparing to stand before the judgment seat of Christ (v. 10)? We will surely stand there.

• Am I actively persuading others with the gospel message (v. 11)? Those who trust God look for ways to engage others in gospel conversations.

• Do I understand and affirm that through Jesus' death on the cross, my allegiance is to Christ (vv. 13-14)?

• Have I died to self (vv. 15-16), seeing all persons through the eyes of Christ? The Christian believer looks at others through the eyes and heart of Jesus Christ.

• Am I living my life as a new creation in the reconciling love of God (v. 17)?

The life and death of Jesus has ushered us into a new way of being and living. "There is a new creation"—and we are part of it!

Loving God, give us the undying desire to surrender all we are into a trusting relationship with you. May we live out our lives as new creations. Amen.

The Best and Worst in Us

JUNE 18–24, 2018 • BRADFORD BOSWORTH

SCRIPTURE OVERVIEW: As children of God, we will face opposition; but God will ultimately give us victory. The psalmist cries out to God asking for deliverance from oppression at the hands of his enemies and concludes the psalm with the assurance that God will do so. Tradition credits this psalm to David, who as a boy had risked his life against Goliath based on that same assurance. Goliath mocked the Israelites and their God, but God gave the victory. Paul recounts his sufferings for the gospel, yet he is not overcome or in despair, for he trusts in God. Jesus calms a storm and is disappointed that the disciples show so little faith. Why do they not believe in God's deliverance? And what about us? Do we still believe in God's deliverance?

QUESTIONS AND THOUGHTS FOR REFLECTION

- Read 1 Samuel 17:1a, 4-11, 19-23, 32-49. How do you stay grounded in the knowledge that you are part of the people of God? How does that knowledge sustain you in trying times?

- Read Psalm 9:9-20. When have you been provoked to cry out, "Rise up, O LORD?" On whose behalf did you cry?

- Read 2 Corinthians 6:1-13. When have you allowed your discipleship to become lax? Can you sense Paul's urgency in his appeal: "*Now* is the acceptable time" (emphasis added)?

- Read Mark 4:35-41. How do you find the quiet center when the storms of life rage around you?

Writer who worships and serves at Smyrna First United Methodist Church, Smyrna, Georgia.

Our first image of the Philistines is that of an unsettled, wandering, irritable, and discontent people—like me for a long period of my life. What is likely to happen to us when we do not have any internal grounding? We nominate and elect a champion to go forth and represent us. Suddenly we are victims of injustice, and the champion comes forth on our behalf to attack and chide in a loud, grating voice everything and everyone, even our closest, those we love.

The image of Goliath—a big bully—resonates with us, striking an obscure vein flowing rich in truth and images of sticks and stones laid out in front of us as we recall a familiar childhood playground rant. This champion of the untethered Philistines is a picture of ourselves when we fail to mature as God's chosen people, a characterization and example of who and what is the worst in us.

What in the world is wrong with the people of Israel? It seems like only yesterday God was guiding them through parted waters to the Promised Land. Do we have to establish some kind of concussion protocol for these folks? An army of them stands quaking in its boots while a big blowhard continues to shout obscenities. Don't these folks know they are the people of God?

Well, no, they have forgotten. This revelation is our dilemma, you and I together. Daily we need to return to our grounding call in the Lord our God—not to forget. Furthermore, we serve as the guiding wire for those in our midst who have not yet found their own grounding point! Then we will find Christ, the best in us.

Guiding God, may we turn toward you daily so that we remember you have brought us through troubled waters before and will do so now and forevermore. Amen.

This scripture is a treasure trove of truth about ourselves. Here we have the example of what we can become when we are unsure of ourselves as Goliath was when he shouted, "Am I not a Philistine?" We can imagine the Philistines feel less esteem as a group than the Israelites but not because the Israelites treat them that way. Certainly the actions of the Philistines cause Israel to view them as the enemy.

What happens when we begin to view ourselves as part of a segmented group, which in my case could be WASP, jock, senior citizen, or Georgia Bulldog? We may lose sight of who we are as individuals and take on the group's identity. In these verses, we witness the concept of posturing—the grand ploy of the ego—on full display. The Philistines and Israelites engage in childhood playground antics by yelling dares and double-dog dares back and forth at each other. And the elected representative has a uniform of armor second to none.

This stage production begins to border on comedy. On the one hand, we have all this noisy chaos with two groups screaming at each other. Surely this image is the worst in us. On the other hand, the youthful David walks in calmly, fresh from tending his flock. He shuns elaborate war dress for five smooth stones, providing a picture of divine assuredness, comfortable in his own skin.

When David arrives, he greets his brothers and hears Goliath's challenge. His reply, "Your servant will go and fight. . . . The LORD will save me." We learn then that the best in us can rise above and overcome the worst in us with God's assurance!

Father, may we be aware of the hope of glory and the five smooth stones that turn back our egos. May we also seize the day! Amen.

The Best and Worst in Us   207

Today's scripture provides a striking contrast in tone. We are lifted up with affirmative praise and reminded of the reward for those who seek God (vv. 9-12). Then just as quickly and abruptly the tone changes to an admonishing lament (vv. 12-17). When we contrast the hardened young man who would be king writing this psalm alongside the innocent shepherd boy with sling in hand, the polarity provides glimpses of the incongruence that underpins this week's theme.

The psalmist speaks of the involvement of three parties: the enemy, the oppressed (of whom the psalmist is one), and God. The psalmist faces an adversary stronger than he can singlehandedly take care of, but God delivers him. He invokes the singing of praises to God. And just when we think all is well, the psalmist raises his voice to God again: "Be gracious to me, O Lord." And he speaks again of his complaint: "See what I suffer from those who hate me." For the psalmist, it is God who has the final word, God who holds sway over the nations and executes judgment and justice.

This psalm gives us pause when we consider our nation, or the world for that matter. In recent major election seasons, we have witnessed deep division in countries around the globe. We may wonder if we "have sunk in the pit" of our own making. Could it be that we do not stand on the side of the oppressed, the needy, the poor? And if that is the case, shall we raise our voices to God for help: "Rise up, O Lord!" God, "do not let mortals [the best of us or the worst of us] prevail." Only the Lord remembers the needy and upholds the hope of the poor. The Lord is a "stronghold in times of trouble."

Yahweh, when we are oppressed, be our stronghold. May we rejoice in your deliverance. Amen.

The Best and Worst in Us

Mark's few verses are consistent with the theme of contrasts this week. Perhaps we need these opposites to remind us of life's ebb and flow. Today is the summer solstice, the longest day of light, a midpoint, a celestial high tide! The tide comes in, bringing the best and worst; the tide goes out, taking the best and worst. Phrases like "across to the other side" and "leaving the crowd behind" or "just as he was" foster feelings of solitude and the peaceful calm of that which is eternal. Then suddenly we face phrases like "a great windstorm" and "already being swamped." We in our everyday existence strike a balance between peace and calamity. Then here "in the stern" we are most likely to find Jesus.

But what about Jesus' response? Maybe like some of us when awakened from a nice nap, he seems a bit grumpy. He "rebuked the wind." We may consider this a rather harsh reaction. I struggle in visualizing Jesus being as abrupt as is the connotation of this word, being more comfortable with the word *rebuke* taking on the meaning of "to correct," one of its root meanings. And this writer believes most of the time Jesus employs this method of rebuke as a teaching tool. *Rebuke* is a word that describes Jesus' response to more than a dozen Gospel situations.

What did Jesus come into this world to do? Was it not to correct and change the course of humankind? Was it not to show us the power of still and quiet in the center of the storm and draw our attention to the question of our fear? With that in mind, we come to understand that right in the middle of our successes and failures, we find our faith, ourselves, and our peace—when we turn to him and allow him to calm the storms.

Prince of Peace, may we always turn to you when we find ourselves in the middle of life's storms. Amen.

The Best and Worst in Us

I grew up in Miami, Florida, on Biscayne Bay. Water became an integral part of life. Pier fishing after school became Saturday surfing, turning into full-moon catwalk shrimping. The influence of the Atlantic Ocean permeated the soul; the tide came in and the tide went out. This boy learned to be—by the water, on the water, in the water. Among the disciples in that boat on the Sea of Galilee were some Biscayne-boy types.

Time and again I have been on boats with groups of people when there have been rough seas, watching the progression of sea sickness like a contagious virus spread from one individual to the entire group. It never fails; one will lose a bit of equilibrium and get dizzy. Then you can see doubt in the eyes of the next person. Uncertainty sets in and fear takes over. Multiple people end up hanging over the side of the boat.

If we are Peter, Andrew, or a Biscayne boy, what is the virtue or salvation in dropping our nets to follow, if we lose our perspective on faith? Think of all the healing and teaching these disciples have witnessed leading up to this storm. Yet it took no time for doubt and fear to set in and throw their collective faith overboard. We can find solace in this story; we are the same disciples today as those in the boat with Jesus on the Sea of Galilee two thousand years ago. We may readily throw our strong faith overboard daily when storms arise and we forget God is in the boat with us. Then we allow self-doubt to spread until we glance over to the stern to see Jesus just as he was and is and will forever be: God with us, Lord over the storm.

Abba, we pray that our periods of doubt and fear will become fewer and farther between and that we will be at peace in the certainty of Emmanuel. Amen.

Our time together closes in the port of Corinth with an ETA on the sabbath. We are beginning to identify with the Corinthians much the same as we viewed the Israelites: a people off course looking to navigate their way back.

We can almost feel the gentle rocking motion as if we are back in the boat on the Sea of Galilee as Paul in subsequent verses reels off life's juxtapositions: honor/dishonor, ill repute/good repute, well known/unknown, sorrowful/rejoicing, poor/rich, and nothing/everything. We find ourselves reaching out, looking again for that stable place to recover our balance. Yet, to be without these variances in our daily experience means we are not living. And if we look back to 2 Corinthians 5:20, we note the place of balance as Paul advises us to "be reconciled to God." For Paul, this reconciliation is a matter of urgency: "Now is the acceptable time."

As a boy transitioning into manhood, I cannot forget the nights sometimes turned into morning, full moon hanging over Biscayne Bay, me leaning over a bridge catwalk railing with a long dip net. If my shrimping mates and I were fortunate to have the high tide turning and subsiding under the full moon, we would bring up a bounty of shrimp in our nets. I know that in those moments between the bay's ebb and flow, some neighborhood boys found themselves "in the time of [God's] favor" between the frontiers of life's extremes. God continues to offer the gift of reconciliation, but we must choose to accept it and acknowledge the greatness of the gift.

God, may we accept your offer of reconciliation that helps keep our lives in balance. Amen.

We would think that the presence of the new covenant in Jesus might draw Christian communities back toward God and away from their wandering pattern. Looking at the church of Corinth, apparently not. Despite the efforts of an apt ambassador in the apostle Paul, the congregation loses its bearings like a boat listing in the harbor.

I meet with a small group of men on a regular basis, and I shared today's scripture with that group. The group offered up this summation:

> It is not easy being a Christian. Don't let anyone convince you falsely that it is supposed to be easy. Serving God requires great perseverance and a wide-open heart. We are at our worst when we receive God's grace in vain and at our best when we accept and receive God's grace as offered in the ultimate gift of the Son. Discipleship is serious business. We are talking life and death—don't blow it! Now is the time to get our act together.

I've spent many years in retail frequently working on the sabbath, lamenting the practice in our culture of business as usual on Sunday. Keeping pace with the competition is always the argument for opening on Sunday. My small group meets at a business establishment that holds true to its Christian principles. The business is closed on Sunday so all employees can celebrate the sabbath. Yet, that business remains number one in their business market segment. "Now is the acceptable time; see, now is the day of salvation!" Let us not delay taking each other's hands with affection and opening wide our hearts, forevermore finding the best in us: Jesus the Messiah.

God, may we keep our hearts open so that your Son may make a home here with us now. Amen.

Waiting with Hope

JUNE 25–JULY 1, 2018 • DEMÉTRIO SOARES

SCRIPTURE OVERVIEW: David is remembered in scripture as a mighty king but also as a great poet. Many of the Psalms are ascribed to him. In Second Samuel we find a poem, a song of lamentation over Saul and Jonathan. Saul was violently jealous of David, yet David still honored Saul as God's anointed king. Jonathan was David's best friend, and David bemoans Israel's loss of these two leaders. The author of Psalm 130, although probably not David, appeals to God in David-like fashion. The Gospel reading takes us in a different direction, showing the power of a woman's faith. In Second Corinthians, Paul deals with practical matters. The Corinthians had promised to send financial help to the believers in Jerusalem. Now that pledge needs to become a reality.

QUESTIONS AND THOUGHTS FOR REFLECTION
- Read 2 Samuel 1:1, 17-27. When have you acknowledged, upon his or her death, the value of a person you deemed an enemy?

- Read Psalm 130. When have you cried out to God from the depths of your despair? What was God's response?

- Read 2 Corinthians 8:7-15. When have you lost enthusiasm for a project that had originally ignited your interest and best efforts? How did you rekindle that interest?

- Read Mark 5:21-43. What has been your experience with God's plans and timetable?

Lay member of the Methodist Church in Brazil; coordinator of International Relations of the Methodist School of Theology in Sao Paulo, Brazil.

We are always preparing for something in this life. We prepare for the arrival of a baby. We prepare for the end of college. We prepare to move to a new house, a new city, or even a new country. But we never seem prepared to be separated by death. The first book of Samuel ends where the second one begins, with the death of Saul. David feels the pain of saying goodbye; in his mournful words, David declares what his heart feels. He uses instruments of war to bring to memory the meaning of Saul and Jonathan in his life. Saul and Jonathan used bows and swords with accuracy and efficiency; Jonathan's archery skills helped David escape the wrath of Saul. (Read 1 Samuel 20:35-42.)

David's generous praises, that include Saul, whom he had previously tried to kill, show that forgiveness is part of David's life, since he himself had received God's forgiveness and enjoyed God's merciful love. In this text, David expresses a deep compassion and forgiveness for Saul, acknowledging his value to Israel as a leader, "who clothed you with crimson, in luxury." He also expresses his love for and friendship with Jonathan.

Farewells awaken in us a variety of feelings, and it is no different with David. Although he recognizes the shortcomings of Saul and holds Jonathan in high esteem, he turns this moment of pain and memory into a song for a lifetime. Many times when we experience goodbyes in life, we encounter a myriad of feelings. Sometimes they help us grow; other times they continue to pain us. Our greatest challenge comes in dealing with each feeling in due time, taking it in and growing.

Lord, help us embrace the emotions of saying goodbye. Like David, may our memories move beyond pain to the joy of here and now. And in the midst of these feelings, may we find the certainty of your presence. Amen.

Psalms 120–134 are known as Songs of Ascents, psalms sung by pilgrims on the way to the Temple in Jerusalem. Along the way, people sing their pain and praise. From the depths of despair, someone cries out. The people of Israel make the climb, singing their story of gratitude. So take note of these pilgrimage or climbing songs. In their verses we find sadness, crying, praise, gratitude, and security.

These people, although at times rebellious, know whom to seek in difficult times. In the early verses of this psalm, the writer states that in the depth of his despair he cries out to the Lord. He cries out, despite his iniquity, acknowledging God's forgiveness. And he walks on.

The psalmist yells out from his soul: "Listen to me." Perhaps after days or even years, he finally has the courage to ask God to listen. Not that God does not know his feelings, but he has never spoken so honestly to God as he does now.

Likewise, God knows our pain and what we have been through. To whom do we turn in difficult times? Do we bring to God our anguish and recognize our weakness? Maybe God awaits our cry from the depths of our being, thereby allowing God to work within us.

Father, sometimes we believe we can resolve all our burdens alone. How wrong we are when we don't talk with you about what you already know! So often we lack the courage to acknowledge our flaws and our need for forgiveness. From the depths of our souls, we cry out to you. Hear our cry. Amen.

We do not always wait with hope. Often we wait for something, but our unbelief does not allow for hope. The psalmist hopes, since the word of God does not fail. The psalmist's hope in the word of God parallels Israel's hope in the Lord—the certainty that the God who delivered the people from Egypt and the desert is the same One who hears their voices. We can trust in God's word.

The psalmist waits for the Lord and hopes in "his word." He places his confidence not in things that satisfy anxiety temporarily but in the Lord, who gives certain and long-lasting answers even in difficult times. Only the Lord offers mercy, redemption, and true forgiveness.

Waiting is not always easy because we live in an immediate world where matters have to be attended to yesterday. We are easily disappointed and quick to lose heart. Hope fades from our lives when we do not immediately receive what we hope for. Unlike the psalmist, all too often we look to human action and response rather than the will of God—and so we lose hope.

God, how anxious is my heart! When I am required to wait for something, I confess to you that I do it without hope. Forgive me! Help me, O God, to put my trust and hope in you forever. So I pray. Amen.

The apostle Paul begins this chapter by talking about the Macedonian offering for the poor in Jerusalem. The Macedonian churches of Philippi and Thessalonica have eagerly responded to the invitation to share financial resources. They want to set out for Jerusalem with offering in hand. The Corinthians, however, after their initial eagerness to participate, have not come forward with a commitment.

Paul encourages the Corinthians by reinforcing their stellar qualities, noting their excellence "in faith, in speech, in knowledge, in utmost eagerness." Paul reminds them of their spiritual "debt" to the saints in Jerusalem. Their love and generosity stems—not as an obligation—from Jesus himself becoming poor for their sakes. Their giving is a matter of grace. Paul recalls the Corinthians' initial desire to participate in the offering and rather than commanding they give, suggests they give out of love.

God rejoices in a grateful and willing heart; in this particular case, Paul opens the eyes of these Christians with regard to their coldness in rejecting the needs of others. He points out that Christ, being rich, gave up everything for love—and that through Christ's sacrifice, we become spiritually rich. Paul does not ask for a specific amount—only a generous donation from grateful hearts.

For the Corinthians and for all Christians, giving is more than a financial exercise. It is an act of love in response to Christ's giving of self.

Great God, your love exceeds our understanding. In Christ we can enjoy the proof of greater love. Teach us to love, even as you first loved us, and awaken in us a grateful heart. Amen.

Have you ever experienced an initial burst of enthusiasm about a project, gotten a good start, and then stopped along the way and wanted to give up? Sometimes we find ourselves pausing without finishing. The Corinthians needed to finish what they started and complete their harvest for the mission in Jerusalem. They needed this reminder, since for various reasons they had stopped the mission.

Paul speaks to them about their willingness and rush to collect an offering; they have begun the collection and done that out of their own eagerness. He highlights the fact that God's concern focuses on the giver's heart and attitude. The giver's motivation makes the gift acceptable or unacceptable, and he does not want to pressure them. However, he points out that God's purpose is to help them understand that money is not real wealth nor the only reason for living. The exalted Christ became human, became poor, and lived and died that they may be rich. Christ completed his task; he finished what he proposed. For that reason, the Corinthian Christians and the Christian church today must act.

God does supply our needs. When we understand that we are part of the mission, we do not stop on the way but continue forward. The One who called us is the one who sustains us, who strengthens our tired feet so that we see our commitments through to the end!

God, I often feel tired in my journey, and I confess that sometimes I think about stopping here and not going on. I recognize that I am not always grateful. Forgive me, Lord. Renew my courage and strength to continue in the knowledge that I am not alone. Amen.

When I consider Jesus' miracles, a single word comes to mind: *resolve*. Most of the people who received miracles in their lives decided to leave their homes and come to Jesus. They did not remain stagnant in their records, diagnoses, or cultural impositions but faced the challenges head on.

The woman in today's scripture knows that simply being female prevents her from approaching Jesus. But she does not care. She has reached the end of her resources—financial, mental, spiritual. The medical professionals have exhausted their efforts at a cure. People who suffered from illness found themselves marginalized because people believed them to be ill as a result of sin. The woman's need for acceptance by her community is as compelling as her illness and greater than her fear. The healing that she and others sought involves not only physical wellness but the desire to experience acceptance by and integration into society. So she leaves her house to seek out the one who can heal her pain and restore her life.

Jesus' public declaration, "Your faith has saved you," expresses the faith of the woman, as well as the result of her faith. The Greek translation of the expression "saved you" is the same as "healed you," which denotes a holistic healing: physical and spiritual. In a society for which disease is a manifestation of sin, Jesus publicly forgives the woman's sins.

Father of love, your presence transforms our lives, and we begin to see differently. Just as this woman's healing brought new meaning to her life, may we focus more on you than on our problems, more on our possibilities than the difficulties of life along the way. So we pray and believe. Amen.

The miracles that we expect from God in our lives do not always come according to our timing, nor do they always look like we want them to. How often do we desire God's quick action rather than trust God's timing? Surely Jairus has this same feeling; after all, his daughter is dying. He needs a miracle *now*—before it is too late.

Jairus is an important man. Perhaps in his mind or even in the minds of others, his situation would take precedence over others in need. But as Jairus and Jesus travel to his house, a woman in the crowd makes a risky decision and acts on it. Jesus stops to converse with the unclean woman. He heals her; he does not go immediately to Jairus's house.

As Jesus' encounter with the woman comes to a close, people arrive from Jairus's house to relay the bad news: His daughter is dead. There is no point in taking Jesus any farther. The funeral is already being planned; the mourners are in place.

Jesus now faces another situation that seems to be beyond help. The miracle Jairus needed was waylaid; Jesus' help comes too late. But the case is not closed. Jesus can still heal, even in this situation. When he arrives at the house, Jesus contradicts the logic of the people, takes the daughter by the hand and orders her to stand up, "'Talitha cum,' which means, "Little girl, get up!'" She arises and a miracle comes to her family. Even though the miracle does not follow Jairus's timetable, the result is perfect. God does not always act according to our plans or timing. But our faith opens the door for healing action.

Lord, teach me to wait on you, to trust that at the right time and in the right way, your miracles happen. Amen.

The Everyday and the Holy

JULY 2–8, 2018 • LYNNE M. BAAB

SCRIPTURE OVERVIEW: The readings from the Hebrew scriptures this week celebrate the city of Jerusalem. This was the capital of the great King David, who united the ancient Israelites and built up the city. The psalmist praises Jerusalem using the image of Zion. Zion is a name used for earthly Jerusalem, but it is also a gesture toward a future day when God's people will abide in a heavenly city. In Second Corinthians, Paul explains that even though he is an apostle, he still struggles like everyone else. Wild speculation surrounds the "thorn" that plagued Paul, but his point is that when he is weakest, God is strongest. In Mark we see God's power working through Jesus, who sent out others to expand God's healing work.

QUESTIONS AND THOUGHTS FOR REFLECTION

- Read 2 Samuel 5:1-5, 9-10. The king of Israel exhibited the qualities of a shepherd. How do those qualities square with your experience with those in power?

- Read Psalm 48. Bring to mind a place where you experience God's presence. Do you find yourself drawn there? Why?

- Read 2 Corinthians 12:2-10. When have you experienced a weakness becoming a source of power?

- Read Mark 6:1-13. When have you limited God's power through your disbelief?

Author of numerous books and Bible study guides, living in Seattle, Washington; blogs at www.lynnebaab.com.

In David's time, shepherding was an everyday task. Even children were charged with tending sheep and goats, and David himself had been a shepherd as a child. When the leaders of the tribes of Israel call David to be their king, they say that God called David to be the shepherd of Israel. The leaders use the words *shepherd* and *ruler* synonymously.

These leaders tell David that he has already demonstrated characteristics of a shepherd ruler by leading Israel, even during the time Saul reigned. As they make these statements, the people draw on their everyday knowledge of shepherding; they know that leading the sheep is one task of a shepherd. Ezekiel 34 names some other tasks of shepherding: feeding the sheep, strengthening the weak, healing the sick, binding up the injured, and searching for lost sheep. This is an astonishing list of characteristics to associate with kingship. Ezekiel 34 links these tasks to human leaders and to God. The notion of a king who fulfills the tasks of a shepherd foreshadows Jesus as both King of kings and Good Shepherd.

One of David's most significant and lasting achievements as king was the establishment of Jerusalem as the city of David. This city became the place of worship for the people of Israel, particularly after David's son, Solomon, built the Temple there. The name of the city mentioned in this passage—city of David—holds particular significance. The people attribute David's greatness to the fact that God is with him. The city of David represents Israel's foundational, guiding truth that God resides with the people God chose. The city has a close tie to our Shepherd God, the God-With-Us who chose David to be shepherd and ruler.

Shepherd God, thank you that David's greatness came from your presence with him. May I live that way too. Amen.

The moods of Psalm 48 are like a sandwich. The opening and closing verses resound with joy and exultation, while verses 4-7 describe astonishment, panic, and trembling. The source of these varied emotions is God's powerful presence in Jerusalem, referred to as the city of God and Mount Zion in this psalm.

For the people of Israel, the city of God is a source of joy and wonder because it reflects God's very nature. The city's elevation is a marvel, giving beautiful views of the surrounding hills, providing safety from enemies, and reassuring the people that God is the city's defense.

The city inspires its inhabitants' awareness of God's greatness; they cannot help but tell their children and grandchildren about God's acts. God has been faithful to the people of Israel, and God will continue to guide them, their God forever.

Sandwiched between words of joy and exultation is a description of what the kings of invading armies felt as they approached the holy city. The strength of the city is visible to these kings as soon as they see it, and they panic. The aspects of the city that comfort its residents affect outsiders in a very different way.

This holy and everyday place, the city of Jerusalem, spoke in different ways to residents and to foreign kings. In the same way, many ordinary events and places speak in various ways about God to us. We may find ourselves in a joyful place like the people of Israel or trembling like foreign kings; either way, we look to God as protector and guide.

Loving God, help me to see you clearly in everyday events and places. Give me moments of exuberant joy in who you are and what you do. Amen.

The Everyday and the Holy   223

The city of God, Jerusalem, and the Temple are inextricably connected in the minds of the people of Israel. Some beauty of the city emanates from the wondrous reality that God dwelled in the Temple (though not exclusively). The Temple served as a place to remember and recount God's victorious deeds as God established, protected, and guided the people of God.

The people of Israel viewed those powerful deeds of God as a sign of God's steadfast love. Translations of verse 9 employ a variety of verbs to describe the act of remembering and recounting: *ponder, meditate, contemplate, reflect, have thought of.* All the actions imply a sense of active waiting, which may seem hard to do. Choose one of the verbs that feels comfortable to you and consider when and where you find it easiest to practice.

This process of reflection connects to what God has done in the past. Looking back with the intent of seeing God's hand at work plays a role in the kind of pondering that took place in the Temple and that we are invited to do today. Connecting God's past actions with God's love is another aspect of contemplation.

Some people ponder best when their hands are busy, perhaps with gardening, knitting, or washing dishes. Some people reflect most easily when their bodies are engaged in walking, running, swimming, or biking. Others reflect by writing journal entries or poetry, or through music and other creative activities. The psalms result from such pondering. Individuals thought about God's actions and love and sang of what they had been thinking about. The psalms offer an excellent aid to pondering because they give us language to express the connection between God's action and God's love.

Guiding God, help me reflect on your love and your action in my life. Amen.

All too often people have trouble perceiving brilliance in ordinary people and everyday situations. We get in ruts in the way we think about people. "I know that man. He's just Joseph's son, an ordinary carpenter." Or, "He's only Mary's son. I know his family."

Jesus, of course, wasn't ordinary at all. However, we know little about his life before his baptism. He apparently lived a fairly simple life as a carpenter. His parents undoubtedly recall the Temple incident when Jesus stayed behind to talk with the teachers of the law. (Read Luke 2:41-52.) In that instance we glimpse his depth of understanding and his clear devotion to God. What was he like as a teenager, learning the craft of carpentry? What was he like as a young adult, working with his father? Surely some of his goodness and devotion to God would have been visible to those who looked closely.

People, however, seldom look closely. We find it hard to see the unique gifts in the people around us. Perhaps we're busy, preoccupied with the next thing to do. Perhaps we're concerned about our own image, what people think about our competence or how we appear. Perhaps we simply don't care enough to take the time and effort to look carefully at the personalities and characteristics of the people we know.

Jesus could do few miracles in his hometown because people took offense to him. Their perception of him limited his ability to minister. We sometimes place similar limits on people in our own lives. We overlook their skills and talents, pronouncing them ordinary rather than precious individuals created in the image of a loving and amazing God.

Loving God, help us see your image and your Spirit at work in the people around us. May we pay attention and affirm and value what we see. Amen.

The Everyday and the Holy

In the first five chapters of Mark's Gospel, Jesus' ministry consists of preaching the gospel of repentance for forgiveness of sins, performing miracles of healing, and casting out demons. Here, for the first time, Jesus encourages his twelve disciples to do the same. He sends them two by two to do the same work he has been doing.

The theme of being sent into the world as Jesus was sent into the world is common throughout the New Testament. The Latin word for "sent" is *missio*, and we get our words *mission* and *missionary* from that Latin word. In the last century or two, Christians have often adopted a perspective that only missionaries are sent to minister like Jesus did, and the rest of us lead ordinary lives.

In the early centuries after Christ, Christians knew that all who believed in Jesus were sent into the world as Jesus was sent (see John 17:18). Ordinary, everyday life as a Christian meant being sent, just like Jesus. In our time, with the growing secular culture around us, Christians are rediscovering the "sentness" of every believer. All of us are called to follow Jesus' model and become more like Jesus in every way.

Some Christians read the four Gospels and primarily see a man who performed healings. Others read the Gospels and see a man who showed love to the outcast and marginalized people. Yet others see Jesus as a great moral teacher or a man who spoke prophetic words to powerful people. The way we view Jesus' priorities and ministry influences the way we define our call to be sent into the world as he was sent. Whatever our view of Jesus' priorities in ministry, we model our understanding of our "sentness" after Jesus.

Jesus Christ, help us see the variety of ways you ministered, and help us follow you into this hurting world. Amen.

Paul mentions a man who received such a powerful vision of God that he actually experienced Paradise. This would seem to be exactly the experience the super-apostles in verse 11 would look to as evidence of true apostleship. And such visions would confirm Paul's apostleship to the Corinthians who are looking for miracles and power. While scholars believe that Paul is actually the man in the story he narrates, Paul chooses to boast only about his weakness.

Why does Paul boast about weakness? His experience with his "thorn" in the flesh, given to humble him, teaches him much about God's power and what is worth boasting about. Christians have long debated what Paul's thorn is: a physical disability, chronic condition, or some kind of addiction. Paul's brief but vivid description of this weakness includes a feeling of being tormented. People who struggle with many kinds of physical or relational limitations identify with Paul's situation.

Paul asks God three times to remove this thorn. God's response to Paul includes two components. The first part of the answer is God's grace, which God says is sufficient—enough. The second portion of God's response to Paul juxtaposes power and weakness. Power in light of the Christian gospel is somehow—mysteriously and wondrously—perfected in everyday weakness. Jesus on the cross is the quintessential model of this unexpected and baffling juxtaposition, and Paul says he boasts in his weakness because he is eager to know God's true power. Paul offers a provocative view of power: True power for everyday living comes in our weakness because God transforms our weakness into strength.

God of grace, teach me about the connections between my weaknesses, your grace, and your power. Amen.

The Everyday and the Holy   227

As Paul describes his thorn in the flesh, his words are quite countercultural for life in the second decade of the twenty-first century, when materialism and financial success are honored in so many settings, when political and military power plays such a role in the news, and when self-promotion is viewed as necessary for success. Paul adamantly asserts that his weakness was given to keep him from being arrogant and thinking of himself too highly. Paul boasts in this weakness so that Christ's power will be real in his life. Paul's perspective sometimes seems incongruous and a bit hyperspiritual. Yet I find his humility appealing. The daily news gives many examples of the ways arrogance can result in short-term success but damage relationships long term.

I also find Paul's contentment appealing. In verse 10, he mentions being content in the midst of weakness and obstacles because the challenges force him to rely to Christ. His weakness reveals Christ's strength to him, a true gift he takes great comfort in. This reliance on Christ in the midst of everyday challenges shifts his focus from his immediate situation to God's goodness, generosity, and bountiful gifts, which are all the more visible to him when his life is not going smoothly. Paul frequently urges the Christians in young churches—who have their own share of hardship—to shift their focus from human wisdom toward Jesus' love and God's unexpected way of doing things. In these verses, Paul models a profound shift in perspective: a move from pride and outward success to a focus on God's gifts, goodness, and strength.

God of power and presence, help me be honest about my weaknesses and see your blessings and gifts in the midst of my everyday life. Amen.

Connecting with God

JULY 9–15, 2018 • GORDON A. R. EDWARDS

SCRIPTURE OVERVIEW: Two readings this week focus on welcoming God's presence. David does this by bringing the ark of the covenant into Jerusalem. As the ark arrives, David dances with all his might, worshiping God with reckless abandon. In Psalm 24, the author poetically calls a city to open its gates and welcome the great king. These passages invite us to consider how willingly we receive God into our lives. The reading from Ephesians speaks of God's eternal plan. While circumstances may seem chaotic from our perspective, God holds an eternal perspective and has sealed us with the Holy Spirit. Mark tells us the sad story of the execution of John the Baptist, yet another example of a righteous person experiencing persecution.

QUESTIONS AND THOUGHTS FOR REFLECTION

- Read 2 Samuel 6:1-5, 12b-19. How do you bless others in your daily life?

- Read Psalm 24. How do you evidence your willingness to be a steward of God's creation?

- Read Ephesians 1:3-14. When have you experienced a "hiccup" on your journey and found God ready and willing to assist? How did that help come?

- Read Mark 6:14-29. When have you experienced a guilty conscience? What triggered it?

Pastor, Westchester United Methodist Church, Bronx, New York; licensed psychotherapist.

In chapter 5 we learn David has covenanted with all the tribes of Israel to be their king and has made Jerusalem the capital of Israel. David's relationship with God sustains him and proves to be a critical asset at those pivotal moments in David's life and the life of ancient Israel.

After defeating the Philistines, David reaches into Israel's past to reconnect with God. David goes with thirty thousand Israelites to retrieve the ark from the house of Abinadab, where it has been residing. David resolves to take the ark of God to Jerusalem, a move that solidifies his political power with spiritual power. The ark of God symbolizes God's constant presence. And so David and the entourage process with the ark to Jerusalem accompanied by music and dancing.

As human beings, we tend to keep moving forward without consulting God, giving little thought to how the past informs the present. We may not raise the question: "Where is God leading me?" In the midst of life's busyness we may forget who has brought us this far along our way.

David's behavior advocates a different posture toward God and our personal and collective history. We can ask ourselves questions David may have asked: What are the symbols of God's presence in my life? What role does my past play in reconnecting me with God? How do I carry God and history with me as I move forward?

Lord God, help me remember that I did not get this far on my own. Use the symbols of your presence to remind me of our life together. Amen.

David retrieves the ark from Obed-edom before recommencing the celebration. Elaborate celebrations accompany the journey to Jerusalem: David dances "with all his might" and dresses the part too. He engages fully in praising God. His linen ephod signals that the ark's procession is not only a celebration but a ritual act, an act of worship. And as the ark enters Jerusalem, David ritualizes the event, offering sacrifice, blessing the people, and feeding them.

The entire city turns out for the celebration, but one lone person stands apart: Michal, Saul's daughter and David's wife. She herself serves as another piece of David's consolidation of his kingdom—a wedding of convenience. That bit of information may justify our raised eyebrows at David's religious fervor and cause us to doubt his motives.

Yet David's celebration can teach us how to connect with God and one another. It may call us to assess our own religious fervor. When has our love of God resulted in actions of wild abandon? When has our zeal isolated others from worship?

David's actions after arriving in Jerusalem show us that we can extend God's blessing to others through word and compassionate action. How do we expand our thanksgiving for God's presence to all?

After the blessing and food distribution, the people return to their homes. After we worship God and bless others with God's blessing, we also return home—to the places where we live out our stories and our relationship with God.

Lord, teach me how to celebrate you, share your blessings with others, and carry my faith into my daily life. Amen.

Today's verses illuminate three aspects of creation theology: the earth belongs to God; we who live in the earth belong to God; God is the source of life. The psalmist sees them as inextricably linked to one another and imperative in our relationship with God. These three observations have serious implications for the ways we connect to or disconnect from God.

The earth with everything in it belongs to God. God is the only one who can claim power or possession of the earth. As created beings, we cannot master the earth; but God calls us to be its stewards. Stewards take their direction from the master, who holds them accountable for their work. How we treat the earth reflects how we view our role as the stewards of God's creation. God will hold us responsible for the state of creation because the earth belongs to God.

As beings on the earth—as part of creation—we also belong to God. We live here because God lets us. How we treat others reveals whether or not we view ourselves and others as created beings who belong to God. God calls us to care for one another as God cares for each of us—with compassion and love. Because we are part of creation, God calls us to invest in rather than exploit one another.

The earth and everything in it—including us—belong to God because God created us. God is the source of life. The psalmist states it clearly: Everything belongs to God. Though technological advancement allows us to feel entitled to and in control of everything within our grasp, we cannot forget that our very existence and our relationship with God depend upon our care for God's creation.

Lord, teach me that belonging to you means caring for your creation and all that is in it. Amen.

Today's reading celebrates God as the King of glory and reminds us of a crucial element of practicing faith—ritual helps us reconnect with God. Psalm 24 may have been used in the ceremonial entrance of God's ark described in our reading from Second Samuel earlier this week. Today's verses help us imagine and experience what a ritual of bringing the ark into Jerusalem or a ritual reenacting that event by bringing the ark into the Temple may have looked like.

Both this passage and the ceremony it illuminates center the "King of glory" present on the ark, God's earthly seat. It celebrates the Lord's strength and might. When we find ourselves in situations greater than we can handle on our own, we know God's capabilities outstrip our own. Recognizing God's ability to help us implies God's availability to us. God who is mighty stands with us through the thick and thin of life.

The scripture encourages us to ask, "Who is the King of glory?" when we find ourselves needing to recenter God in our lives. These verses remind us that mentally recalling God's power and presence often is not enough; rituals help us reexperience God and renew our faith. The ritual this passage reveals carries God's earthly seat back into the physical center of life and worship in Jerusalem. Even the gates lift their heads to recognize God's strength and welcome God's presence. When our past stifles our relationship with God or we allow the ardor of that relationship to wane, rituals help us reconnect with God's glory and constant presence.

Dear God, Lord of hosts, help us experience your presence with us anew. Amen.

Connecting with God   233

The heart of this text tells us that in Christ we are in right relationship with God: Jesus Christ is God's all-sufficient pledge that we may inherit redemption as God's people. The first verse reminds us that God "has blessed us in Christ with every spiritual blessing." God chose us in Christ to be distinctly different, to be holy and blameless before God in love—unconditional, unrelenting, and nonreacting love. Through Jesus Christ, God adopts us into the family, redeemed by Jesus' blood and restored through grace. We cannot earn our way into God's family; God bestows love on us through grace.

Today's passage assures us that we are destined to be God's. Our relationship with Christ helps us connect with God, whose claim on our lives extends "before the foundation of the world." Paul assures the church at Ephesus and us that the Holy Spirit marks us as God's when we hear and believe the truth of our salvation in Christ.

When we struggle through difficult experiences that threaten to unhinge us from our relationship with God through Jesus, we can rest assured that God has placed at our disposal all the resources we need to get through life's hiccups. Jesus helps us remain connected to God. When we get in our own way, we can know that God has gotten us to this point, and we can rely on God to guide us and make known God's will. Our relationship with God continues to improve as we remain connected through Jesus Christ.

Lord God, keep me grounded and connected through Christ so that I never stray too far from you. Amen.

Remembering reconnects us when we have been disconnected or cut off. Anything can trigger a memory, a remembering: a story, word, sighting, or experience. Psalm 24 shows us that ritual experiences help us reconnect with God. But we cannot always control what memory may arise. It could be something we have forgotten completely, and it may haunt us.

In today's text, Herod hears rumors of Jesus' teaching and healing. People speculate about Jesus' identity, and Herod latches onto the suggestion that Jesus is John the Baptist raised from the dead. This triggers Herod to recall in detail his disposal of John. The deed long-buried comes flooding back. He also remembers his complex relationship with John, whom he both feared and enjoyed listening to. Remembering his choice to behead John must have been difficult. When he remained cut off from the memory of his role in killing John, John's death seemed all right. Herod's memory of the man did not haunt him; his guilty conscience haunted him.

What happens when we remember events that cause our conscience to haunt us? Feelings of guilt can bring suffering or keep us from meaningful relationships with God and others. A guilty conscience provides another way of remembering; to suppress it only causes it to become more persistent. It can even reconnect us to others, which may free us from the memories that caused it in the first place.

Guilt often stands in the way of our relationship with God. However, as Christians, we can confess our actions to God. God offers us forgiveness through Jesus Christ, and we can be set free and re-membered with God.

Dear Lord, give me the courage to seek release from guilt so that nothing keeps me from being re-membered with you through Christ. Help me face my struggles and seek you. Amen.

Connecting with God   235

Throughout the Gospels, the writers give us clues about Jesus' nature, miracles, birth, and death—even when they're not writing explicitly about Jesus. Mark lets us know this story will reveal something about Jesus' nature or foreshadow something in Jesus' life by mentioning him while introducing Herod's relationship with John the Baptist.

The story begins by denying specific rumors regarding Jesus' identity: He is not John the Baptist raised from the dead, through this primes us to think Jesus might rise from the dead. Jesus is not Elijah—who did not die but went up to heaven—though this plants the seed that Jesus might ascend directly to heaven. Jesus is not a prophet like the prophets of old, but he could be a different kind of prophet, the promised one who offers redemption and brings us closer to God.

Herod's words again foreshadow Jesus' resurrection as the narrative of John's death opens. Then, as the scene closes, Mark draws us back to his ongoing Jesus narrative with another clue about Jesus' death. The disciples take John's body and lay it in a tomb as Joseph will lay Jesus' body in a tomb.

Mark surrounds Herod's memory of John's death with details of Jesus' identity, death, and resurrection to prepare us to remember better Jesus' story when we finally hear it. We believe that God has destined us to be God's people. When we look back on earlier stages in life—even before we knew Christ—we can often see evidence of God's role in situations that eventually led us to accept Christ or to deepen our relationship with God. God's perhaps unseen presence in our lives prepares us to know God and to see or remember God's role in our lives when we finally reconnect through Christ.

God, help me remember your presence in my past as I seek to reconnect with you. Amen.

Naming Our True Identity

JULY 16–22, 2018 • JENNIFER COPELAND

SCRIPTURE OVERVIEW: David was God's anointed king over Israel. He believed God desired a house, a Temple worthy of God. But God wanted David to understand that only God can build things that truly last. Thus, God promised to construct a dynasty from David's family. From this line will eventually come the ultimate King, the Messiah, who will rule God's people forever. The Messiah will complete God's work of uniting all people as children of God, and the author of Ephesians declares that this has happened through Christ. All God's people—Jew and Gentile—are now part of a holy, spiritual temple. In Mark, Jesus shows that part of being a great king is showing compassion. He puts aside his own desires to help those in need of guidance and healing.

QUESTIONS AND THOUGHTS FOR REFLECTION

• Read 2 Samuel 7:1-14a. Do you prefer stability or flexibility? What are the advantages of each?

• Read Psalm 89:20-37. What has been your experience with organizations or churches that are leader-dependent?

• Read Ephesians 2:11-22. When have you found yourself employing binary thinking: black and white with no shades of gray? How has that limited your focus?

• Read Mark 6:30-34, 53-56. When have you had an experience of illness or accident that left you isolated from community? How did that increase your awareness of others in that situation as you moved to health?

Executive director, North Carolina Council of Churches; adjunct instructor, Duke Divinity School.

An old saying goes like this: "History predicts the future." Today's psalm is betting on that probability. God is lauded as one who is righteous, just, steadfast, and faithful. To validate this extraordinary list of attributes, the psalmist rehearses God's promises to King David. While King David is no longer with us, the promises made to David continue into the present and, presumably, the future. Even when current events show no similarity to the promised forecast, the promises still hold.

Leaders come and go, and some leaders are better than others. Still, the psalmist declares that God's promises supersede leadership particularities. David certainly had his list of foibles—adultery (2 Sam. 11:4), murder (2 Sam. 11:15), and poor parenting skills (2 Sam. 13:21) just for starters. And yet David was remembered as "a man after my heart, who will carry out all my wishes" (Acts 13:22).

Years later, the psalmist reminds us that as leaders come and go, God's promises are not leader-dependent. They are faith-dependent. They depend on people of faith who believe the promises, recognize the vision for righteousness and justice, and live accordingly regardless of current events. For a nation that purports to be founded on "Judeo-Christian values," we would do well to heed the psalmist's advice. The leader we have, no matter how popular or dominant, will not accomplish God's purpose without the faith-filled actions of people who practice righteous behavior, seek justice for all, and offer their lives for the betterment of others. Even David could focus on those principles once he understood that God's purposes would always win the day.

God of grace and God of glory, on thy people pour thy power; crown thine ancient church's story; bring her bud to glorious flower. Amen. (UMH, no. 577)

Enabling good health is a community restoration project. It's really not about prescription plans, copayments, individual deductions, out-of-pocket expenses, or any other cost-benefit analysis. It's about community. When people are sick or hurt, they usually don't feel like getting out much and, depending on their illness or injury, they sometimes can't (think contagious). This means they are hostages to separation, whether confined to their home, sequestered in facilities, or shunned by family and friends. The greatest gift Jesus offers people through his healing is restoration to community.

Mark tells us in a few swift verses, without enumerating their ailments, "all . . . were healed." He does not record that those with full coverage were healed, those who qualify for Medicaid were healed, those who receive Medicare were healed. Just *all*. Such healing restores them to the touch of a loved one, the rapport of friends, and the company of neighbors. Today these illnesses of isolation have names like cancer, diabetes, kidney failure, heart disease. Some of them could be treated early or prevented altogether with access to preventative care. Other ailments and injuries can be treated, restoring people to community. *All* deserve access to healing services.

Jesus used the means at his disposal to restore people to community. We can do no less. We must use the means available to us as followers of Christ, and when those channels do not flow freely, we must unstop the dam. Human dignity requires the option to be made well, to be healed. Individual healing leads to communal wholeness.

Grant us wisdom, grant us courage, for the facing of this hour, for the facing of this hour. (UMH, no. 577)

Things are rosy for leader David. The ark is home, clearly identifying Jerusalem as the matrix of all things powerful: religion, politics, and the military. What more could a king want? Nothing, it seems; so this king wants a house for his God.

The temples we build reflect less on our admiration for our gods and serve more as a mirror of our own prestige. American religious architecture bears out this axiom through a simple recitation of names. We name our landmark worship sites for ourselves. Churches dot the American landscape carrying the names of their benefactors as often as they bear the name of faith, making it mostly about us.

God knows this about us and says as much to the prophet Nathan, instructing him to remind David that God will dwell where God will dwell. David doesn't need a big building to remind the world that God is on his side. Clearly God is on David's side, but conditions may arise that preclude God's support of David; then the building will be exposed for the sham it is, a shell of misplaced trust.

Eventually, there will be a temple, though not David's to build, and eventually it will be destroyed after misplaced trust. God sides with the righteous, and when the people who build the temple—or the nation—are not righteous, the temple does not protect them. There's a lesson in this for us all. We may build the temple or the nation on righteous ground, but unless we diligently preserve that righteousness, we command no assurance of God's allegiance. God aligns with the poor, hungry, mourners, and those reviled for God's sake, regardless of nation or name.

Lo! the hosts of evil round us scorn thy Christ, assail his ways!
Fears and doubts too long have bound us; free our hearts to
work and praise. (UMH, no. 577)

These two scripture segments from Mark 6 sum up the heart of Jesus' ministry—teaching and healing. Other fascinating action items fill chapter 6, and they all serve as supporting evidence for the importance of today's revelation.

A careful reading of the first three Gospels—Matthew, Mark, Luke—exposes the reality that Jesus' teaching and healing lead to his crucifixion. The inevitability of Jesus' death is less about divine justice—dying for our sins—and more about human brokenness. If sin is a synonym for brokenness and the brokenness of people is manifest through fear and greed, then listening to what Jesus tells us is a real threat. Imagine the occupants of gilded towers on 5th Avenue in New York City hearing it's easier for a camel to go through the eye of a needle than a rich person to enter the kingdom of God. (See Mark 10:25.) Imagine Wall Street tycoons being told not to store up treasures on earth where moth and rust destroy (See Matthew 6:19.) Imagine the banking barons learning they should not loan money with interest. (See Luke 6:35.) No wonder the people with power had Jesus killed!

The society Jesus describes is a place where everyone has enough and no one has too much, a place where the sick and infirm are restored to wholeness regardless of ability to pay, a world where hard work is rewarded with fair pay. The society Jesus describes can come into being, but it will require confessing the truth about ourselves. We don't really want to share our abundance, and we fear those who suggest we do. No wonder Jesus was killed. And for that reason Jesus died for our sins.

Grant us wisdom, grant us courage, for the living of these days, for the living of these days. (UMH, no. 577)

Binary thinking defines most of our cultural world: black and white, boys and girls, Democrats and Republicans. We fall into believing only two ways of thinking exist and that we must choose one or the other of them. Paul suggests only one way of thinking about the world, and that one way frees us from the limitation of choosing between two. In fact, in the one way, our binaries give way to multiple ways of thinking. As the one way, he offers Christ Jesus, the Cornerstone. This Cornerstone erases categories like circumcised and uncircumcised, near and far, aliens and citizens. It replaces them with the household of God.

The household of God does not erase our differences but enhances them and celebrates them. Now we can be black and white and all shades in between as members of the household of God. We can be boys and girls, men and women, gay and straight as members of the household of God. We can even be Democrats and Republicans as members of the household of God. Identity politics give way to the Cornerstone that is our primary identity.

It's all a matter of perspective. If I always look at the world through my straight, white, female eyes, I will always see a certain kind of world. But if I look at the world through my faith lens, particularly my Christian-tinted lens, I will see the household of God. When I look out on that household, I will respond differently to every person I meet, every decision I make, and every event I witness. Now my choices are limitless because I stand firmly on the Cornerstone.

Cure thy children's warring madness, bend our pride to thy control; shame our wanton, selfish gladness, rich in things and poor in soul. Grant us wisdom, grant us courage, lest we miss thy kingdom's goal, lest we miss thy kingdom's goal. (UMH, no. 577)

From tent to Temple: This oft-used cliché captures what is lost and what is gained in moving from provisional to permanent, from flexible to rigid. There is much to gain from the stability of staying in one place. If we doubt the advantage of such security, we can ask a few of the world's sixty-five million refugees how they feel about tents. However, consider the growing popularity of tiny houses that can be packed up and moved with minimal effort, which allows flexibility.

God likes the flexibility of moving where the Spirit blows and sends Nathan to tell David as much. Later when God has a Temple, God refuses to stay put, moving out with the people of the diaspora, off to Babylon with the exiles, and to the ends of the earth once the Gentiles are grafted onto the stump of Jesse.

David, however, has a house of cedar and reigns from a fortified city. Such fortification isolates us from the winds of change and the possibility that God will do a new thing in our midst. We must stay open to the winds of change, also known as the Holy Spirit, and to God's new possibilities in our midst. Perhaps this is why God eschewed the offer of a temple: to show us divine possibility measured against human probability.

Humans are more likely to resist change, even when that change is good for them. Humans choose to play it safe, even when doing so compromises their values. Humans will more likely avoid conflict, even when speaking up can address dissension. Divine possibility welcomes change that enables justice, forfeits safety for faithfulness, and speaks the truth in love. When we choose the temple, we cannot allow it to box us in. More importantly, we can never allow it to wall others out.

Save us from weak resignation to the evils we deplore; let the search for thy salvation be our glory evermore. (UMH, no. 577)

Naming Our True Identity   243

Choosing teams on the playground was the most stressful part of my school day. Read aloud for the class—got it. Recite the "times table" for twelves—got it. Color the picture of a rainbow—got it. Wait to be picked for a thirty-minute game of kickball—anxiety abounded. Truth is, I was never picked last. For a girl, I was considered pretty good by the boys who were always the choosers; and because everyone had to be chosen, I would be among the first girls to land safely. But I watched as the numbers dwindled, and the last person standing (not always a girl) would end up on the team that got last pick. There's not much joy in going where you are unwanted, and it wouldn't be too many weeks into the year when those last picks would opt out of being not picked—"Naw, I don't want to play" and go off in search of an empty swing.

Paul has watched this scene play out among his own people for much higher stakes. He knows that while we remain locked in competition with one another, there will always be "strangers and aliens." There will always be people who are not picked. Paul explains the new rules, the promise to all of us through Christ Jesus: We have already been picked. We are chosen. Such knowledge frees us to grow together into "a dwelling place for God," and such a dwelling place is absent of hostility, exclusion, or rejection.

Paul reminds us what the prophets have always known— God's presence is manifest through the people and the places that live into God's hope-filled future. To break the hold of hostility clouding our vision for this future, we can begin with some simple goals: Stop choosing sides; stop keeping score. Focus on the One whom we adore.

Grant us wisdom, grant us courage, serving thee whom we adore, serving thee whom we adore. (UMH, no. 577)

244   *Naming Our True Identity*

Mea Culpa

JULY 23–29, 2018 • BOB SITZE

SCRIPTURE OVERVIEW: The Bible is filled with the stories of imperfect people. David is a classic case. In Second Samuel he commits adultery, tries to cover it up, and then plots a murder. How can this be the same man who penned this week's psalm, which decries the foolishness of people who act in a godless way? Like us, David was a fallen person who needed God's extravagant mercy. In Ephesians we read of this same extravagance given through Christ, whose power can do what we cannot—namely redeem all of us who are also foolish and fallen. The Gospel author demonstrates the power of Jesus through what he describes as "signs," which Jesus performed not primarily to amaze the onlookers but rather to point them to his identity as the Son of God.

QUESTIONS AND THOUGHTS FOR REFLECTION

• Read 2 Samuel 11:1-15. How often do you consider the ramifications of your decisions and actions on the wider body?

• Read Psalm 14. How frequently do you find yourself envisioning a life free of constraints? What does that life look like?

• Read Ephesians 3:14-21. How does "being rooted and grounded in love" manifest itself in your life?

• Read John 6:1-21. When have you tried to force God into a mold of your own making to serve your needs?

Author and church consultant with more than four decades of congregational and denominational service in the Lutheran family; lives and works in Wheaton, Illinois.

Davidʼs sexual dalliance or his murderous plot? There were good reasons to justify himself just like any other self-made person: "Iʼm in charge here, and I deserve to do what I want." Consequences? Easily arranged—in order to avoid the lawʼs death sentence for adultery. Victims? Hardly noticeable.

Under the sometimes lurid exterior of King Davidʼs adultery is another sad story: the moral descent of a person who yields to the temptation of thinking that he is god. Theologians call this "self-idolatry." Today we meet an apparently righteous guy who is slowly decaying inside his own self-image: a man of unquestionable authority, a man unafraid to use that power to satisfy his own urges for pleasure. King David is a person who can do no wrong, someone privileged—in literal Latin, "operating according to a private law." No *mea culpas* for David.

Sometimes not for me, either.

Iʼve never stolen another personʼs spouse, and I donʼt recall having arranged for anyoneʼs death. My sins are small, economy-size. Sure, there are lots of them, but theyʼre easily admitted. So I can rest easy because I think Iʼm basically a righteous guy. I deserve to be forgiven, right? No foul, no problem.

But inside that unrighteous notion is this dangerous notion: I also have trouble admitting that Iʼm *not* god. I think I can do whatever I want simply because it pleases or entertains me. I donʼt always count consequences or victims of my small-and-continuing sins. I sometimes believe that *mea culpa* does not apply to me. In the long run, this does not make for easy—or righteous—living.

Lord of life, bring me up short when I think that my self-idolatry is not obvious. Lead me to confession. Amen.

Mea Culpa

In the rite of confession—Confiteor—the admission of guilt is followed by the phrases, "Through my fault, through my fault, through my most grievous fault." In these words—*mea culpa* in Latin—the repentant sinner acknowledges responsibility for confessed sins. Today's reading tells the story of a man who did not consider the victims of his most grievous fault and how his irresponsible self-idolatry crashed into others' lives.

We can easily name the apparent casualties: Bathsheba and Uriah. A short list at first glance. But what about Bathsheba's immediate family—her soldier father Eliam and her grandfather Ahithophel (one of David's close advisers)? How about David's trusted ally, General Joab, or the servants who first bring Bathsheba to David? Those who relay messages? The Thirty, Uriah's elite warrior compatriots?

Think of the sins these persons add to David's original transgression—their required complicity in this horrific crime. Consider how their loyalty to David tamps down their apprehensive consciences. Think how they are compelled to put their own good names on the line to cover the sexual abuse of this self-absorbed king—a self-righteous man who has no regard for the lives he is wounding.

This situation calls to mind how my self-idolatries may appear at first to have no consequences that tangibly harm others. In my skillful self-justification mode, how easily I overlook the lives I'm trampling on. How quickly I minimize or redefine as normal the hurt I've caused. How I even name the gathering results of my supposedly small-scale sins as something that could *benefit* unnamed others. My most grievous fault may resemble David's: creating victims.

Truth-insistent Lord, lead me toward another **mea culpa**— *naming the victims of my self-idolatry. Amen.*

Mea Culpa   247

Raw atheism—"there is no god"—can be an easy target for theists like us. How nice it can be to mow down opponents with verse 1's wonderful insult! After all, who wants to be a fool? Extracting this passage from its context, we can relish the implied assurance—you're not a fool if you believe in God—and claim our imagined reward for faithful worship of the true God. And the psalmist draws a distinction between the foolish, whose denial of God results in immoral behavior, and the wise, who seek after God.

Something else is going on here, though, that takes us away from intellectual skirmishes with God-deniers. The psalm grapples with the question of evil's existence and invites us into yet another set of frontal-lobe activities that involve mental processes as we ponder difficult questions that we hope pure brain power can answer.

Standing on the sidelines of this tussle is another question. This passage takes us back to the self-congratulating possibility that we are actually gods, or at least godlike, with all attendant privileges. Journeying down to the heart of our self-image, past rationality or logical cognition, we come to a secret room inside our souls. There we take comfort in soaring feelings about living above or beyond the rules that ensnare other people. No imperatives claw at us; no rulebooks keep us chained to low self-image. We relish the emotions that come with being totally free of constraints that keep other people moored to laws—other people or even God. We are righteous because we are gods!

What's unwise and evil here? Believing that this way of thinking could work out for us, now and into the distant future.

Ever-powerful God, help me keep my foolish self-idolatry at a manageable level today. Amen.

Since this psalm is attributed to David, we may wonder if he composed these lines before he ruined his and others' lives with adultery and murder. Or did this psalm come from his ongoing reflection about righteous living after his ruinous behavior and later repentance? Clearly David wants to transcend the foolhardiness of disregarding God's presence.

After its terse beginning, the psalm reveals something else about both foolishness and evil: If you think there is no God—or that you are godlike—you eventually come to disregard others. You are beyond them, so they are beneath you. By comparison, they are now literally "low-lifers"—they don't count. Worse yet, they can become fodder for your appetites, your whims, or your supposedly godly wishes. (The Contemporary English Version refers to the poor as the ones evil people "gobble down.")

What makes this kind of self-idolatry really reckless? Disregarding the God who cares for the poor. Verse 7 makes a veiled reference to the Exile events as reminder and proof of God's providence: "The LORD restores the fortunes of his people." It seems like he's directing worshipers: "When you're indifferent about those who are poor, you're showing disdain for the God who protects them." And for a refrain, these words, "God does not take kindly to contempt for the poor." (In Romans 3:10-12, Paul quotes these thoughts to remind early Christians of their need for divine grace.)

The measure of my personal foolishness? Any time I discount or neglect those who are poor, I will be singing only my own praises! *Mea culpa.* . . .

Caring God, don't allow me the foolishness of ignoring the poor. Refresh me with your song. Amen.

Today's reading is part of a longer narrative that stretches over two days of Jesus' ministry. Right in the middle of the action we note a significant event—the people want to force Jesus to be their king.

The crowd's reaction to the feeding of the five thousand with twelve baskets left over seems understandable: Deliverance is at hand. Jesus is just the man to overthrow the Roman occupiers and reinstate a kingdom bound by the law. Here is a king who can also take care of the physical needs of his loyal subjects—Jesus has bread-making on his resume! Why not force him to accept their adoration, their followership, their willingness to fight alongside him? What could go wrong, given the power of this convenient neighborhood messiah? No fault here!

One large problem: These newly zealous believers are trying to force him into their mold, to fit their preconceived notions of what God desires. Forged by years of revolutionary theology, these people remain self-serving with narrowly conceived notions of messiah. Perhaps unknowingly, they are trying to put God into a box by determining God's nature and priorities. Another way of describing self-idolatry!

I understand their impulsive semi-adoration: How easy it is for me to recast Jesus into the kind of Savior I need just for myself! If it was only "me-and-you, Jesus," and this salvation thing was some kind of game, I could get away with that attitude. But Jesus came to redeem the *entire world* for all of time. My self-idolatry is petty compared to the needs of the cosmos and the scope of God's all-encompassing love for the world.

How dare I remake Jesus into a Bread King to serve only me! A grievous fault that requires yet another *mea culpa!*

Almighty and all-loving God, forgive me for missing the point:
You love far more people than simply me! Amen.

This scripture offers some answers to a nagging question: How can self-idolatry ever end? Paul's rhapsodic exultation about Christ's love opens the window to a satisfying, lasting remedy: Replace your self-adulation with worship of God!

Paul suggests that we can correct the critical error of naming ourselves as our own god by replenishing ourselves with "all the fullness of God." The moment self-idolatry runs out of gas—when enough *mea culpas* finally convince us that this isn't going to work much longer—then God's love and power can replace the tawdry idolatries we have constructed.

How can that work? We start by assessing our most grievous faults. We admit to our emptiness, our inadequacy, our selfishness. We repent of this most basic sin, this acting as though the universe centers on us. We surrender false notions of superior control, power, or worthiness. By the Holy Spirit's influence, we come to see that Jesus can save us from ourselves.

This God-filling is more than an aggregation of neuronal firings—something more mysterious and wonderful is going on. (Paul measures this state of mind as wide, long, high, and deep.) A Spirit-enabled identity helps us daily to push aside the recurring temptation to name ourselves preeminent. The love of Christ overflows and washes away again and again our knee-jerk immediacy of watching out for Number One.

We will always be sinners—that part of us remains—but the saint part of us will have the opportunity to transcend self-idolatry more often. And our faults, our faults, our most grievous faults will be forgiven. Assuredly, completely, graciously.

Gracious Lord, send your Spirit into my life and replace my self-idolatry with your fullness. Amen.

Mea Culpa   251

This has been a tough week for self-concept. We've begun to understand how thoroughly self-idolatry creeps into so many nooks and crannies of our identity. And perhaps most difficult is the realization that self-idolatry colors the souls of everyone. This is a good time to close with a hopeful note from Paul's letter to the Ephesians.

In this epistle, Paul writes to folks who know a thing or two about idols, about serving idols—even about taking advantage of idol-worshipers! To these people, he writes these encouraging words: "I pray that, according to the riches of his glory, he may grant that you may be strengthened in your inner being with power through his Spirit, and that Christ may dwell in your hearts through faith, as you are being rooted and grounded in love."

These words offer a doxology (a praise hymn) and a benediction (good words for living):

- Thinking of God's glory as the primary source for our own, smaller significance.

- Gaining strength for our inner being—the place where self-idolatry tries to insinuate itself permanently.

- Being *rooted* and *grounded*—sturdy words that plant us firmly in a good place.

Each of these ideas reassures us that we continue to grow in faith throughout our lives. We are not permanently condemned to a self-image that destroys itself in ultimate futility. We serve the will of God, not our own, and are infused with God's love.

Most grievous faults? Self-idolatry? *Mea culpas*? Rites of confession? Still necessary ideas to consider; but with God's grace, they're not as tough to swallow. Good news!

Loving One, I am glad to find my identity in you. Amen.

Deeper Issues

JULY 30—AUGUST 5, 2018 • CINTIA M. LISTENBEE

SCRIPTURE OVERVIEW: David thinks he has gotten away with adultery and murder, but God sends Nathan to tell David a story. The story angers David, but Nathan reveals that the story is really about David's own sin. Indeed, it can be tempting to condemn others' sin, while we justify our own sin. Psalm 51 is David's appeal to God for forgiveness and restoration. If we want to please God in our own lives, what does this look like? Ephesians tells us that the signs of a redeemed life include humility, love, patience, and building up one another (the opposite of what David displayed). In John, Jesus has crowds following him because they want a free meal. The lasting nourishment they truly need, Jesus teaches, comes through believing that God has sent him.

QUESTIONS AND THOUGHTS FOR REFLECTION

- Read 2 Samuel 11:26–12:13a. The Lord has put away your sins. How has God's forgiveness changed your life?

- Read Psalm 51:1-12. When have you felt "unclean" before God? How did God restore you?

- Read Ephesians 4:1-16. Who has been essential in your walk with Christ?

- Read John 6:24-35. God's presence in our lives is as important as food. How do you feed your soul?

Wife of worship pastor, Zeke, and mother of three world changers; a journalist who blogs at SimplyCintia.com and enjoys running marathons for fun; member of Braeswood Assembly of God Church, Houston, Texas.

My kitchen was clean. The pile of papers and kid toys that often rested on the table were gone. Only an unidentified sour smell remained, but I had no time to deal with it. Guests were arriving soon, so I pretended the bad smell did not exist. Then I opened the refrigerator, and the smell became unbearable. It turns out, the black beans were spoiled. Now that I knew the source of the problem there was no escaping it; I was compelled to deal with it. I threw away the smelly beans, washed the container, and hoped the awful smell would dissipate quickly.

Today's scripture helps us understand that we can look clean on the outside while "smelling" dirty on the inside. David has become so familiar with his sin that it no longer bothers him. In his mind he is a king who simply welcomed another wife and baby into his palace, but David's actions displease the Lord. Despite David's moral failing, God loves David and sends Nathan to deliver a parable capable of provoking David's basic human senses to see the gravity of his sin. As a former shepherd boy, David understands how humans can grow fond of animals under their care and the great injustice the poor man suffers. The parable infuriates him. At this point, Nathan breaks the news: David is the sinner. Now he has the opportunity to repent and reconnect with God.

When sin settles in, we risk becoming familiar with it. But God's love always makes a way for us to live free from the sting of sin. David receives a parable to reveal his wrongdoing; we have been given Jesus Christ.

Loving God, open my eyes to see the gravity of sin in my life. Open my ears to hear the forgiveness you freely give through the work of Jesus Christ. May I walk in the freedom you purchased for me on the cross. Amen.

A few times a year my electronic devices experience what I call "the upgrade syndrome." Suddenly, apps and programs that once worked perfectly start to slow down. My work becomes unfruitful, and I get frustrated. When Instagram goes through the upgrade syndrome, I can no longer take photos, share my videos, or see what my friends are doing. I rejoice when an upgrade is about to happen. Once the upgrade is complete, I can use the app to its full capacity.

Forgiveness works in a similar way. Once we confess our sins, God gives us a forgiveness upgrade and we can live up to our full potential as the people we are called to be. God put away David's sin because God is good and because David's life needed to work at a greater capacity. Sin separates us from God; God takes sin seriously. But God offers forgiveness.

God offers David forgiveness but notice that David's sin still has consequences—consequences that will be lived out through his family and household. "The sword shall never depart from your house." The ramifications of his sin will carry through successive generations.

However, once David confesses his sin, God gives him a forgiveness upgrade. Nathan tells David, "Now the Lord has put away your sin." Forgiveness is a benefit worth embracing with thankfulness. I wonder if any area of your life could use a forgiveness upgrade. If we confess our sins, God is able to forgive us and cleanse us. (See 1 John 1:9.) Forgiveness restores us to our full capacity in our relationship with God and in our ability to serve others as followers of Christ.

God, you see in secret and you forgive openly. We confess our sins and ask that you restore us. Thank you for the abundance of life we enjoy. Help us to remain thankful all our days. Amen.

I grew up in Rio de Janeiro, Brazil. My family's relatives lived in a state less humid than Rio, and part of the wonder of our childhood was the number of showers our relatives took when they visited—five per day to be exact. We did not have air-conditioning, and we used one fan only at night as everyone settled down to sleep. Now I know their motivation was not only cleanliness but also refreshment. Today's psalm reminds me that just like showering, asking God for forgiveness is something I need to practice often—several times a day if needed.

The superscription ties this psalm to David as he reflects on Nathan's visit. The visit assured David that God saw his sin and that God required truth from David. Notice how David acknowledges his sinful state; he writes in detail about his need for a deep cleansing from God. His sense of brokenness comes through each line. David recognizes that—Uriah and Bathsheba notwithstanding—his transgression is against God: "Against you, you alone, have I sinned." Only God can restore him to right relationship.

We also hear David's desire for restoration. He asks God to create in him a clean heart. Psalm 51 is a good model to follow as we seek forgiveness. We move beyond the simple "I am sorry" to the root of our problem: our need for a clean heart and a right spirit that only God can give. As we ask God to forgive our sins, we can remember that God's love is steadfast, God's mercy abundant. Joy and gladness come in God's ability to make all things new.

God, you desire truth in the inward being, so I come to you in transparency and humility asking for forgiveness. Restore to me the joy of your salvation. Amen.

When marathoners go on long-distance runs, we carry a few essentials. I take a headlamp because it is dark when I run at 4:30 A.M. I need to see the path in front of me, and I do not like to fall. I always take water because my body needs to be hydrated. I take food to refuel my body on the three-hour journey. I like to wear a hat because when the sun rises, I can use a little shade in front of my eyes; the hat eases the effects of the sun. The most essential thing is an encouraging attitude. I train with a group of runners who, like me, use encouragement to persevere and complete the run.

Every life journey requires its essentials, and our faith journey is no different. Paul, in his letter to the church at Ephesus, teaches us to live a life worthy of our calling. Paul lays out the essentials we carry with us as we run our journey of faith. Humility helps us relate to others. The gentleness we wear in our attitudes helps us serve our neighbors as Christ would serve them. Patience is a disguised way of expressing our love to those around us, and a loving attitude is the way Jesus told us others would know we are his. Most significantly, we can't forget to make every effort to maintain unity through the bond of peace.

As we embrace these characteristics, we are reminded of our need for one another within the body of Christ. I am glad that we do not walk alone in this Christian journey. I rejoice that God has given us one another as partners in this worthy calling of faith.

Lord, today I embrace a humble, gentle, and patient attitude as I seek to live a worthy life. It's not always easy to love and live with my brothers and sisters, so I ask that I will bear those difficulties in love. May unity be evident through the peace I carry in my heart. In Jesus' name. Amen.

Construction sites interest me. I like them so much that they become tourist attractions to friends and family who visit me from Brazil. There are several stages in the home-building process. The foundation always comes before the roof goes up. Plumbers, masons, and electricians all help build the homes we admire so much. In the same way, apostles, prophets, evangelists, pastors, and teachers help build the body of Christ. Each one of these gifted people is important and necessary to equip us for the work God gave us. When I was a child growing up in Brazil, my Sunday school teachers laid a strong foundation of Bible knowledge. Each Bible story and song taught me about God's love and helped build my faith. We would learn a new Bible story and talk about how to apply the truth of scripture to our lives.

I see those years as the foundation stage of my faith. As an adult, I still rely on spiritual leaders to help me continue building on my childhood foundation. Because the foundation has already been laid, I can go on to different stages in my faith-building process. Just as building a home takes time and many stages, so does building a disciple of Christ. God provides people who help us grow in the knowledge of God in each stage of discipleship. I am grateful for those who equip us with what we need in each stage of our faith-building process so the truth of God's word will be evident in our lives.

Today, O God, we remember those who work diligently to fill our lives with your goodness. Bless them and fill them as they pour out the wisdom and love you have given them. Help us share your love with others, as well. Amen.

The crowd cannot get enough of Jesus. They have never experienced anyone so wonderful! And he is right here, walking among them! He heals the sick and multiplies bread and fish so thousands can eat and be satisfied. Being present at the amazing multiplication of food and being physically filled must have felt incredible.

The next day the crowd finds him and ask many questions. Jesus knows they are looking for yesterday's miracle again, but the satisfaction of physical hunger was meant to go beyond meeting the present need for food. Jesus intends the miracle to point toward himself as God's gift of life. So he offers the people a different type of bread, the bread of life that satisfies not physically but far more completely.

The crowd knows their ancestors experienced daily manna from heaven in the desert, and so they expect this miracle of sustenance to be the same. Jesus promises more. When Jesus declares, "I am the bread of life," he promises a spiritual sustenance to those who believe in him so they will never hunger or thirst for truth. Jesus uses the language of daily physical need to show us how integral our relationship with God is. Jesus offers to meet our constant need for God's presence in our lives. Just as bread and water sustain us physically, Jesus—the Bread of Life—offers divine sustenance for our souls.

Will we accept Jesus' invitation? Believing is not always easy; but when we do, our Savior promises to satisfy us and give us life. All we need to do is come to him and say, "Sir, give us this bread always."

Jesus, bread of heaven, guide me as I walk through my life circumstances today. I come to you, and I believe in you. Amen.

Researchers say that women speak around twenty-thousand words a day. By the end of a year, the average woman will have spoken 7.3 million words! Unfortunately, not all the words that come out of our mouths come from a heart of love. I have spoken in haste and regretted my words many times. Have you ever regretted any words you've said? I'm assuming we all have. Words are tricky: Once we say them, we cannot unsay them. For some reason, when I was a teenager, I expressed many harsh words. My comments may have been truthful, but I did not say them in a loving way. I had learned the "speaking the truth" part of today's reading, but I was yet to discover the revelation that we do so "in love."

Truth without love hurts others. Wisdom comes when we speak in a way that allows others to receive our words well. Before we speak the truth, we ask ourselves whether our words are motivated by the kind of love Paul mentions in these verses, which he explains in his first letter to the church at Corinth: Love is patient, kind, not jealous, not proud, not self-seeking, not angry, and keeps no record of wrongs (1 Cor. 13:4-8).

When we speak the truth in love, our words can build up our brothers and sisters in the body of Christ. The good news today is that we can speak the truth with God's kind of love. As we do so, we grow in Christ and become more like him.

I don't know your word count for the year, but I pray that all your words come from a heart committed to God's kind of love, love that builds up community in the body of Christ.

O Lord, fill my heart with your kind of love. Help my words be truthful and loving so that they build up my brothers and sisters in the body of Christ. In Jesus' name. Amen.

Transitions and Transformations

AUGUST 6–12, 2018 • KATHRYN HAUEISEN

SCRIPTURE OVERVIEW: David's family was a mess. Among his children there was rape, murder, and a plot to overthrow him by his son Absalom. Violence followed, and Second Samuel tells the story of Absalom's death. Even though Absalom had betrayed him, David still loved his son with a parent's never-ending love—the kind of love that God demonstrates perfectly for us, as David celebrates in Psalm 34. The author of Ephesians warns against acting out of anger, wrath, and malice (the very things that tore apart David's family). We should instead forgive, as God in Christ has forgiven us. In John, Jesus restates that he is the path to God because he teaches God's truth. Jesus will give his own life but then raise up those who believe in him.

QUESTIONS AND THOUGHTS FOR REFLECTION

- Read 2 Samuel 18:5-9, 15, 31-33. When have you been called to "deal gently" with a loved one?

- Read Psalm 34:1-8. Reflect on a time when you were able to intimately "taste and see" God's goodness in your life.

- Read Ephesians 4:25–5:2. Are your words and actions imitating Christ?

- Read John 6:35, 41-51. God comes to us in unexpected ways. Who have you discounted as a servant of God? How can you support their ministry?

Retired pastor, Evangelical Lutheran Church in America; lives the ecumenical life with her husband in Houston, Texas; enjoys gardening, writing, reading, and blogging at www.HowWiseThen.com.

Absalom's life seems to consist of one crisis after another, many brought about by his own decisions. We would expect his father, King David, to use the battlefield as a way to be done with this rebellious and dangerous son. Instead, King David instructs his military leaders to "deal gently for my sake with the young man Absalom."

As human beings, we usually do not respond with such grace to deceit and ruthless recklessness. We're more likely to go for revenge and retaliation. The actions of David as Absalom's father gives us a small glimpse of how God the Father prefers to operate.

After his sister was brutally murdered, John Sage founded Bridges to Life, an in-prison program that gets prisoners talking about what went so wrong in their lives that they wound up serving prison terms. Trained leaders meet with them in small groups each week to explore their past. Part of the program includes listening to stories from crime victims. Perhaps for the first time in their chaotic lives, these inmates are treated with kindness and respect, in spite of what they've done. They are transformed in the process. Participation in the program does not shorten their prison time, but it does change how they behave for the duration of it.

God's grace transforms people. Wars like the one between David and Absalom continue to kill thousands of people and destroy communities. Yet, God's grace manages to find footholds in the midst of destruction and despair. We may never put an end to war. However, we can choose to be partners with God in making grace known in the midst of conflict.

Gracious Lord, help me do my part in showing your grace to those in desperate need of a kind word and good news. Amen.

King David tries to protect his son on the battlefield, but his plans are thwarted in the heat of battle. When messengers tell King David about the defeat of his enemies, David can only focus on the death of his son. He cries out in anguish, wishing he'd been the one to die instead. He experiences the bitter consequences of his own sins. (See 2 Samuel 12.) Nothing Absalom did kept his father from loving him. David, though a flawed man himself, loved his son—perhaps in part because David knew firsthand the consequences of a life gone astray. David wanted desperately to protect his son but in the end could only express his love by grieving for him.

My friend John's son Fred cannot stay sober long enough to get his life on track. Fred has tried various programs and pills to get and stay sober. Time after time John, himself a recovering alcoholic, learns his son is again living on the streets or in prison. This has been going on for decades, and John grieves for Fred each time. Yet John continues reaching out to Fred and praying he will find his way to sobriety and a better life. John desperately wants Fred to kick the addiction that keeps him homeless and too often hopeless. Meanwhile, John prays and waits.

Not all parents are capable of the passionate commitment to their children demonstrated by King David and my friend John. However, parents like David and John reflect God's eternal love and devotion to us. God knows us and desires that we be in good relationship with one another. These truths give us hope that God will intervene.

Gracious Lord, help us to trust that your love for us is stronger than any wrong steps we take. Amen.

King David was known for many things, including being a poet and songwriter. Though David's life belies such pronouncements as "I will bless the Lord at all times," or "Let the humble hear and be glad," today's psalm does reflect David's overall desire to magnify the Lord. Like David, we sometimes struggle to keep our focus on God. We have all experienced moments of shame and forgotten to seek out the Lord when we're in need of deliverance from our fears. However, as we learn to turn to God, we begin to tip the emotional scales of our lives away from emotional turmoil toward inner peace.

Many years ago, while I was going through an especially difficult chapter of life and experiencing depression, I turned to a spiritual director for insight and encouragement. Initially her advice didn't seem helpful. She sent me to a well-appointed bed and breakfast in the middle of nowhere and told me to "be still." She admonished me to just sit and be quiet for a while. I am used to going full speed ahead day after day, so this was difficult for me. However, with little to do other than walk in the garden or sit on the porch, my anxiety and pain began to diminish. So I sought the Lord, and a sense of hopefulness for the future began to displace my fears. "This poor soul cried, and was heard by the Lord." I doubt I'll ever master the art of "bless[ing] the Lord at all times." However, taking time out to be still and focusing on God's mercies once in a while helps us "taste and see that the Lord is good." I am happier when I take refuge in God.

Gracious and all-powerful Lord, help me allow the psalms to guide me when I struggle to find insight. Thank you for spiritual directors who lead us back to you. Amen.

The situation kept deteriorating. Pastor Seth accepted this call to ministry two years ago, trusting his skills could meet the congregation's needs. A few members were still upset over the departure of their previous, much-beloved pastor, and some members left during the uncertainty of the yearlong transition.

Disgruntled former members encouraged others to join them in their new church homes as Pastor Seth tried valiantly to diffuse lingering hard feelings. He worked diligently to introduce new ideas and programs. Yet, attendance and financial support kept dwindling as unresolved issues continued to undermine meetings and mission efforts.

One day, Pastor Elliot, a colleague from a neighboring congregation, invited Pastor Seth to lunch. A veteran of thirty years of ministry and many congregational challenges, he sought to give grace to his young pastoral neighbor. He asked Pastor Seth what he most enjoyed doing.

"Hiking," Pastor Seth answered. As gently as he could, Pastor Elliot suggested it was time for him to do just that. "Go take a hike. Let this go. It's not working. It's hurting your health, and it's not helping the congregation either."

Pastor Seth left six months later. He used those months to groom a few leaders to handle the next transition and then spent a few weeks hiking part of the Appalachian Trail.

Sometimes God needs us to hear a hard message; other times God nudges us to deliver the hard message. Pastor Elliot's words were hard to hear and hard to speak. Sometimes the truth is both. When we do either with grace, the truth can set us free.

Lord, help us hear and speak your truth to one another in kindness and love. Amen.

In his letter to the church at Ephesus, Paul offers sound advice on how to oil the wheels of human community. It sounds much like my insistence to my daughters when they would quarrel, "You don't have to like each other. But you do have to be kind to each other."

A little kindness goes a long way in defusing tense situations. As followers of Christ, we know that kindness is more than a social advantage. It is one of many marks that indicate a follower of Christ. And Christian culture is hardly unique in promoting the benefits of treating others as we want to be treated. Most cultures and religions emphasize the need to treat people with kindness and fairness.

As Christians, this way of living becomes who we are as we imitate the ways of Christ. In Christ we become new creations, and this transformation comes from the inside out. Eventually, we don't have to consciously decide to behave in Christlike ways—doing so becomes our very nature. Of course, being human, we sometimes slip back into less Christlike behavior; but the more we grow in Christ, the quicker we realize this and make amends.

Sometimes I sit in public places to watch strangers interact. When persons go out of their way to be Christlike to others through actions or words, I see an immediate transformation in attitude and demeanor. Smiles replace frowns, and people *look* at one another rather than *past* one another.

It is popular to ask, "What would Jesus do?" Perhaps it is better to ask, "How am I imitating Christ? Am I walking in love, demonstrating the way Christ loves us and gave his all for us?"

Gracious and loving Lord, thank you for those who live out the way of Christ among us. Help us do the same. Amen.

I've been in ministry long enough that some people I first worked with in youth groups or as a camp director are now married with children or serve congregations as pastors or youth leaders. It is rewarding to watch these young people take their places in leadership, but sometimes I am surprised by the high levels of responsibility entrusted to them.

When I see these men and women handle situations differently than I would as they go about serving Christ, I try to avoid grumbling at their approach. Yet I understand the tendency that the Jewish leaders fall into in today's reading. We can easily dismiss the capabilities of those we have known since they were young. The Jews who complain about Jesus' words remember him as the child they knew in need of parental care and religious training. How could Jesus have come down from heaven? How is that possible when he is the son of Joseph and Mary? His claim infuriates those who have known him since childhood. They know his parents, after all.

Sometimes we too express skepticism of people who don't fit our image of how we think a religious leader should look, think, talk, or act. But God reaches out to us through people of all ages, all ethnic groups, all levels of education, and all levels of capability.

As we grow in our understanding of this mysterious One who claims to be "the bread that came down from heaven," we can set aside our skepticism and accept that Jesus is who he claims to be. God continues to come to us through some pretty unlikely people today as well. How does our skepticism limit our ability to see God at work in our lives?

Lord God, Bread of Life, help us grow in our understanding and acceptance of who you truly are. Amen.

There is a phenomenon among babies and infants called "failure to thrive." This may happen when newborns or infants have their physical needs met but do not respond normally. Sometimes the bond between child and caregiver isn't strong enough. Orphans raised in institutions with overworked staff also suffer from failure to thrive. It is not enough to fill our stomachs with nutrients. Food keeps our bodies alive, but it does not meet our deeper needs for affection, human contact, compassion, and finding a purpose in life. When caregivers have little time to engage with the children under their care, the children begin to suffer from lack of human bonding.

Jesus knows our spiritual well-being is as crucial to our overall health as our emotional well-being is crucial to our physical health. Jesus goes beyond meeting our needs for belonging, security, community, and purpose—he provides eternal life.

God provided manna for the Israelites in the desert—physical sustenance, but they died. Jesus is the living bread from God who sustains us spiritually so that we can experience fullness of life on earth and in eternity.

Through Christ, God is always ready to feed us. God comes to us in many ways—intimate relationships with family and friends, worship, service to others, scripture, and the incredible world all around us. Our ritual of Holy Communion regularly reminds us to pause and partake of Christ, the Bread of Life.

Lord God, you provide for all our needs. May we turn to you to address our spiritual needs even when our physical needs are being met. Amen.

The Quest for Wisdom

AUGUST 13–19, 2018 • KYNDALL RAE ROTHAUS

SCRIPTURE OVERVIEW: If you could ask God for one thing, what would it be? God offered this chance to Solomon, and the king asked for wisdom to rule God's people well. God honored this request by giving Solomon many other gifts too, as long as the king followed God's ways. (Later on, unfortunately, Solomon lost his way.) The psalmist tells us that wisdom begins with understanding who we are and who God is. Ephesians addresses practical implications of wise living: follow the will of the Lord, be filled with the Spirit, encourage one another, and be grateful to God. The Gospel passage continues Jesus' metaphorical description of himself as the bread of heaven. Here Jesus anticipates the sacrament of Communion, in which we partake of his body and blood by faith.

QUESTIONS AND THOUGHTS FOR REFLECTION
- Read 1 Kings 2:10-12; 3:3-14. Why are you afraid to ask God to meet your needs or show you your call?

- Read Psalm 111. What actions dominate your quest for God? Do you remember to stop and delight in God's love for you?

- Read Ephesians 5:15-20. How do you make the most of your time with God? How do you show others that you are filled with the Spirit?

- Read John 6:51-58. In Communion we recall Jesus' offering of his body and blood. How has that concept been a stumbling block to you?

Pastor, Lake Shore Baptist Church, Waco, Texas.

Solomon follows his father's instructions with one notable exception—King Solomon offers sacrifices and incense in the high places. In most biblical contexts, such sacrifices were not acceptable, but here Solomon takes it upon himself to diverge and ascend the high places—a syncretism with Canaanite religion we would expect God to condemn.

Contrary to expectations, God appears to Solomon, and Solomon appears to have pleased the Lord. "Ask for whatever you want me to give you," God begins—which is a rather generous offer, even from God. Could it be that location and form are not as important as the sincerity and intention of the seeker? Perhaps an idolatrous place for one person is a portal of divine access for another. We do not usually think of the God of the Old Testament as being loose with the boundaries, and yet here God is, showing up in the forbidden place without reservation and bearing unrestricted gifts.

Sometimes when we need an answer, we feel we must know the right way to ask or the right place to look, and we end up paralyzed by our own uncertainty. Instead of climbing the mountain to pray, we stay in bed and hide. We'd rather avoid success than risk retribution.

When we feel disposed to hide, we remember the rookie king who breaks from his father's tradition to do his own kind of search and to offer his own kind of prayer. To his great surprise, God answers. What drives Solomon to depart from the way set before him by a "man after God's own heart?" Is it curiosity? adventure? discontent? The most important step in the quest for wisdom is to begin.

O God of surprise appearances, help me ascend to the high places of the heart to search for you without fear of judgment or failure. Amen.

We could paraphrase many of our prayers in this way: "God, get down here and fix it." We commonly plead for God to end our pain, suffering, conflict, or threat from an enemy. These prayers can build up a lot of spiritual resentment in us when God fails to appear on command like a genie out of a lamp to give us what we want.

However, Solomon does not ask to get out of anything. He does not bemoan the difficulty of the work or request a rescue. He doesn't seem to expect miracles or even special treatment as king. He does not lash out at God because his father is dead or because his father wasn't around enough when he was alive. Instead, he expresses gratitude for the many kindnesses God has shown him, and he asks for wisdom and discernment to face the challenges ahead.

While I am certain God can handle it when we rage at God because of unanswered prayers and while I believe it is better to be honest with God than untruthfully modest and compliant, we may be better served to pause our demands of God and reevaluate our expectations. Is God the giver of an easy life or the giver of strength and wisdom? Is God is in the business of making shortcuts or making hard things possible? In this moment, will I ask for deliverance or for wisdom?

God of wisdom, I do not know how to carry out my work in the world. Give your servant a discerning heart to distinguish between right and wrong. Help me to seek not only solutions but wisdom. Amen.

Ponder, delight, remember, extol. The psalmist employs these four verbs (as translated in the New International Version) in today's psalm. Do these encompass what it means to fear the Lord? To fear the Lord is to ponder and wonder about God's presence in the world; to suspect that behind every blessing, every sunrise and budding flower, God works. To fear the Lord is to delight in every gift, however small or predictable, and not to take for granted our ordinary and daily gifts. To fear the Lord is to remember and call to mind God's wonders—whether it be a story or a place in nature or a memory of feeling most alive. To fear the Lord is to extol, to celebrate all that is good. When we extol the Lord, remember God's wonders, delight in the Lord, and ponder God's power, we begin to find wisdom.

When searching for wisdom, it is counterintuitive to stop in the middle of the hunt and throw a party. But the psalmist reminds us that celebration and praise are essential to life. In order to continue growing, we remember and name what we have learned already. To find our way out of the dark, we give thanks for the light we have been given. To be wise, we embrace the vulnerability of joy. Grief expands the contented soul while joy enriches the soul that is in turmoil.

O God of magnificent works and tiny miracles, I pause and give thanks for the wisdom, the mercy, and the gifts you have already given. Your grace has carried me before, and your grace will carry me again. For the moment, that is all I need to know. When I look back, I remember that I did not blaze that trail alone. Though I cannot see more than a step ahead, I know you are clearing the way for me. Amen.

Often in life, our fears obstruct our wisdom. Fears—flaming, screaming, whimpering distractions—keep us from our path. Fear is so often the enemy of what is good. This is why the scriptures tell us, "God has not given us a spirit of fear, but of power, and of love, and of sound mind" (2 Tim. 1:7, NKJV). We are assured that "perfect love casts out fear" (1 John 4:18).

Yet we know the brave are not always fearless. They are often very afraid and for good reason, but they act upon their conviction anyway. Perhaps wise people simply know how to prioritize their fears. They are not fearless, but they fear some things less than others.

A wise person may think, *I fear the loss of my integrity more than I fear the loss of a job. I fear the loss of self more than I fear the consequences of being true to myself. I fear a loveless life more than I fear the pain of loving. I fear the regret of not doing this brave thing more than I fear the risk of doing it. I fear being silenced more than I fear being disliked.*

Perhaps the beginning of wisdom lives in an explicitly Christian version of these statements: I fear denying God, not because I am afraid of punishment or wrath but because I know I could miss out on adventure, meaning, and purpose.

Courageous God, it is scary to follow your way of radical love. Help me to be less afraid of the consequences and difficulties of fidelity to your path and more afraid of missing out on what is good and right and true. If there is no escaping fear in this life, grant me the wisdom to know which fears can guide me and which fears obstruct my walk of faith. Amen.

It is difficult to make the most of every opportunity when we worry about the future. It is difficult to make the most of every opportunity when we spend time reliving the past.

Wisdom requires that we be present, that we show up—not in a perfunctory way but in a fully engaged way that reveals our understanding of the Lord's will. The wise are awake to the presence of Christ in world around them. Ephesians 5:14 calls to us, "Sleeper, awake! Rise from the dead, and Christ will shine on you."

Today's passage does not mean that we have to squeeze every last ounce of juice out of life or else we've wasted it. We could expend so much energy squeezing that we never taste or savor or admire! Rather than "making the most of every opportunity" by measuring how much we accomplish, we can mark our time by how we seek to understand God's will. Production and achievement don't necessarily indicate that we're living well. Even Jesus rested, prayed, and broke bread with his disciples. He could have spent every spare moment healing others, but his more reflective actions show us another way to make the most of our time.

Making the most of our time is unique to each opportunity—sometimes we have the opportunity to be silent, sometimes the opportunity to speak. We can take the time to rest well when we are given the opportunity. Seeking to understand the Lord's will helps us discern the way to make the most of every opportunity: whether to rest or to work, to play or to create.

O God of opportunity and giver of choices, help me discern your will. Free me from enslavement to automatic impulses and unexamined habits. Grant me the freedom to be fully alive. Grant me wisdom. Amen.

Get drunk on God, on music, on conversation—this is what God's word recommends, especially when the days are evil. Unlike being drunk on wine, this sort of intoxication isn't a form of escapism but a form of engagement, a way to resist, and a communal pledge to keep going. Think of African American spirituals—which are scripture and music and Spirit and community and resistance all rolled into one—and hear them bellowing through the streets during the Civil Rights Movement. Then you can see what I mean about empowerment versus escapism. The days indeed were evil, but God's people "spoke to one another with psalms, and hymns, and songs from the Spirit," and God's people prevailed.

Recently after a national tragedy that left many of us rattled and afraid and feeling betrayed, some friends gathered together and made handmade love notes for our congregation. Men and women cut out hearts, glued construction paper, and wrote messages using words of scripture or song lyrics or simple declarations of love. We ate cookies and listened to music and sipped a bit. But mostly we filled up on love, hope, resistance, friendship, and Christ.

We didn't change the world that day or overturn the days of evil. But we faced the times with heart and compassion and creativity, which felt a whole lot like understanding the will of the Lord.

God of justice, we know you see the suffering that exists all around us, and we confess there are days we feel swallowed up by it all and wish for a means of escape, a way to feel numb, a place to hide. But with music and song, community and friendship, you draw us back into the world to do our work. Thank you. Amen.

When Jesus starts talking about his body as bread and his blood as drink, the people are understandably perplexed, and perhaps a bit mortified. The apostle Paul explains it this way, "Jews demand signs and Greeks desire wisdom, but we proclaim Christ crucified, a stumbling block to Jews and foolishness to Gentiles, but to those who are the called, both Jews and Greeks, Christ the power of God and the wisdom of God" (1 Cor. 1:22-24).

Indeed, the Cross is where we are likely to trip up on our quest for wisdom because it is all so odd, and yet believers find the center of faith and a deep source of wisdom in this mystery. It is illogical and nearly incomprehensible that God would become flesh, that God would empty Godself of glory, that God would willingly suffer and die, and that death would become the portal to life everlasting. Yet we reenact and celebrate this process again and again in the life of the church. God's seeming recklessness initiates our salvation.

The church's practice of Communion is one of the more peculiar activities we participate in together as we receive God's mystical gift by approaching the table with our bodies. Most days we try to approach God with our minds, and wisdom escapes us. During Communion we approach God with our full and humble selves, and the wisdom enters us through the flesh and blood of Christ.

God of Mystery, I may never fully untangle who you are or why you do as you do. Grant me not the answers I want but the wisdom I need. O Christ, help me understand what it means for you to be human not so I can master knowledge but so I can live as you lived. O Living Spirit, guide me down the right path, even when I do not understand the instructions or perceive the reasons. Amen.

Standing Firm within the Word

AUGUST 20–26, 2018 • JOHN A. BERNTSEN

SCRIPTURE OVERVIEW: God had prevented David from building a temple in Jerusalem but then permitted David's son, Solomon, to build it. In First Kings, Solomon places the ark of the covenant in the holiest place, and God's presence descends. The psalmist rejoices in the Temple and would rather be in its courts than anywhere else because that is where God dwells. The New Testament readings remind us that the people of God have always met with resistance. The author of Ephesians compares living the Christian life to going into battle, so we must be prepared. Jesus also meets with resistance in John. His teachings are too hard for many to accept, so they abandon him. When we face resistance, therefore, we should not be surprised; but we are also not alone.

QUESTIONS AND THOUGHTS FOR REFLECTION

- Read 1 Kings 8:1, 6, 10-11, 22-30, 41-43. How does your faith inform your sense of hospitality to friends and strangers?

- Read Psalm 84. Is your joy in the Lord? How does your relationship with God help you through times of sorrow?

- Read Ephesians 6:10-20. How do truth, righteousness, peace, faith, salvation, and God's word help you live boldly as an ambassador of the gospel of Jesus Christ?

- Read John 6:56-69. God came to us in a messy human body. How does your embodiment help you understand what it means to abide in Christ?

Retired Lutheran (ELCA) pastor; living in Bucks County, Pennsylvania.

Jesus' forbears had an ambivalent relationship with temples and houses of worship. On the one hand, the human impulse to "contain" God led to shrines and tabernacles on a grand scale. On the other hand, as King David was to find out, God challenged the very notion of permanent sanctuaries: "Did I ever ask you for a temple? From the beginning, I have lived in tents as my people have wandered" (2 Sam. 7:6-7, AP). Because of his vanity, David never sees the Temple. It was left to Solomon as an engineering feat. Today we read Solomon's prayer of dedication.

The great mystery of God's presence is that even though the "highest heaven cannot contain" God, this very God chooses to stoop down and "dwell on the earth." The One who is great becomes small and makes a home in a "down-to-earth" dwelling.

Even so, nothing made by human hands is permanent. God's presence is always hidden in things that are transitory. The saying "this too shall pass away" applies to all our temples and monuments. The only remnant of Solomon's great Temple complex is the Western Wall in Jerusalem.

My home church burned to the ground in January 2009. Because the congregation had already dwindled in size and shared a pastor with a nearby church, the members decided not to rebuild. Instead, they donated the insurance money to a variety of missions. All that remains on the site is a small memorial of park benches, a garden, and the relic of the bell tower. And yet, like the faith of the ancestors of Solomon's Temple, the church's ministry lives on through those who carry out God's work in the world.

God of hosts, you alone have been our dwelling place through all generations. Hide us in the shelter of your tent until the day we see you face-to-face. Amen.

Solomon is wise enough to know that the house of prayer receives blessing only when it opens itself and welcomes the "foreigner" and outsiders from "a distant land." For Israel, this is never easy, since neighboring kingdoms threaten its sovereignty. Fearing invasion doesn't encourage a climate of hospitality. Still, hospitality remains a promise and a spiritual mandate.

When we let people into our homes, they can get messy. The only way to stay spick-and-span is to live in a bubble. Yet as soon as we welcome others, we welcome all that comes with them. I once read of someone who said that even as she cleans her home left in shambles the day after a party, she remembers the joy of the night before shared with people she loves.

Our homes may be our castles, but unless we welcome the stranger, they remain museums gathering dust. The image of a mansion turned into a museum comes to mind—a place where rooms are roped off and for viewing at a distance only, lest priceless heirlooms are damaged. Do we want to live in such "perfect" spaces? Today's text reminds us that hospitality is part of our call as we seek to worship fully in God's presence. Welcoming others into our homes and into our places of worship invites God into our midst as well. It is better to huddle together in a hut and share God's joy with one another than to live in a pristine world alone.

God of welcome, bless the mess that comes with our togetherness; while we tidy up, teach us to pray. Amen.

This psalm is a song sung by pilgrims who yearn for God's presence. After a long and arduous journey, what can be better than to arrive in "the courts of the LORD" for respite? The joy of worship in the Temple serves as the reward for the hardship of prolonged travel.

The psalmist twice uses the familiar phrase "happy are those." The declaration stands in the long tradition that culminates in Jesus' Beatitudes from the Sermon on the Mount. (See Matthew 5:1-12, CEB.) While *happy* is the repeated word, singing "for joy" more fully expresses the outburst of praise by the weary traveler.

The difference between happiness and joy is a great discovery on our journey. Happiness can pass quickly, dependent on the winds of circumstance. After a while, the pilgrim learns that pursuit of happiness leads to a fretful soul. Joy, however, is ongoing, described elsewhere as what "comes in the morning" after a long "night of weeping." Happiness is only part of joy. The pilgrims have joy as they seek the happiness that comes in praising God in God's house and find their strength in God. Though their journey has surely been tough, the pilgrims already have joy. They understand that joy relates to overcoming sorrow; joy is a reversal of the grave. Joy comes from living life devoted to God, from whom all happiness and joy come.

Johannes Brahms expresses the nature of our pilgrim yearning in his serene *German Requiem*. The fourth movement, *Wie lieblich sind deine Wohnungen* ("How lovely are thy dwellings") is based on this passage. Listening to this piece of music may help you find rest for your soul.

Lord of hosts, my heart and flesh sing for joy to you, the living God. Amen.

The second part of the psalm mentions "a doorkeeper in the house of my God." I think of doorkeepers as a cross between ushers and custodians.

While I was in seminary, I worked as a custodian in a church. I lived in an old Tudor mansion that had been converted into the parish house. When you are a janitor, you basically hear complaints. The floors aren't waxed to a shine. A dust bunny hides in a corner. The furnace cuts off early on Sunday morning before people arrive. A restroom runs out of paper towels. Custodians can be forgiven if they develop a grouchy, defensive demeanor because it is a thankless job.

In today's reading, the pilgrims would rather serve in this thankless job and be in God's house than to live in the comfort that would be theirs within the tents of the wicked. The pilgrims, who have longed for the courts of the Lord, would rather be there for only one day than to live a thousand elsewhere.

Today's passage prompts us to ask ourselves: What are we willing to do to seek the joy of the Lord? In what ways are we willing to serve to be continually in God's presence?

Ever since my behind-the-scenes experience as a janitor, I have made a conscious effort to compliment custodial staff on their good work. When I meet with staff or leaders, I make it a point to tell them how welcome I feel when I cross the threshold of their facilities. I note that theirs is no small service. The Lord withholds no good thing from those who serve.

Lord of hosts, your sanctuary is the place of welcome. May I be a willing doorkeeper for all who enter to praise you. Amen.

A spate of ads on TV has promoted home security systems. An intruder gets scared away by a siren and a recorded warning voice. I have at times thought of investing in one. Yet not long ago I read a statistical study about gated communities versus those in similar neighborhoods that are not gated. Oddly, the crime rates were the same! Are we at times deluded in what we think will protect us? Granted, it is a good idea to have a backup system for your basement sump pump, but perhaps you don't need a castle moat with crocodiles swimming around!

When I hear the writer of Ephesians call us to "put on the whole armor of God," I easily think in military terms. Indeed, I can mistake the summons here to become like some spiritual survivalist living in a fortress or bunker crouched in battle readiness for we know not what.

Except for the "sword of the Spirit" (which is about boldness of witness), all the pieces of armor named in the text are defensive, not offensive. The point is not lost upon the Ephesians, who experienced military threat. Yet Paul calls them to arm themselves not against physical enemies but against evil. He encourages them to "stand firm"—to stand together as Greeks and Romans stand shoulder to shoulder in military battle—in order to resist the dark forces of a broken and often unjust world. Our togetherness is not rigid but flexible in its firm resolve to proclaim the good news.

How can I remain steadfast yet open in my witness?

Holy Spirit, strengthen me to fight the wiles of the evil one by making me pliable to your firm but gentle leading. Amen.

Jesus feeds a crowd of five thousand, and then he walks on water. When he calls out to the disciples, "It is I; do not be afraid," we know Jesus offers something more than bread alone. The people had their fill of the loaves, but what they still lack is Jesus himself. "It is I."

The crowd chases after Jesus clamoring for more bread and more miracles. But since Jesus refuses to be their king, they want to know how they can become miracle workers on their own. "What must we do to perform the works of God?"

And Jesus answers, "This is the work of God, that you believe in him whom he has sent." In other words, the true work of God is the work of believing, the work of faith. This is no ordinary work, either. Indeed, this "work" means to receive on his terms Jesus' offer of himself, "I am the bread of life."

Then the religious leaders weigh in: Who does he think he is, this Jesus? Isn't he the kid we knew from down home? How can he be from God? Aren't the things of God extraordinary and spectacular, not lowly and common? (See v. 42.)

Yet Jesus doubles down: "Whoever eats of this bread will live forever; and the bread that I will give for the life of the world is my flesh." And by flesh he means his humanness in all its stark reality.

Spirituality doesn't seek God in high and lofty places, but in the ordinary, the lowly, and the commonplace. We may come to church to be "uplifted," but Jesus offers us his flesh as the place where heaven and earth dwell. God leads us from the heights of heaven back down to earth to meet us in a body, from a manger to a cross.

God of miracles, you abide with us in Jesus, the Word made flesh. Feed us with the bread come down from heaven so that we may serve a hungry world with your love. Amen.

Standing Firm within the Word 283

Jesus doesn't shy away from speaking graphically. He says to his listeners: "Unless you eat [my] flesh and drink [my] blood, you have no life in you." This language and idea really offends the religious folks. "How can this man give us his flesh to eat?" Even his disciples plead, "This teaching is difficult; who can accept it?"

At last, Jesus reveals his point. He wants the people to "abide" in him. He wants people to live in him and to do so continuously—at all times. He draws people to himself and invites their dependence on him.

Today we tend to scorn dependence. Yet isn't that the challenge of the Christian life—to find strength in our very weakness? Why are we so proud? What do we fear? Why do we persist in the fantasy that we are self-made men and women?

Could it be that our real issue is one of trust? Like our forebears—the disciples, the crowds, and Moses' people in the wilderness with their manna—we find it hard to trust that God will take care of us. Sure, Jesus provided five loaves and two fish, but will he provide for us today and tomorrow and the next day? Dare we "abide" in him for our very lives?

When many turned away, Jesus asks Peter, "Do you also wish to go away?" Confused and doubtful though he was, Peter finally confesses, "Lord, to whom can we go? You have the words of eternal life."

This is our choice too. When Jesus promises, "I will be your bread of life," will we go away? Or will we dare to abide—to live in dependence on him?

Eternal God, give us the courage to accept our dependence on Jesus as our true daily bread. Amen.

Love Comes

AUGUST 27–SEPTEMBER 2, 2018 • MARY C. LINDBERG

SCRIPTURE OVERVIEW: The poetry of Song of Solomon is thick with romantic imagery, and most scholars agree that these lines mean what they say on the surface; they are written from the author to the beloved. Psalm 45 echoes the refrain of admiration and desire. Such desire is not wrong if it is awakened at the proper time, as the author of Song of Solomon says elsewhere. James argues that ethical living is done not in word but in deed. True religion is not putting on a show but displaying mercy and controlling the tongue. Jesus rebukes some of the religious leaders in Mark on this very account because they talk of obedience to God but do not live it out. What we say and what we do should match.

QUESTIONS AND THOUGHTS FOR REFLECTION

- Read Song of Solomon 2:8-13. The narrative poetry of Song of Solomon invites us into the Bible in a way that differs from other texts. How does God speak to you through this poetry?

- Psalm 45:1-2, 6-9. Intimate human love can reflect God's love. How do your relationships honor the gift of love?

- James 1:17-27. How do you bring God's love to those who need it?

- Mark 7:1-8, 14-15, 21-23. Are you simply going through the motions of faith, or is your heart close to God?

Lutheran pastor (ELCA) and freelance writer of children's and adult curriculum, as well as articles, book study guides, and blog posts; living in Seattle, Washington.

"Pay attention to the words people speak as you get ready to walk out the door," our chaplain supervisors advised us during our training as student chaplains. And sure enough, they were right! No matter how long we sit with patients and no matter how many topics we talk about, they often share the crux of what they want to say just as we prepare to say goodbye. With a hand on the doorknob, a chaplain may suddenly hear the words, "I am a little scared," or "My children haven't come to see me." At that point, the chaplain may sit down and enter a new and deeper conversation.

This passage from James both hints at the power of casually spoken words and saves its deeper message for the end. James touches on themes of speaking, listening, and acting as he recommends a way of life for Christian followers. In his plainspoken style that translates fluidly across the centuries between us, James includes coping strategies for spiritual tests and the rewards for faithful endurance.

Finally, at the end of the passage, James reveals what really matters. Before we go out the door of this scripture, James reminds us of the "why" of what we do as disciples. Our mission isn't about justifying or saving ourselves. Rather, God seeks to work through us to serve all those who depend on us. James and other biblical authors use the phrase "orphans and widows in their distress" to refer to the most vulnerable of God's beloved children who receive few resources and fewer rights. Come back and sit down, James reminds us. Don't go out the door before you hear this deeper truth—our actions, inspired by God's love, matter the most.

God of truth, remind us that love comes in quiet moments of relationships. Give us ears to hear and courage to turn and listen to what matters most. Amen.

James speaks as a realist. He recognizes the specific hindrances that block our faith, and he calls them out for us. Ego and anger, James knows, are two serious impediments to doing God's will. Today's verses move from God's action to the action expected of us. The author addresses the importance of listening undergirded by moderate speech and slowness to anger.

James would probably advocate for anger management classes. But he would have a different purpose in mind than those we name in our day. We attend anger-management groups so others won't be hurt by our out-of-control anger. But James takes this idea a step further by reminding us that our "anger does not produce God's righteousness." What a great insight!

New Testament experts typically interpret "anger" in the Bible as a sign of sin. But James explains anger even more profoundly. He insists that our behavior begin with God's righteousness, rather than by trying to earn God's righteousness. But how can we rely on God's righteousness to eclipse our anger when we are so painfully human? James is a realist about that question as well. Go back to the beginning of the passage to find his answer. Do you see it in verse 17? Every generous act of giving, with every perfect gift, is from above. When we choose forgiveness over anger and stop trying to use our anger as self-righteousness, we surrender to the gift of forgiveness that we first received in Christ Jesus.

God, who is slow to anger and abounding in steadfast love, we know your love comes through your grace. Help us learn how to manage our anger and how to surrender it to the hope that only you provide. Amen.

The Pharisees and scribes are Jewish religious leaders who hold tradition in high regard. In the missing pieces in between the portions of this text, Jesus points out that these leaders even give precedence to some traditions over God's commandments.

Today's reading describes the Pharisees and scribes reprimanding Jesus because his disciples have eaten with unwashed hands. Jewish tradition required that practitioners ritually purify both their hands and their cooking utensils.

Despite the leaders' ritual cleanliness, Jesus smells hypocrisy. Isaiah's prophecies were right, insists Jesus. The people perform their religious duties properly, but their hearts are no closer to God for following the rules of tradition. They have forgotten God's commandments from which the traditions arose.

Jesus points to another way: Right relationship with God comes not through ritual purity and tradition but through a heart set on God and relationship with others. Nothing outside us by going into us can defile us. Sin separates us from God and comes from within us—from our humanity and our capacity for evil. The sins God warns against in the Ten Commandments defile us, and they come from within our hearts.

So how do we avoid sin? A few chapters later, Mark gives us Jesus' answer: Love God with all our hearts, souls, minds, and strength, and love our neighbors as ourselves.

Dear Jesus, love comes through God's commandments. Write the greatest of these on our hearts so that we may better love you and others. Amen.

Fifty kids and leaders tumbled out of the minivans and car pools that carried them to the Bible school field trip at the community garden. Half an hour later, after instructions from the garden stewards, the kids busily harvested ripe carrots out of the ground for use at local food banks. In an effort to teach kids more about where our food comes from, the stewards invited them to taste the produce. Of course they also mentioned washing the veggies first. But the line for the water hose got very long, and Ben couldn't wait. "Ewwww!" responded Sam when he saw Ben take a bite of his soil-encrusted carrot. "You're going to get dirty inside, Ben!"

Like Sam, the Pharisees and scribes worry that ingesting unclean food with unclean hands is a big "Ewwww!" Not because it is disgusting but because it defiles—it is ritually impure. Rules of ritual purity—especially related to food preparation and consumption—separated Jews in Jesus' time from people who practiced other religions. The rules remind practitioners of their differences from others because they follow God. Jesus and his disciples would have known this well.

But Jesus comes along with radical news. Like Ben, Jesus can't wait to take a bite and get to the heart of the matter. What goes into us does not separate us from our neighbors; our hearts make us different from those who do not follow God. What we put into our bodies cannot cause us to stumble, but what is already in our hearts can. Only our love for God and our neighbors can cleanse our hearts.

Gracious God, love comes from the inside out. Please come into our hearts with your love. Amen.

The heading of this psalm titles it "a love song." In actuality, it is a royal wedding song. When read in its entirety, the psalm elaborates on the fine clothing of the bride and groom: robes fragrant with myrrh and aloes and cassia for the king; gold-woven robes for the princess. I suppose this is a bit of a Bible version of a royal wedding that people around the world might watch for entertainment. The pageantry of a royal wedding draws us in, and we get a chance to imagine a very different life as we gaze at stunning characters carrying out ancient traditions.

Verse 7 illuminates an aspect of an ancient royal wedding we might not see today. The psalmist proclaims that *God* has anointed the bridegroom—the king. We have not read or seen this in photos of royal weddings in *People* magazine!

The proclamation of the king as "anointed" shapes how Christians read this psalm. The Hebrew word for anointed can also be translated "messiah," and the Greek word can be translated "Christ." Ancient Israel identified many leaders as anointed, but for Christians our true anointed one is Christ. Because of this and because it is odd to have a psalm simply about a king, some Christians interpret Christ as the king in this passage. The New Testament begins this tradition. Hebrews 1:8-9 quotes Psalm 45:6-7 and demonstrates how early Christians made this psalm their own. The author of Hebrews simultaneously shows Christ's relationship to God and claims this psalm as about Christ rather than simply a secular king—Christ is anointed to bring God's reign and loving righteousness to the earth.

God of all, love comes in your Anointed One. May we worship him in truth. Amen.

"Please don't ask me to officiate any more weddings," I begged my two clergy colleagues on our church staff. After a string of wedding mishaps, I needed a break from less-than-ideal experiences. I had recently performed a ceremony for a couple who forgot to get a marriage license, and I had to marry them again officially after their honeymoon. Then I officiated at a wedding during which the bride talked to her attendants throughout the ceremony, even during the Lord's Prayer. Things were not going well for me in the world of weddings. But our large church received so many wedding requests that all of us had to step up and preside over our fair share of ceremonies.

After my grumbling, God surprised me with a wonderful blessing in the next couple I worked with. They were friendly, upbeat, and committed to spending a life together that included practicing their faith. We met several times before the ceremony to talk about marriage and pray together. When their wedding day arrived, I felt as excited as others in the church—not just because my disappointing wedding streak had passed, but because of my excitement about their sharing a life in Christ as married people. This rewarding experience and today's reading describe weddings that exemplify why many Christian traditions call marriage a holy sacrament: They point us to God's holiness. No matter how quirky a wedding can be, marriage reminds us of God's covenant and the abundant, sturdy grace it requires of those who would join their lives together.

God of surprise, we know your love comes through marriage. Be with all the couples and officiants celebrating weddings today. Amen.

Song of Solomon is one of the briefest books in the Old Testament with only one hundred seventeen verses organized into eight short chapters. However, as its other name, Song of Songs, implies, this book is treasured as one of the loveliest in the Bible. Perhaps because it focuses on the theme of love as our highest calling or because the springtime story of a young couple's romance engages us. Today's passage in particular evokes spring's contribution to the couple's love. And as the man invites the woman to "come away," his words draw us deeper into their love story.

In whatever way the text draws us, we cannot help but notice its difference from the rest of the Bible. Take a moment simply to lay your thumb on the outside of the pages of your Bible and gently fan through them. As you glance at the pages that pass by, you'll see many pages covered with text. But in the middle of your Bible, you'll glimpse white space. That's where the poetry lives. Song of Solomon appeals to us not just as a story but as a book of poetry.

While the psalms carry a didactic quality, Song of Solomon presents narrative poetry. Poetry in general, and this text in particular, can open us to the renewing power of love. It invites us to look more intimately at ourselves, our relationships with others, and our relationship with God. And what better place than a holy text like the Bible to discover the mysterious power and presence of poetry!

God of mystery, your love comes in Bible poetry. May we hear your sacred language. Amen.

Love Comes

Love Your Neighbor as Yourself

SEPTEMBER 3–9, 2018 • ROY L. HELLER

SCRIPTURE OVERVIEW: It has become an uncomfortable subject for many in our society, but God does have ethical standards. The author of Proverbs declares that those who act unjustly, particularly if they oppress the poor, will provoke God's judgment. The psalmist repeats the refrain that God blesses the righteous but is not pleased with those who choose a consistent lifestyle of rebellion against God. James challenges us practically on this point. Do we judge people by their wealth or status? This is not from God. Truth faith shows no partiality and prompts action. Jesus models this in Mark when he heals two Gentiles. Jews and Gentiles generally remained separate (an ancient form of racism), but Jesus did not discriminate based on their ethnicity. He cared only about their hearts.

QUESTIONS AND THOUGHTS FOR REFLECTION

- Read Proverbs 22:1-2, 8-9, 22-23. How has God shown you that there is no difference between persons who are rich and persons who are poor?

- Read Psalm 125. When have you seen righteousness in someone your church or community has labeled "wicked"?

- Read James 2:1-17. How do your works support your faith in God?

- Read Mark 7:24-37. God calls us to love all our neighbors, no matter their abilities or place of origin. How can you be a good neighbor to those your community has excluded?

Associate Professor of Old Testament, Perkins School of Theology, Dallas, Texas.

In our twenty-first-century world, e-mail, social media, and 24-hour news sources connect us in ways unimaginable to previous generations. Our technologies and online lives bring us seemingly closer to one another than ever before possible. On the other hand, our hyperconnected digital lives often separate us from our physically closest neighbors and deepen labels of "us" and "them." These categories are often purely imaginary; sometimes, however, they highlight deep differences between us. This week's readings will help us navigate both our real and fabricated differences as we learn the answer scripture gives to the question posed to Jesus long ago: "Who is my neighbor?"

The book of Proverbs helps us tease out the difference between illusion and reality, between what appears to be true and what is true. Today's readings hold to the light a common pair of labels—rich and poor—and show them to be an illusion in measuring our worth to God.

As humans, we often fall for the illusion that a person's life or worth is found in the things he or she possesses. We see those with great wealth as "important" in society because of the influence and power their wealth seems to bring, while we overlook or completely ignore persons without power and money. But today's readings make the point clearly: Whether we have or lack wealth, we are all created as children of God. We share common human experiences: our need for love and care, our knowledge of what it is like to be frightened or lonely, our ability to feel both despair and joy. At the end of the day, whether we lay our heads on silk pillowcases or a canvas bag on a curbside, God loves and values each of us. We are truly alike.

Lord, help me know that my neighbor is just like me: known and loved by you. Amen.

Yesterday's reading from Proverbs revealed that measuring people's worth by their wealth is an illusion. God created all of us, and our common humanity can bring us together. Today's reading from James illustrates a particular situation in which we may confuse wealth with importance. James chastises favoritism based on economic status. He writes with a parable: The host provides the best seats to those who have wealth while simultaneously telling those who have no financial resources to "stand there" or "sit at my feet," automatically placing them on the lowest rung in the group.

James argues that the leaders making distinctions about people based on wealth indicates that they have become "judges with evil thoughts." One valuable quality that a judge in a court of law needs to have is the ability to distinguish between facts, between arguments, and between people. The ability to distinguish truth from falsehood, or good from bad arguments, is critical to a judge's fulfilling his or her role. When, however, a judge distinguishes facts or arguments based on random or trivial details, then he or she can become dangerous.

And so it is with James's hearers. Because they decide people's worth based on their wealth, they have become like dangerous judges. Doing so, of course, causes division within the group but, even more so, calls into question whether the leaders actually believe in Christ, who, as James points out, has called all of us to honor the poor. While the rich find ways to oppress and blaspheme, God chooses to bless the poor with the inheritance of the kingdom of God.

Lord, help us to know that wealthier does not mean worthier as we seek to love all your children. Amen.

Ahealthy relationship with God requires both faith and works. Faith acknowledges the relationship we have with God, both individually and as a community. It understands and holds dear the privileges that such a relationship brings, as well as the responsibilities that such a relationship requires. Faith is simply a way to talk about a healthy relationship with God.

But how can we know that our relationship with God is, in fact, healthy and not presumptuous, prideful, abusive, or guilt-ridden? James gives us a litmus test: the way we interact with others in our everyday lives. Do we have a firm, true grasp on the privileges and responsibilities that our relationship with God has on our relationships with one another? The individual in the reading seems to assume that a relationship with God involves using religious language ("go in peace") and a certain level of hope for others ("keep warm and eat your fill"). But James asserts that this type of relationship with others is incomplete. It lacks the works necessary to support the words.

The way we treat others tests the health of our relationship with God because it reveals whether we see all people as created by God, choosing to meet their needs as they are set before us. At the end of the day, mere words, even religious words, do nothing to alleviate physical needs. It takes action, born of compassionate faith, to help and to heal.

Lord, may we not only see and speak about the needs of our neighbors but work to alleviate their needs. Remind us that our faith dies when we do not support it with loving works. Amen.

We often differentiate among people by focusing on national borders. The question of the status of immigrants or refugees is a daily discussion on news programs and in the halls of Congress. The question of how "they" are supposed to relate to "us" and vice versa is posed in simple language that assumes national borders can give us essential information about what is in another person's heart and mind. Unfortunately, these ways of thinking are nothing new.

Jesus himself crosses a border at the beginning of today's reading as he leaves Galilee and enters the Phoenician region of Tyre. There he is a stranger and a noncitizen. A woman—a citizen of the nation where Jesus is visiting—asks him for help. Jesus, surprisingly, relates to her through the usual differentiation based on region. He claims that her daughter has no share in his healing ministry because she is not Jewish.

The woman, however, knows that borders have little to do with loving a child, with knowing heartache, or with needing help. These qualities are part of being human and do not depend on nationality, ethnicity, or race. She contradicts Jesus' assessment of the situation, and he eventually capitulates. Her only concerns are her daughter's needs and Jesus' ability to heal. Nothing else matters. Nothing.

We erect walls and borders and designations to separate ourselves from our neighbors, but our relationship with God demands that we see one another as persons with needs. As Christians we claim to follow the works and teachings of Jesus. We are called to act as Jesus does in this passage: to accept criticism, recognize our mistakes, and meet the needs of those in front of us.

Lord, help us to learn what Jesus learned: Borders do not separate us; we are all your children. Amen.

Love Your Neighbor as Yourself   297

We may also find ourselves "labeling" people based on their physical ability—like seeing or walking or comprehending. We use the terms *disabled* and *whole* to divide people. We lump all those who cannot participate in certain activities due to varying degrees of capability into one group. "We," on the other hand, who may be unable to do many other things but can hear or speak or read do not consider ourselves disabled but "whole" people. This way of separating people is as irrelevant in assessing a person's worth as considering financial status or documenting someone's birthplace.

Today's story concerns Jesus healing a man who cannot hear or speak. A group brings him to Jesus and begs for his touch. Jesus takes the man away on his own and commands him, "Ephphatha—be opened!" The man can hear and speak. Yet the story is not over. Jesus goes on to command both the man and his friends to be silent and tell no one. But they disobey Jesus. They tell everyone about it, and the more Jesus implores them to be silent, the more they proclaim it.

The irony of this story is hard to miss. Those who were already "whole" by our standards are lacking; they fail to obey Jesus' commands. While their epithet that Jesus "does everything well" may be correct, they do not understand it—they refer only to his ability to bring hearing and speech. Being able to speak well or to hear is not fundamentally good or bad. Our goodness and wholeness stems from our ability to obey Jesus' commands. Being a good neighbor is not about bringing others to Jesus for healing; what truly differentiates us as followers of Jesus is our obedience.

Lord, we know that wholeness comes not from our abilities but from our willingness to follow your commands. Amen.

All religions attempt to instill a sense of right and wrong into the hearts and minds of their followers. Although we can think and discuss ethics without considering religion, it is difficult to discuss any religion without, at least partially, recognizing how the followers of that religion live out their faith. It is, therefore, understandable that one way religions generally, and Christianity particularly, have divided humanity is by sorting them into "good people" and "bad people."

Psalm 125 comes from a time when the inhabitants of Jerusalem feel confident in their safety, security, and place in the world. They believe that God protects their holy city from all enemies. For their part, the inhabitants have to make sure that no "evildoers" or people who "turn aside to their own crooked ways" or any "wickedness" find a place within their blessed, protected, and holy city. Furthermore, clearly the psalmist views himself and the people who agree with him as decidedly *not* in the group of "evildoers" but rather in the group of "righteous" and "good" people who are "upright in their hearts." All that needed to be done is to round up all those "bad people" and remove them so the "good people" can remain and be assured of God's protection.

This way of viewing life does not match the way the world is. While there may be a few true saints and a few true devils scattered here and there, the vast majority of us are a mixture of both. Being a creature of God means we have within us light and darkness, evil and goodness, hope and fear.

Lord, help me recognize my own virtues and vices before I label others as "good" or "bad." Show me how to love all my neighbors as your children. Amen.

Love Your Neighbor as Yourself

So many factors in the human experience can serve to separate us. Governments, societies, and even religions seem intent on erecting walls and boundaries that divide us based on any number of characteristics. Wealth (or lack of it), devotion (or lack of it), health (or lack of it), national origin, and even questioning an individual's goodness or badness have all been used to divide us and to set us against one another. The many qualities that often fuel discord among us has little if anything to do with what it means to be created and loved by God.

This week's final reading from James undercuts all that separates us from one another. Jesus' primary call is to love our neighbors, but that love must be based on a strong foundation: our awareness and acknowledgment that our neighbors are human, that God created them, and that God loves them in just the same way and to the same extent God loves us. Jesus calls us to love our neighbors not out of pity or condescension but rather from a deep knowledge that each of them is as capable of human failing and as worthy of love in God's eyes as we are.

And what should our attitude be toward those who perpetuate those divisions? The end of the reading provides a clue: Know that we ourselves will be judged mercifully by God, judged by a law of liberty. As we come to know God's merciful attitude toward us more fully, we, in turn, will show mercy to all and, by that mercy, triumph in the end.

Lord, help me recognize that loving others is the only way to be in good relationship with you. Amen.

Heed the Calling

SEPTEMBER 10–16, 2018 • STEPHANIE GATES

SCRIPTURE OVERVIEW: Through the scriptures and the guidance of the Holy Spirit, God shows the paths of righteousness and warns against the ways of destruction. The writer of Proverbs describes this as the voice of Wisdom crying out, yet some refuse to listen—to their peril. The psalmist rejoices in the law of the Lord, for God's decrees teach us how to live well. Living a godly life includes paying attention to our speech. How can we, James asks, praise God with our lips and then curse others with those same lips? Peter is tripped up by his words in Mark. He declares Jesus to be the Messiah, yet in the next scene he recklessly rebukes Jesus for speaking of his death. Our words matter, and God desires purity and consistency.

QUESTIONS AND THOUGHTS FOR REFLECTION

- Read Proverbs 1:20-33. How clearly can you hear Wisdom's call? What keeps you from answering?

- Read Psalm 19. How do your words and your heart's meditations reflect your faith? Do you think God finds them acceptable?

- Read James 3:1-12. Consider your words. Do they honor the image of God in those to whom you speak?

- Read Mark 8:27-38. When has God called you to be silent? Were you better able to hear an unexpected call from God?

Lives with her family in Denver, Colorado, where she writes and edits; find more of her work at awidemercy.com.

This week's readings center around hearing God's voice and heeding the call to faithfulness. Each scripture bears witness to the power of God's presence in the words and an invitation to respond.

Words can both harm and heal. They can usher peace and new life into a soul, or they can strip a soul of hope and freedom. Even the right words offered at the wrong time can have dire consequences. In Mark 8, Peter recognizes Jesus as the Messiah. However, Jesus quickly tells Peter to keep his knowledge to himself. He doesn't just tell, he warns the disciples not to share what they know. Indeed, if Peter had proclaimed Jesus as the Messiah prematurely, he would have cut Jesus' earthly ministry short and hastened his death.

Sometimes God calls us to be silent. When we see persons struggling because of poor choices or when we watch them repeat harmful patterns of behavior, we may be tempted to highlight exactly why they are in their current predicament. Our motives are good. We all want the people we love to experience a joyful life, free of suffering. Yet sharing even a truthful message at the wrong moment can further harm the people we most want to help.

Sometimes kind silence or a word of encouragement is much more beneficial than sharing facts. God's calling to speak will always be led by grace, gentleness, patience, and—above all else—love. If we speak outside of such motivations, we may speak the truth, but we do so outside of God's calling.

As we approach our communities with our own confessions of Christ, may we recognize who Jesus is and when to share our message of hope.

Jesus, give us the wisdom to recognize when you call us to speak the truth and when we should refrain. Amen.

Today's scripture recounts a notable interaction between Jesus and Peter. When Jesus shares a message of suffering and death with his disciples, Peter rebukes him. Jesus replies, "Get behind me, Satan" and warns that Peter's mind is not on the things of God but on human things. How shocked and embarrassed Peter must have been at Jesus' response!

Often, Jesus' message did not conform with the disciples' expectations. Throughout the Gospels we see other moments where Jesus' actions and teachings do not line up with what the disciples believe their rabbi's next steps should be.

We often experience the same internal conflict as did the disciples. We may feel a spiritual nudge to take an action that runs counter to our ideals and common sense. Perhaps we feel a growing passion for a specific political or social issue. Or we sense a pull toward a person in need, though their life path is out of sync with our personal values. We may feel drawn toward a kindness that is completely illogical. Perhaps we feel compelled to extend grace that comes at personal cost.

Others—even other disciples of Jesus—may warn us not to pursue the matter that weighs on our hearts. Logically, we may even agree with them. Yet we can't deny what we feel compelled to do. In such moments, we must decide which voice to follow.

Today's scripture reminds us that Jesus' ways are not like ours. Though many of us have followed Christ for most of our lives, heeding God's call can lead us in surprising directions. God's voice is more reliable than our own common sense. When we act outside of our own logic and trust God's Spirit within us, we follow in the footsteps of Jesus.

Help us, Holy One, to follow your voice and trust your ways, even when they don't make sense. Amen.

Heed the Calling

When my daughter was two years old, she enjoyed two activities: playing outside and removing her clothes. More than once, she sprinted out the front door and down our quiet residential street completely nude. Neighbors peeking from behind their blinds saw a tiny girl squealing with glee barreling down the road with her mother chasing her and yelling, "Come inside! Put on your clothes!"

Shortly after one of my daughter's joyful escapes, a police officer rang our doorbell. "There's been a report of a naked child in the streets," she said. "I'm here to make sure she's okay." One look around our living room confirmed my daughter was well loved and nurtured, and the officer soon left, reassured. But clearly my daughter's outdoor shenanigans had caught a neighbor's attention!

Today's proverb tells us Wisdom calls from the streets, and in this passage, she speaks loudly and clearly. Much as my neighbors could not help but see my jubilant toddler, Wisdom is hard to miss. Her voice is God's voice, and the way forward is clear. Why, then, do we struggle to make decisions? Why do we worry and fret? If Wisdom is calling with all the clarity of a naked child in our front yards, why does she feel so complex and elusive?

We know what we've been called to do, but we fear trusting God or ourselves. We're afraid of failure and humiliation, so we listen for a different answer. However, as today's passage warns, we need not fear the call but rather the consequences of refusing it. God will allow us to reap the disastrous rewards of our complacency, but we can live at ease if we choose to follow God. What we need now is the courage to heed Wisdom's call.

Lord, when Wisdom is in plain sight, please give us the courage to follow her. Amen.

Today's psalm describes something every one of us has experienced: The heavens declare the glory of God. Whether we're captivated by a mountain on the horizon, early mornings on a beach, or a sunset from our backyard, each of us has felt God's presence in the beauty, holiness, and majesty of the natural world.

Nature isn't the only thing that offers a glimpse into God's character. Many of us know persons whose lives bear a similar witness to God's presence. We can see a consistent, humble picture of kindness and grace in the daily lives of faithful people living out their call in our communities. They are not celebrities, nor have they chosen extraordinary paths. But day after day we observe their faithfulness to God and their goodness toward their neighbors. They leave us in awe as they evidence God's glory as fully as a beautiful sunset or gorgeous mountain view.

Often faith can feel complicated. We struggle with how to navigate the details of life in the most faithful way. As we consider how best to love God and neighbor, we can take great encouragement from the truth of these verses. We don't have to know the exact words to heed God's call. Nor do our lives need to be extraordinary to point others toward Christ. Our everyday routines share the grace and kindness we've experienced with our communities just as loudly as our words ever could. Simply by living out the goodness we have experienced, we bear faithful witness to Christ. In the same way a sunset draws us to the beauty of God, a faithful life can speak volumes.

Loving God, may my quiet habits reflect your glory as beautifully as your natural world. Amen.

Heed the Calling   305

In today's passage, James uses strong words to describe the tongue. He says it's a match that can start a wildfire—a fire that originates in hell. He warns that our "tongue," or speech, is the one animal that can never be tamed.

Is James right? Are we unable to control ourselves? Is our language doomed to be as damaging as he describes? Certainly our language has the power that James suggests. Language has the power to create new emotional realities and to rip all hope of peace from us. The language we use to describe events creates the framework through which our spouses and children view the world. Words are incredibly powerful.

If our primary objective is to stop the flow of negative words, then, yes, James's images ring true. When we harbor ill feelings toward others but try to hold them back, in time the dam will burst; we will spew bitterness and frustration onto those around us. Alternatively, we may successfully control our words, but our negative emotions will smolder internally, fueling deeper anger and poisoning our own souls. If we want to control our tongues, we must first address our hearts.

Luke 6:45 tells us that out of the overflow of the heart, the mouth speaks. To change our words, we must address the deeper emotions of our hearts. Are we speaking from a place of pain or out of the longing of an unmet need? Let us reflect on our emotions and make peace every way we can, first with God, and then with our neighbors.

We can heed James's call to tame the powerful beast that is our tongue. But first, we must resolve the undercurrent of emotions in our hearts.

Lord, heal our hearts so we can control our speech. Amen.

Every Sunday many ministers utter the psalmist's prayer just before offering sermons to their congregations. They have spent the week reading, studying, praying, and writing a spiritual reflection on a passage of scripture. Then, just before they share their thoughts, they pray that their words will please God. The psalmist uses verse 14 for a similar purpose. After creating verses that describe God's glory as evidenced in nature, as well as God's faithfulness to God's people, he asks that his reflections will be pleasing and acceptable to his Redeemer.

Some of us struggle with the idea that God could ever be pleased with us. We've heard descriptions of a fearful or vengeful God and think a misstep will lead to God's wrath. Negative experiences with those in positions of authority can leave us hesitant to believe our thoughts, words, and deeds could ever be useful or pleasing. Even after we devote considerable energy to reflecting on God's grace, mercy, goodness, and kindness, we offer our spiritual gifts with trepidation.

But we can take courage in God's faithfulness. God loves us immeasurably and created us to be in communion with God and one another. When we heed the calling toward love, grace, perseverance, peace, humility, and joy, we can be certain God is happy with our words and actions. The psalmist assures us that God's law is perfect, God's decrees are sure, God's precepts are right, and God's commandments are clear. When we study and follow God's guidance, we can know our words and meditations please God. As we live out the calling of the Holy Spirit, we can trust the voices that tell us we are cherished children of God, who is our strength and our Redeemer.

O God, we know that you love us and have created us for communion with you. Help us to trust in your goodness and to approach you without fear of punishment. Amen.

Heed the Calling

James offers a clear warning: harsh, critical, damaging language has no place in a faithful life. The text suggests it's impossible for the two to coexist: "Does a fig tree produce olives, or a grapevine produce figs?" James asks. Then he answers, "No, and you can't draw fresh water from a salty spring."

No Christian wants to cause harm. Every one of us believes we're doing the right thing or, at the very least, that our responses are justified. None of us sets out to inflict pain or emotional damage on our loved ones or communities. Yet modern American Christianity is characterized largely by infighting, anger, and bitterness. How do we change? When we interact with people who have either hurt us or who we believe are hurting others, how do we move past our indignation to extend grace and compassion to one another?

Even as James describes the problem, he hints at the solution: We can remember that each person is created in the image of God. We tend to see ourselves as complex beings and weigh our motivations as heavily as our results. We view ourselves as capable of love, kindness, faithfulness, and grace, even when we act in a manner that does not line up with such values. Do we extend the same gracious perspective to others? Are we looking for glimpses of God's nature within each person we meet? We hold tightly to the parts of our lives that reflect God's image and judge our misbehavior in their light. Do we look for God's image within others as well, buried beneath their own mountains of pain and good intentions?

God, help us see your reflection within every person we meet. Only then can we change our attitudes and language toward others. Amen.

The Option to Choose

SEPTEMBER 17–23, 2018 • BRAULIO TORRES

SCRIPTURE OVERVIEW: Proverbs describes the noble wife and sets a standard that can seem impossible. This woman is capable and respected but also generous and wise. She serves but is not weak. Is she a "superwoman," and do all women need to be "superwomen"? No, she is noble because she follows the counsel of the psalmist and is deeply rooted in the teachings of God. Therefore, she sets a standard for everyone to emulate, not just women. James, another teacher of wisdom, encourages believers to show these same characteristics by following the wisdom given by God. In Mark the disciples display a lack of wisdom by arguing over who is the greatest. Jesus reminds them that greatness in God's eyes comes through service, not through seeking recognition.

QUESTIONS AND THOUGHTS FOR REFLECTION

- Read Proverbs 31:10-31. How have societal expectations shaped your life? How do you allow them to shape the ways you interact with others?

- Read Psalm 1. When have you had to choose between wickedness and righteousness? What influenced your choice?

- Read James 3:13–4:3, 7-8a. You can choose the way you react to conflict. How can facing your internal struggles help you deal with external conflict?

- Read Mark 9:30-37. With what are you too preoccupied? How do your personal worries constrain your perspective?

Ordained elder, Baltimore Washington Conference of The United Methodist Church; Executive Pastor, Calvary United Methodist Church, Annapolis, Maryland.

We often assume that Proverbs 31 describes the perfect woman or the characteristics a "good" woman needs to possess. However, we need to be aware that this passage is a poem that describes the virtues of wisdom and does not reflect a gender definition. These verses from Proverbs 31 express and celebrate the virtues of wisdom and its character. They celebrate wisdom's capabilities.

The church often employs this passage to encourage women to look on these characteristics or virtues and practice them. This misunderstanding reminds me of a story told by Alan Carr. He wrote, "A teacher gave her class of second-graders a lesson on the magnet and what it does. The next day in a written test, she included this question: My full name has six letters. The first one is *M*. I pick up things. What am I? When the test papers were turned in, the teacher found it astonishing that almost 50 percent of the students answered the question with the word *Mother*.

The children connected the description of a magnet to a role that society has imposed on women. The church often does the same with this passage from Proverbs. We have misunderstood a poetic personification of God's wisdom as an outline for fulfilling the cultural role of "biblical womanhood."

Isaiah 54:5-6 speaks of the Lord as the husband of Israel. From this perspective, today a "good wife" can be understood as the body of Christ, which is the church—a church always ready to serve the Lord; a church with character, integrity, and loyalty.

Father and Mother God, may we be willing to live in harmony and unity, governed by your wisdom. Amen.

Today's passage reminds me of a story from an anonymous author. A little boy named Peter is visiting his grandparents' farm. Peter has a slingshot and plays with it in the forest every day but always misses his mark. One day as he approaches the house for dinner he sees his grandma's pet duck and cannot resist trying to hit it with his slingshot. He accidentally kills the duck and is so sad and scared he hides the body in the forest. His sister Sammy sees everything but does not say a word. When Grandma asks Sammy to help with the dishes she says, "Peter told me he wants to help" and then whispers to Peter, "Remember the duck?" Later Grandpa asks the kids if they want to go fishing. Grandma says Sammy needs to help cook but Sally says, "I can go; Peter told me he wants to help" and again whispers, "Remember the duck?"

Finally Peter cannot hold his guilt in any longer. He confesses his actions to Grandma. She replies, "I saw everything; I forgive you because I love you. I have been wondering how long you would let Sammy use your guilt to control you."

Like Peter, we have a choice: to suffer in the guilt of our mistakes and allow those who recognize our struggle to take advantage of it or to follow not the advice of those with their own motives but rather the path that leads to happiness—the path that meditates on God's word. Sometimes this means confessing actions we would rather ignore or forget. But like Grandma, the Lord is ready to forgive us. Psalm 1 assures us God watches over our path when we seek to live righteously in pursuit of the Lord. The choice is ours.

Lord, help us to follow the path of righteousness as we seek to delight in you. Guide us so that we may flourish. Amen.

The Option to Choose   311

James writes to Christians experiencing conflict. In order to help them, James confronts them with this question: "Who is wise and understanding among you?" In other words, how do you know you are right? Then he moves on to explain the difference between earthly wisdom and heavenly wisdom. Two key words in this passage are worthy of deeper consideration: *show* and *life*. Wisdom is something that can be seen or shown, and our lifestyles will reveal the kind of wisdom we choose.

Like the Christians to whom James writes, we live in conflict with one another for following "earthly wisdom" in many instances. When churches experience change, conflicts can begin when people say, "We have been doing things this way for years." These persons are really saying, "We are comfortable with this approach; this is our preference; don't change the status quo." James calls this wisdom from below. Such earthly wisdom is often based upon envy, self-ambition, or personal preference.

When we decide to follow "wisdom from above," things begin to change—not just for our own benefit but for that of our whole community. This kind of wisdom considers others; it shows respect and listens willingly. Wisdom from above recognizes that it is not about us; it is about God's will. Wisdom is not about receiving recognition but giving honor and glory to God in everything.

James encourages our awareness of motives behind our arguments. He invites us to choose the type of guidance we will follow: earthly wisdom or heavenly wisdom.

God, guide us as we seek to follow your wisdom in our lives and our communities. Amen.

Those conflicts and disputes among you, where do they come from? Do they not come from your cravings that are at war within you?" External conflict often reflects our internal struggles. Sometimes when we are upset or angry at someone, it has nothing to do with what the person did or said. Rather, the person's actions or attitudes have triggered unresolved emotional conflict within us related to pride, hate, ambition, jealousy, and revenge. When our arguments stem from these emotions, we fight only for personal preference or self-promotion.

Today's scripture invites us to look within rather than turning our emotions outward or blaming others when we find ourselves fighting. We question ourselves: What I am fighting about? Is the fight for my desire to have my own way? to gain admiration? to get even? Is it just to fulfill my pride? What personal preference am I trying to protect or seek?

If we pay closer attention to ourselves than to external forces, we will discover that the root of our tensions exists within us. The battle of personal desires is the "war within" that James talks about. Our struggles can separate us from one another or hinder our full relationship with God and with our neighbor. James invites us to discover and accept a simple truth: The fight resides within us. Only an inward focus will move us toward resolution.

Gracious and loving God, help us humble ourselves and face the tensions of our internal desires rather than fighting with our brothers and sisters. Amen.

Obedience to God begins the fulfilling of God's will in our lives. When James writes about submitting to God, he is simply saying: Obey God.

Some of us wrestle with the concept of submitting ourselves because we don't like to be told what to do. However, if we think about it, we submit ourselves every day. We submit when we obey the speed limit or when we slow down to the speed limit to avoid a speeding ticket at the sight of a police car. We submit every year when we fill out tax returns or when we follow what society tells us about what it means to be a good citizen. We submit when we follow the rules and regulations at the airport so we can get on our flight.

James writes about submitting to God to advise us on how to be in good relationship with God. When we draw closer to God, we experience peace, joy, comfort, love, and hope. However, without a close relationship to God, everything we face can trigger fear, anxiety, stress, anger, depression.

God requires submission not to exercise power over us. Instead, God is like a parent who knows what is best for us and wants us to obey so we don't get hurt.

Resisting evil results in opposing our own pride and arrogance that tell us we don't need God because we have everything figured out. We hold the choice in our hands: Resist God and follow our own ways, or resist our self-confidence and vanity and draw near to God. May we choose wisely.

God, help us choose obedience to you so we can follow your ways and draw near to you. Amen.

Why are the disciples afraid to ask? Is it because they cannot conceive that Jesus can suffer death after the notoriety of his ministry and miracles? It seems that their fear reflects more than that. If we pay attention to the scripture, Jesus not only talks about his death and resurrection. He also says, "The Son of Man is to be betrayed into human hands."

I think what sticks out in the disciples' minds is Jesus' use of the idea of betrayal. Today, not so different from Jesus' time, the people we love and trust are those most capable of betraying us. This means that our darkest times of feeling betrayed always stem from people with whom we are in intimate relationships.

It's no wonder the disciples are afraid to ask Jesus for clarification—they know that someone among them will be responsible for events that lead to Jesus' crucifixion. The disciples' strong focus on their own fear makes us wonder, *Do the disciples actually hear the rest of Jesus' declaration?* He tells them he will rise from the dead after he is killed!

When our fear and worry consume us, we may not see other options. Our fear constrains our vision and kills our hopes and dreams. Only when we confront our fears do we discover that everything we feared was an illusion, a product of our imagination. Because, at the end of the day, fear is only False Expectations Appearing Real (FEAR).

God sent Jesus to take away our fear. The victory of the Cross makes it possible for us to face and conquer our fears. We can choose what to listen to: our fears or Jesus' message of new life built on love and forgiveness.

God, help us choose the way of Jesus over the way of fear. Amen.

When I was seventeen years old, I attended a Methodist church where the pastor always encouraged and empowered others. One day I decided to ask him who his favorite student was, expecting to hear my name. So I asked, "Pastor, who is your favorite?" "Why are you asking?" he replied. "I just want to know," I said. "Nobody," he answered. "I have a different relationship with each of you." Then I asked again, "Yes, but who is your favorite? You must have one." He smiled and said, "I know you want me to say that you are the one. I love all of you. I have no special preference for any of you."

I dropped the conversation although I was not fully satisfied by the answer. I did not care about the others; I just wanted to be the "favorite."

Today's passage reminds me that on many occasions we are like the disciples who focus on themselves rather than on others. Despite the fact the disciples don't answer Jesus' question, Jesus gives them the answer to their quarrel.

As I reflect on my experience with the pastor, I remember that I never asked him again about his favorite. I decided to stay with him and learn from him. Twenty-three years later, he is still my pastor. He became my mentor, and I have spent more years with him than anyone else. All this was possible because I stopped trying to be above others. Otherwise, I would not be sharing this story with you today.

Jesus tells us today that we become the greatest not by seeking recognition or being served but by choosing to humble ourselves to serve others.

Almighty God, give us the courage to refrain from seeking to be above others. Remind us that you do not call the best; you call those willing to be servants. Amen.

The Option to Choose

It's time to order!

Upper Room Disciplines 2019

Regular edition: 978-0-8358-1742-4

Enlarged-print: 978-0-8358-1743-1

Kindle: 978-0-8358-1744-8

eBook: 978-0-8358-1745-5

Bookstore.UpperRoom.org

or

800.972.0433

Did you know that you can enjoy

The Upper Room Disciplines

in multiple ways? Digital or print?

The Upper Room Disciplines is available in both regular and enlarged print, but are you aware that it is also available in digital format? Download a copy to your Kindle or choose an eBook version for your e-reader. Whatever your preference, we have it for you today.

What is a standing order option?

This option allows you to automatically receive your copy of *The Upper Room Disciplines* each year as soon as it is available. Take the worry out of remembering to place your order.

Need to make changes to your account?

Call Customer Service at 800.972.0433 or e-mail us at

CustomerAssistance@upperroom.org.

Our staff is available to help you with any updates.

Choosing Life: Being on God's Side

SEPTEMBER 24–30, 2018 • MARY C. EARLE

SCRIPTURE OVERVIEW: The Jewish people have faced possible destruction numerous times. The story begins not with the Holocaust in Europe but far back in history during the time of Esther. The wicked Haman plots to wipe out God's people, but God saves the people through Esther's courage. The psalmist praises God for this kind of salvation from seemingly impossible circumstances. Although we may not face genocide, we have our own struggles. James encourages us to pray with faith, believing that God can and will answer. Our prayers are powerful, James assures us. Jesus teaches us the importance of letting nothing stand between God and us. Using vivid hyperbole, he admonishes us to put the pursuit of God above everything else and to support others in that same pursuit.

QUESTIONS AND THOUGHTS FOR REFLECTION

- Read Esther 7:1-6, 9-10; 9:20-22. What traditions extend your memory?

- Read Psalm 124. God created heaven and earth. How do you choose to be on God's side, the side of creation?

- Read James 5:13-20. When has God's abiding presence allowed you to experience some sense of cheer despite your suffering?

- Read Mark 9:38-50. Whoever is not against you is for you. How can you share God's love with those outside your inner circle?

Episcopal priest, spiritual director, retreat leader, and author of nine books, who also serves as faculty for the Academy for Spiritual Formation; website: www.marycearle.com.

The book of Esther brims with dangerous intrigue. Haman, a courtier consumed by greed, schemes to annihilate the Jewish people who live within the vast Persian realm. He persuades King Ahasuerus to issue an edict against "a certain hostile people," seeking their destruction. Mordecai and Esther, both Jews, attempt to save their people. Queen Esther prays fervently to the God of Israel, asking for guidance. Her inspired exposure of Haman's plot leads to his death.

Mordecai and Esther—outsiders in this kingdom yet trusted by Ahasuerus—become instruments of justice. Ahasuerus rescinds the edict; the Jewish people are protected.

The first time I heard the name "Haman" was in my friend Jill's kitchen. Jill is Jewish, and I spent much of my adolescence in her home. Jill's mom, Esther, always prepared culinary delights for the various feasts of the Jewish liturgical year. One day Esther was baking for Purim, the festival that commemorates the events recounted in the book of Esther. She handed me a cookie and told me that it was a *hamantaschen*. In rabbinic fashion, Esther said, "We might ask why we would commemorate such an evil man. The answer lies in God's goodness, for we were delivered from Haman's scheme. We remember the sweetness of that deliverance."

Central to our way of faith is the practice of remembering. As I savored the sweet goodness of the *hamantaschen* in Esther's kitchen, Esther stretched my memory back to the time of Queen Esther and Mordecai. She led me to see that life is full of those dire times when violence threatens. Esther remembered with me that God transforms despair to hope and death to life.

Gracious God, you meet us in distressing circumstances. Help us trust that you are with us; lead us in the path of life. Amen.

I have received spiritual direction for over thirty years. Each of my spiritual director's guidance has had the same emphasis: God is with us always and in all circumstances. Though I may not perceive God's presence, that does not mean that God is not with me.

The book of Esther reminds us of this eternal truth. God is present through times of trial and through people who are willing to choose life. Mordecai, the Jewish sage close to King Ahasuerus, challenges Haman's plot to annihilate the Jewish people. Queen Esther, who hid her Jewish identity from Ahasuerus, wisely uses her royal status to champion her people. God's desire that we choose life over death lives in these two. Even Ahasuerus creates safeguards for the Jews after Esther exposes Haman's plot.

Esther's story is fraught with abuse of power, consuming greed, and violent intent. Queen Esther's history reminds us that transformation often occurs through human agents. At first glance, neither Mordecai nor Esther seem able to stop Haman's plot. Yet they find a way to create the moment for Ahasuerus to choose life. Inspired and given strength to act by God, Mordecai and Esther upend Haman's machinations.

The mystery of transformation lies within this story—a series of choices on behalf of life and justice. A time of distress becomes a holiday. A celebration of abundant life unfolds, and the celebration of God's abundance becomes a call to celebrate and share our abundance with the poor. We are called to bring God's presence and justice into this world.

God of hope, lead us to bring your presence to others out of our abundance. May we always choose life and justice. Amen.

"Whose side are you on?" My sister would ask me this when we got crossways with our brothers. While my sister and I were trying to do homework or get ready for a date, they were building go-carts and hiding our makeup. We would lay our case before our parents. As in any courtroom, it was important to know which side I represented.

The psalmist is clear: God is on Israel's side. The enemy has not won; God has delivered Israel. "If it had not been the LORD who was on our side. . . . " Israel would have been destroyed. These verses reverberate with relief. This song of God's presence and mercy leads us to remember those times when we've been brought through deep waters.

What is it to know that God is with us, that God chooses us?

So often we subtly assume that because God chooses us, everyone else falls outside the privileged circle of divine protection. Our current social and political conversations are rife with this kind of assumption.

Yet the psalm doesn't take us that far. This poem focuses our attention sharply on the moment of knowing we have come through something awful, through no action of our own. We survived a car wreck. We lived through a tornado. We are still standing after an earthquake. We escaped being blown up by a bomb. We emerged from battle alive.

And yet, we know others did not escape. We know others did not sense the relief that quivers in our limbs. We bow down. We worship. We give thanks and remember.

Loving God, help us to dwell within the mystery of your loving deliverance, giving thanks not only with our lips but with our lives. Amen.

This past spring my husband and I decided to put a sign in our front yard. It is a sign of welcome to our neighbors, written in English, Spanish, and Arabic. I braced for pushback, but none came. Instead, we have been thanked. We have made new friends. We have gotten a "thumbs up" from a couple of young men from Jordan. We have had happy conversations in Spanish. Our neighborhood turns out to be a place where we remember that all people have their origin in God because God made heaven and earth.

Unfortunately, we often struggle to remember this truth. We make the grave mistake of assuming that the life of faith is about deciding who is in and who is out, who is on our side and who is not.

What if we commit to being on God's side? What if we decide to love our neighbors as we love God? What if we live out that call in wondrously varied ways? Imagine a society in which embodied compassion is the norm. Imagine choosing to let go of categories of prestige and privilege. Imagine conversations where we honor the image of God in one another.

Being on God's side means being friends of God, who has befriended us in Jesus, as we proclaim that everyone comes within Jesus' saving embrace. Being on God's side looks like remembering that the Maker of heaven and earth dwells within the cells of every single person and creature on the planet.

In choosing us, God takes the extraordinary risk of hoping we will choose life—not only for ourselves but for our neighbors, our communities, and our earth.

Beloved Friend, lead us to be on your side—the side of compassion and active care. Deliver us from the self-righteous practice of excluding others. Amen.

Choosing Life: Being on God's Side   323

Are any among you suffering?" Suffering manifests in many different ways: illness, depression, loss of work or home, strain in relationships, political and social oppression, the terrible despair that can gnaw away at the roots of living faith.

The world of advertising would lead us to believe that we can alleviate suffering with a new car or a trip or a new lipstick. We constantly receive the suggestion that if we suffer, we must have done something to cause it.

In today's reading, James doesn't seem to care about cause. He focuses on the fact of the suffering and tells us to pray. James does not write this advice in a smug or facile way. He lives in a church facing persecution; he has seen suffering of every stripe. Suffering is real, and prayer offers a means to speak that suffering to God. James's remedy calls for community, anointing, and prayer. This type of communal prayer, praying with and for one another, is both powerful and effective.

In the midst of all this, James asks if any are cheerful. He moves from suffering to cheer in two short sentences. It's as if he believes the two can coexist. In my experience as an Episcopal priest, I've known people who were suffering and cheerful. They weren't full of false cheer. They had the deep and abiding sense of God's presence in and through the pain. I've seen people whose aching loneliness was healed by regular, sustained kindness from friends and occasional wisdom from strangers.

James has confidence that the risen Christ brings life from death. His is a faith that has legs, arms, hands, feet. His is a faith that embodies "love one another."

Healing Christ, may I be honest about my own suffering. Grant me the desire to pray for others and to be a friend to those who hurt. Amen.

The beloved disciple does not start out being gripped by the truth of love conquering death. John, like the rest of us, starts out as a new convert. As a novice disciple, he wants to know that he is doing things the right way, that he is in the inner circle, that there's a clear demarcation between those who are with Jesus and those who are not.

I've been there. Maybe you have too. It's a condition known well by those in the first steps of spiritual formation. This tendency has its usefulness: I know who I am by thinking and acting in this way. Most of us know what this feels like. We prefer simple, clear rules.

Then comes a moment when those simple, black-and-white categories fall by the wayside. For John, it comes when Jesus says, "Whoever is not against us is for us."

What? Doesn't Jesus mean "Whoever is not for us is against us?" That's what we thought was true.

The good news is that those tired polarities no longer work. They did not work for Jesus, nor do they now. Jesus calls us to move beyond simplistic ways of seeing. He asks us to behold the world with his eyes and to discover the truth behind "Whoever is not against us is for us." He is not speaking geopolitically. He speaks from the divine heart, urging John the beloved to wake up and recognize that divine love encompasses everyone and everything.

The good news is that Christ and our Christian communities guide us into deeper, more complex ways of seeing the world. Choosing to be on God's side rarely means excluding those who do not think or act like us.

Beloved Christ, I offer my mind, my heart, my body, my soul, that they may be renewed by your love and life. Amen.

Choosing Life: Being on God's Side　　　325

Jesus offers strong words in today's passage. He cautions the listener to attend to behavior and speech. We could quail in the face of these challenges and assume that going to hell is a given. Yet Jesus, using the colloquial patterns of his culture, loves to overstate in order to make a point.

I am a native Texan, and my own regional sayings have something of this flavor. My grandmothers would say, "Don't cut off your nose to spite your face." Or, "Bite your tongue before you say that." I knew they weren't being literal. I also knew they were trying to make a point. Colloquial speech doesn't beat around the bush.

Jesus desires our awakening from collective slumber. He wants us to notice how we wound one another with unthoughtful speech. Jesus senses that we have fallen into a spiritual narcolepsy. He believes we need strong metaphors. Such serious and yet playful speech can stir our hearts, clear our minds, and kindle our spirits.

After all, we need to have salt in ourselves. As any cook will tell you, a bit of salt brings forth the flavors of a dish. Too much, and you taste only salt. Having a little salt—even through hyperbolic warnings—in the dish of life helps us remember that God created us to live with love, joy, gentleness, kindness, self-control, patience, generosity, compassion, and faithfulness.

Wake up! Be kind! Care for yourself and one another! For heaven's sake, live like you're alive! God calls us to choose life.

Risen Christ, awaken me to this world, to my friends and neighbors. May I know your presence in all places and at all times and be transformed by your Spirit of love. Amen.

Redefining Blessing

OCTOBER 1–7, 2018 • DUANE ALAN ANDERS

SCRIPTURE OVERVIEW: This month we read about Job, an upright man who faces severe trials but never loses his faith. Job's story brings us face-to-face with the fact that living a godly life does not make us immune to suffering. Like Job, the psalmist wonders why he suffers, even though he lives according to God's standards. Hebrews presents Jesus as the ultimate example of unwarranted suffering, yet because of his perseverance he is ultimately glorified. In Mark, some Pharisees test Jesus on the interpretation of the law concerning divorce. Jesus makes strong statements about marriage, but his larger concern is that their hearts have become hard. He contrasts them with little children, who model faith by receiving God with an open heart.

QUESTIONS AND THOUGHTS FOR REFLECTION

* Read Job 1:1; 2:1-10. How do you live with integrity?
* Read Psalm 26. When have you turned to God, fully expecting divine intervention in a tough situation? What happened?
* Read Hebrews 1:1-4; 2:5-12. When has your reaction to God's showing up in unexpected ways resulted in a face-plant?
* Read Mark 10:2-16. How questioning a person are you? When have your questions helped you move below the surface of an issue to see the supporting understanding?

Senior pastor, Cathedral of the Rockies, Boise, Idaho.

My dad accompanied me to get my first-ever car loan at his bank. I was a college student with a part-time job and little money. The interview went like this: "Are you Bill's son?" "Yes sir." "Bill always pays his debts on time. How much do you need?" That was it—no paperwork, no background check. My father's integrity opened the door; I got the loan.

Today's scripture introduces us to Job, one of the Bible's amazing characters who journeys through life's ups and downs. From this one verse we learn Job has a nontraditional Israelite name and resides outside of Israel in the land of Uz. The verse further informs us that Job lives out his beliefs. He is a person of integrity, who seeks God and resists evil.

Life is full of decisions. In our baptismal vows my church asks candidates for baptism to make decisions: Do you renounce the spiritual forces of wickedness, reject the evil powers of this world, and repent of your sin? Do you accept the freedom and power God gives you to resist evil, injustice, and oppression in whatever forms they present themselves? Do you confess Jesus Christ as your Savior, put your whole trust in his grace, and promise to serve him as your Lord, in union with the church which Christ has opened to people of all ages, nations, and races?" (UMH, no. 34). We expect people to live out their responses.

Job's story invites us to ask big questions of God and of ourselves. Can we live with integrity in the midst of chaos? Where is God in the midst of suffering? How does our definition of blessing differ from that of the world's?

God, I want my life to have integrity. Help me make sure that my walk and my talk match. Amen.

What is the nature of relationship between God and human beings? Are we in a symbiotic relationship that rewards behavior? Job is a person of integrity—at least before his life falls apart. But how much integrity does he retain after his losses? In blow after blow, Satan challenges Job with the loss of livestock, servants, transportation, and children. In the face of his world falling apart, Job offers an astonishing statement of faith, "Naked I came from my mother's womb, and naked shall I return there; the LORD gave, and the LORD has taken away; blessed be the name of the LORD" (Job 1:21).

Satan barters with God "skin for skin," and we realize that this is more than marketplace language; Satan afflicts Job's entire body with sores. With his health attacked, Job is left with a ripped robe and a broken piece of pottery to scrape his body. What does blessing look like? Not like this, we say. Blessing looks like Job's prior life when he had health, wealth, and possibilities.

When all four of our children were small and my wife and I took everyone out to eat, calamity and chaos ensued. Often someone would stop by our table and say, "You sure have your hands full." We knew we had our hands full; those words were not helpful. Every now and then a person would stop by and say to our chaos, "You have a beautiful family." Now *that* was a gift of seeing blessing in the midst of calamity.

Job's wife invites him to "curse God, and die." Perhaps that is her way of maintaining integrity. Job replies with words that have changed my life, "Shall we receive the good at the hand of God, and not receive the bad?" Do we perceive God as present in all of life, both in blessing and in calamity?

God, help me bless someone who is in the midst of his or her chaos. Amen.

Redefining Blessing

The Psalms speak with honesty, emotion, and passion. Who prays a dangerous prayer like this? "Prove me, O LORD and try me; test my heart and mind." It sounds like the psalmist is saying, "Look at me, God. I'm doing great! I'm living a godly life and have no sin to speak of. Take a close look at me, and you'll see how spiritual I am."

The Bible ascribes this psalm to David, whose sins we know all too well. His prayers of confession and repentance are some of the most humble, transparent passages in scripture. Not far from Psalm 26 David acknowledges his sin and his need of God's mercy: "Do not remember the sins of my youth or my transgressions. . . . Consider my affliction and my trouble, and forgive all my sins" (Ps. 25:7, 18).

Then it struck me. We also know David as the victim of unjust treatment at the hands of others, being hunted like an animal and slandered, indicted for crimes he did not commit.

Who prays a prayer like Psalm 26:1? One who has experienced false accusation and is pleading the case before God. The psalmist does not brag of spiritual superiority but makes a claim of innocence. He is simply saying, "These accusations are false. I did not do what people are saying I did. I am coming to you, Lord, because you know the truth." The enemies are real, and David turns to a gracious God for redemption, expecting God to act on his behalf.

The psalm ends with a promise of praise anyway. Integrity fosters an ability to bless God and neighbor in all situations.

Examine me, God, from head to foot; fill me with grace that I may praise you and bless my neighbor. Amen.

Learning to water ski requires counterintuitive behavior. Once you get the gear on and you are waiting in the water, some well-meaning "expert skier" will share the following secret, "Let the boat pull you up." This sounds great until you feel the pull of the rope as it begins to tighten between you and the boat. Your first reaction is to begin to pull yourself up. Soon you have face-planted in the lake. The boat now circles back, and the words echo, "Let the boat pull you up." Even though you hear the words, your mind cannot perceive what is being said. Ten or twenty attempts later, as the boat begins to move, you feel the rope tighten and, before you know it, the boat pulls you up.

The author of Hebrews speaks a counterintuitive word to those of us who grew up looking for a messiah but have not yet found one in Jesus. The writer tells us that Jesus not only fulfills the prophetic expectations of messiah but also reflects all that is God. Wow! Our first reaction is a face-plant—so unexpected!

God has used many approaches while reaching out to us. God spoke to Jacob, Isaiah, and Joseph in dreams and visions. God spoke through the actions of leaders like Esther, Ruth, and Daniel. God spoke through words of the prophets like Ezekiel, Amos, and Micah—all were normal, acceptable, familiar ways that God spoke. Now we learn that God is speaking through Jesus, "the exact imprint of God's very being." God speaks "to us" in a counterintuitive way!

Learning new skills and gaining new information takes time and effort. The writer of Hebrews extends an invitation to those who have not fully embraced Jesus to see with new eyes the blessings of God before them in the Son.

Lord, guide my feet as I learn the counterintuitive walk of Christ. Amen.

Who was in charge when you were a child and your parent or parents were not available? To whom were you subject? My wife and I left our children with their grandmother one day. My four-year-old daughter had a meltdown with her grandmother and let her know, "You're not in charge of me; I'm in charge of me." Most of us desire to be in charge of ourselves. Who is in charge of you?

The writer of Hebrews makes it clear that angels are not in charge of the world. The ancient world looked to angels for this service. Angels were thought to be mediators between humanity and God. But the writer of Hebrews argues that angels will never do as mediators. No angel has ever been a human; no angel has ever stood where we stand. But Jesus, the Son, has! The value of his life comes not only through his incarnation but, more particularly, his "suffering of death." Unlike the death of other humans, Jesus' death brings salvation; we find ourselves justified. God, through the very human Jesus, brought divine love to bear.

My church is partnering with many refugee families to serve as advocates, often working as mediators between landlord or agency and the new citizens. Church members have been blessed to get to know our new neighbors. Who in your community has no voice? Is God calling you to listen?

Our mediator is Christ who has been given all authority. Who is in charge? Who will advocate for us? Jesus as mediator will "declare our names" to the congregation. This mediator will let others know that we belong.

Lord, help me be a voice for the voiceless, an advocate for those with no support. Give me eyes to see and ears to hear and feet to move as you call. Amen.

My youth pastor from years ago told me recently that as a student, I always asked "why." I had lots of questions. It's been said that Gentile parents tell their children as they go to school, "Learn something new," while Jewish parents tell their children, "Ask a good question." Questions have the power to open up dialogue, create possibilities, and expand our understanding. Questions can also be used to push an agenda or in this case to "test" Jesus as a leader. The Pharisees test Jesus with this question, "Is it lawful for a man to divorce his wife?"

The challenge of relationships is not new to our time. Jesus responds to their legal question with his own question to point them to the answer they already know. "What did Moses command you?"

Moses allowed for divorce but permitted the women to remarry. (Read Deuteronomy 24:1-4.) Notice that Jesus goes on to speak less of divorce and more about the intent of marriage from the beginning of creation: "The two shall become one flesh." Jesus returns to Genesis to support his understanding of this special union and God's intention for marriage. Nothing shall separate the two. But pay attention to Jesus' disclaimer: Because humankind is not perfect and experiences hardness of heart, divorce still occurs.

The Pharisees do not entrap Jesus with their question. He attempts to deepen understanding by raising a question of his own. He reminds others of God's love and care as revealed through intimate relationship since the start of creation. What questions do you have for God? What questions will give you deeper insight into the grace-filled heart of God?

Thank you, God, that you are big enough for my questions. May my questions draw me closer to you and reveal your gracious intent for all. Amen.

Redefining Blessing   333

We find Jesus angry only a few times in the Bible, and this is one of them. According to custom, parents desired a blessing for their children from the rabbi. But prior to his opportunity to bless the children on this occasion, the disciples have shooed the children away so as not to bother Jesus.

These verses paint a vivid scene in our mind as parents and children, crying babies, squirming toddlers surround Jesus, desirous of his touch. How we all long to be blessed, touched by the Holy. In an attempt to honor and perhaps protect the rabbi, the disciples take decisive action to stop this nonsense. They work to remove this distraction from their real work.

I often work a hard deadline. Sunday keeps coming. My phone rings; even with my office door shut, someone knocks; a person experiencing homelessness wants to talk to a pastor. The request comes, "Pastor, would you pray with me?"

I could shoo people away, not take the call, ignore the e-mail— view it all as distraction from my real work. Yet, interruptions for Jesus often get redefined as blessings: the woman at the well, the one who touches the hem of his garment, the hunger of the five thousand. Each moment becomes a blessing.

Ancient societies did not value children, viewing them as nonpersons, distractions. So the disciples shoo away the insignificant ones. Jesus is angry with the disciples' inability to see the possible blessing. Jesus not only comes to the defense of the children, he advances them as examples in the kingdom. Christ-followers are to help others gain access to the holy, always seeing divine possibilities.

God, forgive me for overlooking and judging people as distractions. Amen.

Redefining Blessing

Spotlight on the Soul

OCTOBER 8–14, 2018 • G. KEVIN BAKER

SCRIPTURE OVERVIEW: Faithful people still have questions for God. Job wishes he could sit down with God and plead his case because he wants God to justify what has happened to him. The psalmist, traditionally identified as David, also feels abandoned by God and wonders why God is not coming to his aid. God can handle our questions. Job wanted an advocate, and Hebrews says that Jesus now fills that role for us. He is our great high priest and understands our sufferings, so we may boldly approach him for help. In Mark, Jesus deals with the challenge of money. It is a powerful force and can come between God and us if we cling to our resources instead of holding them loosely with thanksgiving for God's provision.

QUESTIONS AND THOUGHTS FOR REFLECTION

- Read Job 23:1-9, 16-17. When have you, like Eliphaz, attributed your own suffering or that of others to wickedness on your part or on theirs? How often do you find yourself blaming others for the situations in which they find themselves?

- Read Psalm 22:1-15. How could your prayer life be more honest and transparent? What feelings do you hold back?

- Read Hebrews 4:12-16. When God shines the spotlight on your soul, what does God see?

- Read Mark 10:17-31. How do you square your "wealthy" life with Jesus' call to discipleship?

Lead pastor, First United Methodist Church, Graham, North Carolina.

We easily critique Job's "so called" friends: Eliphaz, Bildad, and Zophar. They work tirelessly to paste neat and easy answers over Job's anguish and pain. For some strange reason, they feel compelled to take turns trying to explain evil, defend God, and unpack the dark mystery of why bad things happen to good people. Eliphaz's words are painfully simple and harsh. Bad things don't happen to good people, which leads him to one conclusion: "Is not your wickedness great? . . . Therefore snares are around you" (22:5, 10).

Job's anguished response bares his soul and the depths of his grief. He is weak from crying and is overcome with fear and dread: "I am scared by his presence. . . . God has weakened my mind; the Almighty has frightened me. Still I'm not annihilated by darkness" (23:15-17, CEB). I believe both Eliphaz and Job have something to teach us about grief and human suffering.

Eliphaz models what *not* to do. I am not sure we have learned much about spiritual consolation over the years. Too often we speak into another person's pain with equally unhelpful and ill-considered words like "everything happens for a reason," "God won't give you more than you can bear," or some other half-truth that does little more than add insult to injury. We all experience moments when we feel like life is nothing but stormy chaos. We desire certainty not ambiguity; we want answers not more questions—and that is precisely where we can learn from Job. It is OK not to have all the answers. It is OK to lament—to express our anger, our confusion, and our fears to God in prayer. There is a time and a place for expressions of joy and praise, and there is also a time and place for lament.

Lord, you are my help even when I become lost in confusion and grief. Encourage me to bare all that is in my soul to you in prayer. Amen.

Some people have heard of the "Jesus prayer," popularized by the Eastern church tradition. It is an adapted form of the tax collector's prayer from Luke 18: "Lord Jesus Christ, Son of God, have mercy on me a sinner." Today's scripture is another type of "Jesus prayer." It provides an example of how Jesus used the Psalter to express his own pain and suffering. It reminds us that when we face situations where we don't know how or what to pray, we can turn to the psalms to help us respond. Even from the cross, Jesus teaches us how to pray and honestly express our sorrow, using the words of Psalm 22 as he hangs on the cross: "At about three Jesus cried out with a loud shout, 'Eli, Eli, lama sabachthani,' which means, 'My God, my God, why have you left me?'" (Matt. 27:46, CEB).

Modern ears may find the words strange on the lips of Jesus. Psalm or not, it is still a bit disturbing to overhear Jesus' gut-wrenching question shouted toward the heavens. It doesn't sound like Jesus. We easily imagine the power of his voice, the thunder of his commands. We like to hear about the power—not the uncertainty, the doubt, and the sense of abandonment. It sounds too much like . . . well, too much like us. And perhaps therein lies the point. If we learn to pray this other type of "Jesus prayer" in moments of grief and despair, we may be empowered to move from the inexplicable pain expressed in this opening line toward the faintly growing ember of hoped-for deliverance and trust that this prayer slowly travels toward: "But you, LORD! Don't be far away! You are my strength! Come quick and help me!" (22:19, CEB).

O Lord, my rock and my refuge, even though I walk through the darkest valley I pray that you will hear my cries and come quickly to help me. Even in places of pain and doubt, I will trust you. Amen.

Years ago, Swiss psychiatrist Elisabeth Kübler-Ross identified five stages of grief: denial, anger, bargaining, depression, and acceptance. Yet long before this modern-day understanding gleaned from psychology, the psalms of lament gave spiritual expression to these deep and dark emotions, including Psalm 22.

Between the opening and closing verses of the psalm we read soul-baring, brutal honesty that we rarely find in the prayer repertoire of the modern-day believer. Perhaps part of the problem with our prayer is not that we pray too little, but that our prayer has become too sanitized, too superficial. We don't have to travel far to come face-to-face with injustice, pain, and evil. We have forgotten that God's word has always been relevant. The problem is not scripture; it is us. We need to rediscover the timeless power and relevance of the ancient prayers of the Psalter and mine the forgotten spiritual treasures that lead to a deeper and more authentic life with God.

Christians have forgotten how to lament. Today's reading invites us to God's original school for prayer. It is not a sin to be angry, but perhaps we sin by removing our anger from prayer. It is not a heresy to name the depths of frustration and suffering, but perhaps we sin when we pretend that everything is OK when it is not. Raw honesty may not be the only thing we need to restore to our prayer life, but it seems a good start for those who desire to follow the rabbi who has nail-scarred hands.

Lord, sometimes it feels like trouble is always near and help is not. Give me courage to pray and express honestly where I am, including my doubts, fears, and anger. Hear me when I cry to you. Amen.

The author of Hebrews states emphatically that God's word is not dead and in the past. It is a soul-dividing, joint-splitting instrument that pierces the darkness of our sin and our disobedience. What happens when you turn on the light in a dark, dusty room? Roaches scurry for cover, cobwebs in the corner indicate inattention, dust on the furniture is made visible, dirt on the floor becomes disconcerting. But what action do you take when these things are brought to light? Turn off the light? Assume the dust and dirt will clean itself?

When it comes to matters of the heart and soul, matters of life and death, I can safely say that ignorance is not bliss. We have another option. The epistle author exhorts us to allow the light to do its work. Let the light of God's living word expose all that hides in darkness. Submit to the soul-cleansing illumination of God's Spirit. Only then can the difficult and healing work of removal and redemption begin to restore the spiritual home that has been left in disarray.

When God's word shines a spotlight on the immensity of our personal brokenness and sin, we have a blessed assurance that God knows and God intervenes. It doesn't matter what you have done or what you have left undone. Journey toward the light. It matters not whether you think you are worthy. Turn your eyes to Jesus anyway. "Hold on to the confession," and "draw near to the throne of favor with confidence" (CEB). Feeling a little exposed and naked? Take off the fig leaves anyway. Quit pretending. No more hiding. It is time to get serious and get real with God and with ourselves. Nothing less will suffice. When we do, we will "receive mercy and find grace" (CEB)—amazing grace!

Lord, shine the light of your living word upon me. Cleanse me, renew me, and remake me that I may find grace and help in you alone. Amen.

Spotlight on the Soul

People find Jesus' life and teaching compelling—compelling enough to cause them to leave their fishing nets at the drop of a hat (or net!), to inspire men and women to ask deep questions about faith and life. Jesus' life and teaching seems to capture people's imaginations. This rabbi and teacher inspires seekers to come from near and far to find out more.

The man in today's Gospel is one of those seekers. He doesn't just look for Jesus—he runs, kneels, and brings heartfelt, probing questions to the traveling rabbi: "Good Teacher, what must I do to obtain eternal life?" (CEB). While the man asks in earnest, he also appears conflicted. Mark indicates that Jesus is aware the man's priorities are out of whack. He has many possessions, which obviously come first. How does Jesus put it? Oh, yes, "You are lacking one thing."

The story is familiar; we know how it ends. But notice what happens *before* the man hears Jesus' charge to "go," "sell," and "give." Before the charge and before the man leaves saddened and dismayed, Jesus sees the man's earnest desire. He "looked at him carefully and loved him." Often I have rushed past this verse to focus on the man's greed, materialism, or inability to take a risk and surrender all. Today, I invite you to pause at this verse with me and ponder the beauty of a Savior who sees our shortcomings, our hang-ups, and our spiritual reluctance. We all have such things in our hearts at one time or another. Yet amazingly enough, Jesus knows us, sees us, and loves us. It is compelling. It is enough to make us want to run, kneel, seek, and, hopefully, with God's help, leave all and follow.

Jesus, I desire to experience the abundant life you taught and preached about. Give me courage to run, kneel, seek, and follow you. Amen.

Jesus said some shocking things about money. I just want to put that out there in case you hadn't run across some of his radical thoughts on the subject. For years I have heard Christians try to explain stories like the one in Mark 10: "It's easier for a camel to squeeze through the eye of a needle than for a rich person to enter God's kingdom." As soon as we read the words, we go scrambling to find a way to justify our lifestyles. Wasn't there an old gate in the wall around Jerusalem that used to be called the eye of the needle?

In truth, Jesus likely means what he says. Imagine a very large camel and then imagine a very small sewing needle. Now imagine trying to squeeze that camel through the hole. If you allow Jesus' word picture to tickle your imagination just a little bit, you will likely respond with the same shock and bewilderment his disciples experienced, "Then who can be saved?" To make matters worse, John Wesley, in his sermon "The Danger of Riches," defined the word *rich* as "whoever has sufficient food to eat, and raiment to put on, with a place where to lay his [or her] head, and something over."

We need not scramble for archaeological evidence for why it is difficult but not impossible to enter God's kingdom. Jesus clarifies matters for us: Entering God's kingdom is humanly impossible. Beware of how easily the things of this world can distract us from the main thing. Then, just when we think there is little or no hope, Jesus reminds us to throw ourselves on the mercy seat of God's grace and forgiveness: "It's impossible with human beings, but not with God. All things are possible for God." Thank God. We don't need an ancient gate; we need grace.

Lord, help me not to trust in things or riches but solely in your love and grace. Amen.

Years ago I remember playfully altering the words of the hymn by Judson W. Van Deventer titled "I Surrender All." I wanted to point out the absurdity of partial commitment to discipleship: "Some to Jesus I surrender; some to him I reluctantly give. I will occasionally love and trust him, in his presence periodically live." The musical meter doesn't fit, but then again, neither does the sentiment. God desires nothing less than all of us, from the top of our heads to the bottom of our feet.

After Jesus makes the costly demand of discipleship clear, Peter longs for reassurance: "Look, we've left everything and followed you." Jesus offers blessed assurance to those who have left family, friends, and livelihoods behind. Jesus promises they will receive much more in the coming age. Our past and present is nothing compared to the abundant life God calls us toward. The call still goes out today. What do you need to leave behind in order to follow Jesus without reservation or reluctance?

The values of God's kingdom turn the values of the world upside down, or perhaps we may more accurately say, right-side up. In God's right-side-up kingdom, the poor have good news brought to them, lepers are invited to the table, and tax collectors and sinners are embraced as friends. In Jesus, God begins the restoration, renewal, and transformation of the world as we know it. Survival of the fittest is the cutthroat call to arms in a world where the strong prey on the weak. Jesus points us away from this lie to the kingdom where the "first will be last" and the "last will be first." That is a vision and a calling worthy of our very lives. It is a calling to which we give our all.

Lord, I pray for the strength to surrender all to follow you. "Worldly pleasures all forsaken; take me, Jesus, take me now." Amen. (UMH, no. 354)

A Sense of Place

OCTOBER 15–21, 2018 • ALLISON RUARI

SCRIPTURE OVERVIEW: At this point in Job's story, God has heard questions from Job and long-winded moralizing by three of Job's friends, who have pronounced that his misfortunes are divine judgment. Now God has heard enough and declares that God's perspective is superior to theirs. God has been there from the beginning, as the psalmist reiterates, so no one should claim to know God's mind or speak on God's behalf. Even Jesus, the divine Son of God, yields to his heavenly Father. Hebrews tells us that Jesus made appeals to God as the ultimate high priest and thereby became the source of salvation for those who obey him. In the Gospel reading, Jesus specifies that his approaching act of submission and service will allow him to become a ransom for us.

QUESTIONS AND THOUGHTS FOR REFLECTION

- Read Job 38:1-7, 34-41. How do you continue to see the goodness of God when you find yourself in situations of intense suffering?
- Read Psalm 104:1-9, 24, 35c. Where do you catch glimpses of God? How significant is God's natural world in your ability to see the holy?
- Read Hebrews 5:1-10. In what ways does the understanding of Jesus' willing vulnerability while serving as high priest affect your interactions with others?
- Read Mark 10:35-45. When have you made a bold request of God? What was God's reply?

Ordained minister in the Christian Church (Disciples of Christ); associate minister for faith formation, First Christian Church, Mansfield, Ohio.

Do you remember a time when you thought you knew everything? When you constantly felt the need to correct or criticize everything? That you knew what was going on in the world, and if everyone could just see it your way things would be better? And then there's a person, a conversation, an experience where you are taken down a notch, put in "your place," and you are forced to see the world in a different way. All of us have at one time or another darkened "counsel by words without knowledge." We've spoken out of turn, out of ignorance.

Being reminded of where our place is can be a humbling experience. When done well it reshapes and reframes our interactions with others and the world. God's conversation with Job does just that. Job's suffering and loss creates discord and chaos. He no longer understands his world; he no longer recognizes or finds comfort in it. Yet God's conversation with Job provides a bigger picture.

How often, in an effort to make sense of the world, do we think so highly of ourselves that we forget all that God has done? When God asks, "Where were you when I laid the foundation of the earth" and "Who laid its cornerstone when the morning stars sang together and all the heavenly beings shouted for joy?" Job (and we as readers) are forced to recognize our place, our limited vision, our smallness. Yes, rules that made sense seem to be broken. Yes, suffering is painful. But the story is not over. God is a God of majesty and mystery. May we remember where God was and is, what God has done and continues to do.

God of mystery and wonder, thank you for all that you have created. Grant us eyes to see your works and your goodness in all the places we go and in all the things we do. Amen.

I've asked "Where are you God?" and "What have you done for me lately?" before. In times of loneliness or loss or impatience, it is easy to doubt God's presence and work in the world. When we move beyond our own situation (even if temporarily) and look around, we see all that God created. We see the clouds that produce rain, and we hear thunder during a storm. We stand in awe of the God who navigates the sand, sea, and skies so that lion and raven have food for themselves and their offspring. The God in Job definitely is a God of power and might. Job questions and God responds with "Here is what I have done. What have you done?" In this scripture, God calls us to recognize God's place in the world God created. This passage highlights God's presence in nature, with the lightning and the lion. With the rain and the raven. God created all these things and continues to be a part of these things. And yet. . . .

And yet, I do not quite resonate with the powerful God depicted in Job. We know Job is suffering and either God doesn't know about it (God does) or God doesn't care (does God?). And this is the heart of the problem for me. I prefer a God who is loving and knowledgeable far more than a God of power. A God of love would answer, "Here I am. I am always with you." A God of knowledge would say, "I understand your pain. I have wept with you and walked with you and given you community to share in your grief." Job doesn't necessarily experience God in that way, but God's love is present: in creation and provision for creation. Divine love abounds, even when we are too wrapped up in our own situation to see it.

God of grief and glory, may we celebrate your power, trust in your knowledge, and lean into your love. Amen.

A Sense of Place

Sometimes we're in the right place at the right time to catch glimpses of the holy. While on a clergy retreat in the Arizona desert, I had some time to sit and meditate. As I sat, I began to be more aware of my surroundings. I heard birds calling to one another and trees rustling in the breeze. I smelled the desert air mixed with rock, dirt, and tree. I noticed a mountain ridge and cacti and flowers falling from trees. I felt the wind and the coolness it brought. It's such a different place than where I call home. And because it is so different, I paid more attention. I saw God's work up close—and it was very good. Prayers of thanksgiving and gratitude flowed abundantly in word, song, and deed.

Being close to nature often requires intentionality. We can easily forget that aspect as we go from home to car to work to car to store to car. And yet when we set aside time to go outside, it is easy to find God. We experience God in all that God created and called good. We can experience more fully the psalmist's words: "O Lord, how manifold are your works! In wisdom you have made them all; the earth is full of your creatures." In that moment and in that place, we utter prayers of gratitude, praise, and awe.

God's creation reminds us that our place isn't in front of a screen or in a vehicle. Our place is to be in community, in creation, in relationship with God. There we recognize all things (including ourselves) as beloved, as wondrous, as good. May we be open to God's messages in all forms and in all places.

Holy God, who speaks all things into creation, thank you. Amen.

Sometimes knowing your place literally means knowing where you are. Other times, it means knowing your roles and responsibilities to yourself and to others. It takes time to realize that your place and role may be bigger than yourself because they reflect a call from God. A high priest fills a large role; he "is put in charge of things pertaining to God." It requires gentleness and sacrifice, communication with the community and with God. This scripture alludes to the fact that being a high priest may not be for everybody. But many traditions ascribe to the notion of a "priesthood of all believers"—that we are all called by God to be gentle with one another, to teach one another, to sacrifice for one another.

The traditions and cultures that celebrate this concept of the priesthood of all believers varies. One example is the Samoan tradition of *ifoga*. After a grave offense occurs, the offender's family takes responsibility to ask for forgiveness, offer sacrifice, and seek reconciliation. The family members act as priests, interceding on behalf of the offender, preparing offerings of food and gifts. They readily offer themselves as penitence for what has been done.

While the offender's family waits outside, the victim's family continues to grieve and mourn and decide on next steps. Retaliation is an option, but usually the families reconcile. The community begins the process of restoration, justice, and healing. The offender's family shares in the other family's pain, loss, and anguish. There are hugs and tears, prayers for the victim and the offender, and, in the end, there is forgiveness.

May we all hear God's call to be priests to one another, offering gentleness and sacrifice.

What wondrous love is this, O my soul, O my soul! (UMH, no. 292)

A Sense of Place

Then there's Jesus Christ, who meets us where we are and deals gently with us. Today, tomorrow, forever. Being a high priest for all and forever is no joking matter. It's not a role anyone would want. Yet, Jesus said yes. With gentleness and humility, Jesus accepted this role given by God because he was God's beloved son. What a succinct Christological statement: Jesus Christ is a priest for all and forever!

Many find it easier to view Jesus as prophet, provocateur, and pastor than high priest. The title itself can carry baggage—abuse of power or holding on to traditions that seem nonsensical. Jesus accepted his priestly role and offered prayers and supplications for all—especially for the least, the last, and the lost. Jesus accepted his priestly title and gave new meaning to old traditions. Jesus accepted his priestly role and met people where they were and ministered to them, not from a place of power but from a place of vulnerability.

This passage reminds us that Jesus didn't challenge his place or his role. He understood his place, as difficult and challenging as it might have been, as listening to God's will and living out God's bigger plan. The plan included a world's salvation, victory over death, and unimaginable and unbounded love. At their best, high priests offer a glimpse of what the reign of God can be: a world of justice, love, and salvific acts done on behalf of others.

What wondrous love is this that caused the Lord of bliss to bear the dreadful curse for my soul, for my soul, to bear the dreadful curse for my soul. (UMH, no. 292)

Sometimes we need to speak up to get where we want to go. James and John do just that. They say point-blank to Jesus words to this effect, "Do something for us. We want to be your seatmates in glory." A pretty bold move on their part. But they know what they want. James and John want to be in a different place, a different stature than they are in, and they are thinking ahead. There's nothing wrong with asking for what you want or need. Most of the time, the worst that can happen is folks say no. But for James and John, the worst-case scenario is for someone (in this case, Jesus) to question their intention, motivation, and capacity. "You don't know what you've gotten yourself into. Can you handle what I'm about to do?" asks Jesus. Even after they reply affirmatively, Jesus says, "Okay. Drink my cup, be baptized in my baptism; but who sits next to me isn't up to me. It might not be prepared for you." Jesus' glory comes with risk and danger through the symbols of cup and water.

James and John's request is bold, to be sure. Yet as clunky and brash as their request seems, Jesus uses this opportunity to imagine a different world where power dynamics have shifted. He answers them, "I can't make that decision. It's not up to me." It's not a no, but it's not a yes either.

Readers are often taken aback at James and John's bluntness. But we could do well to take after them by saying, "This is where I want to go. Help me, Jesus." We simply have to be ready for Jesus' (non)answer and an unconventional path.

Holy One, may we glorify you. May we continue to say, "Yes, we are able" for whatever work you call us to do. Amen.

James and John get a lot of flak from the other ten. Are the ten jealous of the brothers' boldness—their ability to ask the question? Do the other disciples think them arrogant—that James and John are out of place for making such a request?

Jesus recognizes that James and John's request comes from cultural context and from their environment. He gives his disciples a worldview and a practice that subverts traditional power structures. He calls his disciples to live in a way that differs from that of the world. We are not to abuse power but serve our neighbors, the poor, the earth God created.

Jesus knows being countercultural is a hard road in his day. We know that being countercultural is a hard road today. It is fraught with competing values that have louder voices and competing ideologies that have more resources. It is fraught with people peddling fear, anger, and shame.

We stand up to those voices, living calmly, lovingly, and with deep peace. We know our role and our place: to be servants to all, modeling gentleness and love, treating all God's beloved children with respect and service.

Jesus equates greatness with servanthood. May we remember and use Jesus' definition of greatness and live into our own greatness and servanthood. May we continue to know our place and our purpose. May we be surrounded by and participate in communities of care. May it be so.

God of extravagant greatness, may we be your servants in the world you have called good. Amen.

Seeing and Seen, through Suffering

OCTOBER 22–28, 2018 • MARTHA C. HIGHSMITH

SCRIPTURE OVERVIEW: Sometimes we can look back and see why challenging things happened to us, but this is not always the case. Job never fully understood his story but finally submitted his life to God in humility. In Job's case, God restored with abundance. The psalmist also rejoices that although the righteous may suffer, God brings ultimate restoration. The reading from Hebrews continues celebrating Christ's role as the compassionate high priest. Unlike human high priests, who serve only for a time, Christ remains our priest forever. A man without sight in Jericho knows of Jesus compassion and cries out for it, despite attempts to silence him. He asks Jesus for mercy, physical healing in his case, and Jesus granted his request because the man has displayed great faith.

QUESTIONS AND THOUGHTS FOR REFLECTION

- Read Job 42:1-6, 10-17. What are your happy and unhappy endings? How do you acknowledge both?

- Read Psalm 34:1-8, 19-22. When has an obstruction or impediment influenced your relationship with God?

- Read Hebrews 7:23-28. What distinction do you draw between sacrifice and offering? Which do you prefer?

- Read Mark 10:46-52. When have you been unable to see the blessing right in front of your eyes?

Teaching elder, Presbyterian Church (USA); spiritual director; farmer; living near Atkinson, North Carolina.

I heard a story about twin girls, toddlers, blind since birth. As toddlers do, they liked to test their limits. One day as they were headed toward trouble, their mother told them to stop. They did for a moment, and then, very quietly, tiptoed on toward the forbidden activity. They could not understand how their mother knew what they were up to, perceiving their mother to be like them. If they made no noise, she wouldn't know what they were up to. They could not see what they could not see.

In the depths of suffering, Job could not understand God. He cannot see what he cannot see. And even though he does not waver in his belief in God, he begins to question God. Job, while blameless and upright, is also human, and it is the most human thing in the world to ask "why" when things go horribly wrong. Why does God let us suffer? How can a loving God permit calamity? If a hurricane destroys a community or a plane crashes or someone sets off a bomb or shoots innocent people, is that a divine punishment? We, like Job, have those questions, and sometimes we too want to call God to account.

But when Job finally gets to confront God, his questions fall away, and his attitude changes. Once, he carefully tiptoed around God, following the rules, as though he could control God's action by spiritual correctness. Surviving the whirlwind, his eyes are opened, and he is transformed. He acknowledges God's sovereignty and sees what he could not see before: The life of faith is not about blind obedience. Job begins to grasp the greatness of God, the Creator who yet engages with the created. He realizes it is one thing to hear about God and quite a different thing to experience God, to see God.

Holy One, open my eyes to your presence. Help me to see. Amen.

Job's story ends happily. God restores his fortunes twofold, and he is blessed with ten more children: seven sons and three daughters. Job is transformed, a transformation far deeper than the reversal of his woes, more profound than the end of his suffering. He sees the beauty and preciousness of life as he never has and is forever changed.

At the beginning of his ordeal he could say, "Naked I came from my mother's womb, and naked shall I return there; the LORD gave, and the LORD has taken away; blessed be the name of the LORD" (Job 1:21). At the end, he understands what that really means. He sees the grace and extravagance of God's gifts and responds in kind. He gives his daughters names that reflect beauty and pleasure in life. There is Jemimah, whose name means "dove" or "warmth"; Keziah, named for a sweet-scented spice; and Keren-Happuch, which translates as "pot of eye shadow." These lovely and unexpected names convey joy and delight, a father's response to the unexpected gift of their lives. And then he gives each of his daughters an inheritance, also an unexpected gift; traditionally only the (unnamed) sons would have inherited their father's estate.

Not every story has a happy ending. Sometimes suffering continues unabated and without reason. Bad things do happen to good people. Life is not fair. Pain and loss can give way to doubt and anger: doubt about God's goodness, anger at God's seeming absence. We want God to answer to us, to explain, to fix things. We question God. Then, like Job, maybe we come to see that God is beyond our questioning, beyond our understanding. But God is not beyond our experiencing. God is present in all creation, present in our lives—present in our suffering.

All-seeing, all-giving, all-knowing God, may I respond with gratitude and grace to your generosity. Amen.

Seeing and Seen, through Suffering   353

Psalm 34 is an acrostic. With a few exceptions, each verse begins with a letter of the Hebrew alphabet in order from beginning to end. Why did the psalmist shape the poem this way? Perhaps it was a device to help people remember the song, to fix in their minds all that God had done. Or perhaps this scriptural ABC is a theological statement, representing the completeness of God's care, the A to Z of God's goodness.

The psalm begins with an amazing declaration: "I will bless the LORD at all times; his praise shall *continually* be in my mouth" (emphasis added). In times of joy and in times of sorrow, the response to God is blessing and continual praise. To "give thanks in all circumstances" (1 Thess. 5:18), as Paul later commands, is not easy.

But perhaps trouble helps reshape our relationship with God. When the poet Wendell Berry writes that "the impeded stream is the one that sings" ("The Real Work," *Standing by Words: Essays*, 205), he addresses the issue of finding our true way in the world and the role hardship plays in that. Without hardship, we never fully understand our dependence on God. In such a time, when the stream of my own life was impeded by illness and surgery and chemotherapy, I learned how to sing God's praise.

Some of us have been spared from major illness, but sooner or later we will all have our share of trouble. Even the righteous face affliction. Even when we see no way out of suffering, God is still present—watching over us, saving us in God's own way, loving us from beginning to end.

God of the love that is without beginning or ending, when the sorrows of the world and of my own life threaten to blind me to your presence, remind me that you are with me always. Amen.

A few weeks ago, many of us gathered to celebrate World Communion Sunday, in large cathedrals and small country congregations, in storefront missions and suburban churches, in ornate Gothic chapels and outdoors under tents. We were offered a piece of bread—cornbread, matzo, pita, injera, challah, Wonder Bread—and a sip of juice or wine. In the small ordinary actions of eating and drinking, we were invited "to taste and see that the Lᴏʀᴅ is good" or, in the words of the old hymn, "I see thee face to face; here would I touch and handle things unseen" (UMH, no. 623).

A sacrament is a visible sign of an invisible grace. It helps us see that which lies beyond seeing: the extent of God's love. When we eat the bread and drink the cup, those seemingly insignificant tastes open us to the eternal goodness of God.

But what does it mean to taste and see this way? Surely there is more to it than the flavor of yeast and grape on one's tongue. To taste and see that God is good implies a relationship with God, an experience of God's goodness, taking that in and being nourished by it. From the beginning of time, God has looked on creation and seen that it was good. This tasting and seeing invites us to respond in kind: to look on God and see God's goodness.

We may take that goodness for granted when the sun is shining and all is well or perhaps even attribute our good fortune to our own efforts. But when we experience the body's ability to heal, love's power to comfort, a child's smile, or an elder's blessing, then we are fed by the goodness of God; we taste and truly see.

Feed me, O God, with your love. Fill my life with praise for you. Help me to see your goodness. Amen.

Seeing and Seen, through Suffering   355

The writer of Hebrews speaks of a long line of priests endlessly presiding over sacrifices in carefully prescribed ancient rituals meant first to cleanse the priests who prepared and offered the sacrifices and then the people themselves. The priests were only human, after all, sinful and subject to death, so their actions, no matter how meticulous and faithful, were always imperfect and thus never quite good enough.

Jesus changes all that. He is human too—but not *only* human. He was, and is, "holy, blameless, undefiled, separated from sinners, and exalted above the heavens" and "perfect forever." Jesus, who sacrificed "once for all" by offering himself has freed us from never-ending sacrifice.

But what distinction do we draw between sacrifice and offering? To sacrifice is to give up something of value, sometimes out of a sense of obligation or even fear. God's people once thought that proper sacrifices would gain God's favor or appease God's anger. Some may have considered the sacrifice a bribe, an action intended to influence God. An offering, however, is a gift, freely and lovingly given. Embedded in every true offering is an element of sacrifice, and, in every sacrifice, an element of suffering. When we say the Apostles' Creed, we affirm that Jesus "suffered under Pontius Pilate." Perhaps it would be better to put a comma after "suffered." Jesus' sacrificial offering surely involved suffering on the cross. But before that ultimate sacrifice, he must have suffered when he looked on the injustice and pain of the world. That suffering was born of love, God's sacrificial offering of love for the world. The One who has sacrificed and suffered for us sees our suffering—and sees us through it.

Holy and Perfect One, help me offer my life as a sacrifice to you, as you have given yourself for me. Amen.

Some years ago, an unexpected snowstorm left my region of the country without power for almost a week. It was cold, difficult to sleep, impossible to cook. One of the hardest aspects was the darkness. With no streetlights, citizens could not see hazards in the way. At home, the darkness disoriented and isolated. The snowstorm disrupted familiar routines, and moving in darkness required concentration and effort.

I experienced the darkness as a brief inconvenience. But for those with visual impairments, darkness affects everything. Bartimaeus lived in the disruption of darkness, in isolation and helplessness. His blindness had pushed him to the margins of society; he was ignored and invisible, unworthy of notice or attention. Because he could not see, others usually did not see him. But those who are visually impaired often have other highly developed senses, and Bartimaeus heard things that others may not have heard. He knows something about Jesus that they seem not to have noticed: "When he heard that it was Jesus of Nazareth, he began to shout out and say, 'Jesus, Son of David, have mercy on me!'"

Bartimaeus recognizes Jesus as the Son of David, the Messiah. Jesus, in turn, sees the beggar for who he really is, the son (Bar) of Timaeus (honor or value)—a valued child of God. And when Bartimaeus cries out for mercy, for relief from his suffering, Jesus stops in his tracks and has those in the crowd call Bartimaeus to him. I imagine Jesus continues to speak, giving Bartimaeus a word to guide him and help him find his way. And then he asks the beggar a question he has asked others, "What do you want me to do for you?" (Mark 10:36). This time he grants the request. Bartimaeus can see!

Jesus, when you ask me what I want you to do for me, may I respond with humility and faith. Amen.

Seeing and Seen, through Suffering   357

When the crowd calls Bartimaeus to Jesus, the beggar throws off his cloak and leaps up. He leaves behind what is probably his only possession, his means of protection and livelihood—the cloak he uses to keep warm at night and which he spreads out during the day to collect coins and scraps of bread. He leaves everything he has and comes to Jesus. Maybe that leap of faith begins Bartimaeus's healing. Maybe at that moment he is saved. He cannot see the way; he does not know what lies ahead, but he goes. He acts in blind faith.

Faith is the conviction of things not seen. It may involve rising and going blindly in the direction of the Word you have not heard yourself. It is sitting in the ashes with Job, finally seeing and responding as he did, "I had heard of you by the hearing of the ear, but now my eye sees you" (Job 42:5). Faith is going to the cross, watching soldiers compete for the cloak left behind, and suffering and dying and not being able to see God. It is following Christ, even when we cannot see where the way leads, even if it leads to suffering.

We are all beggars, poor beggars lacking sight, dependent on others, struggling along, suffering, and often unable to see the source of blessing right in front of us. But God watches over us; God sees us; God in Christ waits to offer us mercy. All we have to do is get up and go in the direction of the Word. When we can finally see the One who calls us, then we, like Bartimaeus, are to follow—and in our following be made whole.

O God, you have seen me through suffering. May I have faith to see and follow you. Amen.

Seeing and Seen, through Suffering

From Fear to Freedom

OCTOBER 29—NOVEMBER 4, 2018 • BETH ANN ESTOCK

SCRIPTURE OVERVIEW: Ruth and Psalm 146 share a thematic connection. Ruth is a foreigner who decides to follow the God of the Israelites, and the psalmist praises God for being the trustworthy God who cares about the poor, the oppressed, and the foreigner. In Ruth, Boaz will demonstrate this kind of care for her. The New Testament readings focus on sacrifice. Hebrews teaches us that Christ was both the greatest high priest and the eternal sacrifice. A scribe in Mark receives praise from Jesus, for he understands that the sacrificial system was less weighty than the act of loving one's neighbor. Ruth and this scribe are examples of those, named and anonymous, who have come before us in the faith. We celebrate them on All Saints Day.

QUESTIONS AND THOUGHTS FOR REFLECTION

- Read Ruth 1:1-18. When have you left the familiar behind to set out into the unknown? Where did you experience God's presence and help?

- Read Psalm 146. When you have found yourself in despair about the world, where have you witnessed God's work that brings you hope?

- Read Hebrews 9:11-14. How willing are you to release your bag of sins and shortcomings to Jesus?

- Read Mark 12:28-34. In what ways do you understand yourself as a spiritual being having a human experience? What does that mean to you?

Coach for innovative ministries, convener of SpiritSpace (a contemplative practice house church), yoga instructor; living in Portland, Oregon; blogs at www.sacreddirt.com.

I live in a tranquil community with walking trails, bike lanes, and beaver ponds. But when I look out my window I see pain in my neighborhood: One couple is ending a thirty-five-year marriage due to infidelity; another neighbor recently buried his wife; another is going through cancer treatments; a recent immigrant family is feeling isolated as they try to learn English and adjust to a new culture.

I often wonder how any of us do it; you know, get through life—go to work, walk the dog, and put dinner on the table. When life throws us a hard blow, how do we go on?

Naomi had tremendous sorrow in her life after losing her husband and two sons. She felt bitter and forsaken by God. But then one day, after years of suffering, she took a sober look at her life and decided to live.

Naomi's decision helped both her widowed daughters-in-law to find that courage as well. Orpah decided to return to her family; but the other, Ruth, decided to follow her heart. Ruth pledged her love and loyalty to Naomi. Together they put one foot in front of the other and found the will to forge a life in a world where they, as widows, have no sense of safety and security. Together they created a bond of trust that allowed them space to breathe in the midst of their desperation.

When life throws us a hard blow, how do we go on? I think if we were to ask Ruth and Naomi, they would probably say, by the grace of God. They discovered that grace through friendship, honest conversation, and giving each other the space to slowly heal. This gift of grace they could see only in the fullness of time.

Loving God, remind us that your grace surrounds us even in the midst of our sorrows. Amen.

I have a friend who did the unthinkable. Twenty years ago she and her husband were pastors in a highly successful, growing church when they discerned a call to leave everything they knew and begin ministry in a new city. They moved to Portland, Oregon, and started meeting people half their age who were living on the margins of society. They fell so in love with this community that one day they asked some of these young adults, "Will you teach us how to be you?"

So the transformation began. They moved into a rental house, shared food from the food pantry, and found their fashions at Goodwill. She replaced trips to the beauty parlor with the tattoo parlor, and her hair morphed into dreadlocks and his into a mullet. Over these last twenty years of forgoing the "successes" of this world, they have started three churches for people who have been forgotten and forsaken by the city. They have followed their hearts' desire.

It takes tremendous courage to let go of what we know and trust that God awaits us in the unknown. My friends have the persistent faith of Ruth. The journey for Ruth and Naomi wasn't easy. They faced many uncertainties, yet they trusted in their love for each other and for God, and that was enough.

The Bible is full of such stories of people letting go and falling into grace. It is part of our spiritual DNA. My friends knew deep within that their outward transformation marked an inward refinement process—letting go of their fears and falling into trust with God. And like Ruth and Naomi, their light shines brightly! How is God calling you to do the unthinkable? Who will be your people?

Breathe into your heart space and listen. What is your heart's desire? For whom does your heart break? To follow God is to follow your heart.

Sometimes it is hard to sing praises. Whether I am checking my Facebook feed or listening to the latest news, my automatic response these days is more likely to be sadness, dread, or anger. How can we sing praises when changes in weather patterns are creating famine and floods around the world? How can we sing praises when people experience suffering, distrust, and hatred? How can we sing praises when we feel disempowered and hopeless?

So let's put some things into perspective. Remember that neither the trappings of this world nor the shallow promises from the powerful will stave off collective anxiety or create lasting change. That which lasts beyond our lifetimes, God has the sole power to transform. The balance of power tips in favor of God and the socially disadvantaged: the oppressed, the hungry, the prisoner, the blind, the orphan, and the widow. God executes justice.

So sing praises to God! Put your trust in God who created the heavens and the earth and is creating still. The next time despair and fear try to have their way, touch the earth, raise your face to the sky, and breathe in the freshness of the day. Begin by resting in the gratitude of these simple pleasures to remind you that the perfect love of God casts out fear even in the most hopeless situations.

When I despair for the world, I am looking at it from a human point of view. But when I turn to God, I see through the eyes of faith. Beyond my narrative of despair is a larger narrative of God. A God of love who is, was, and will always be in charge. Thanks be to God!

The next time you listen to or read the news, do so through the eyes of God. Practice being a compassionate witness to the suffering of the world. Inhale suffering; exhale peace.

ALL SAINTS DAY

I have sat by the bedsides of many people as they took their final breath. Some of those deaths were slow and agonizing; others were peaceful transitions. All were sacred moments in which time seemed to stop and the veil between heaven and earth opened. The breath leaves the body and with it the spark of life—such a mystery. The soul unites with pure Love; pain and suffering are no longer. However, for those of us left behind, death can bring years of unresolved emotions and grief. Hopefully, death can also be a wake-up call for life.

As a teenager I remember watching a local production of the play *Our Town* by Thornton Wilder. Toward the end of the play the character Emily dies in childbirth. She joins the dead but is granted her wish to return to earth to relive one day. As she relives her joyous twelfth birthday, she is overcome with deep sorrow because she realizes that she should have treasured every moment of her life. When she asks the storyteller if anyone truly understands the value of life while they live it, he responds that maybe the saints and the poets do—but no one else.

Today we sit at the feet of a poet who invites us to wake up to the glory of God's creation and our part in it—from birth to death, using words to this effect, "Drink deeply of life: the love, hope, sorrow, and pain of it all. Ponder the miracle of your being and the web of all living things. Your passion, your gifts, your dreams, and your love are not to be squandered. The king of glory is knocking on your door. Open your heart; it is time to invite him in" (AP).

Open your heart to the treasures of this day.

Growing up, I tried to be a good Christian so that I could squeak by in life unscathed by pain and sorrow. The formula went something like this: Be good, follow the rules, go to church, say your prayers, and God will reward you with a happy life. I pictured God as a stern parent waiting to pounce on my imperfections. I was living like a parishioner of Israel taking my animal sacrifices to the high priest in hopes that God would forgive my peccadilloes and grant me an abundant harvest.

Then along comes Jesus, who changes everything! We no longer have to cower in the dark, fearing our own shadows, afraid to breathe. In a mysterious way, Jesus' death and resurrection frees us from the bonds of fear. The gospel truth is that no one is keeping a tally of our sins or holding us hostage to our shame. On the contrary, Christ frees us to come out of the shadows and live into our fullness.

We are invited to let go of all of our baggage—the regrets, the "shoulds and oughts," and our relentless pursuit of perfection. Christ reveals to us an image of God as loving parent who delights in us and desires relationship. Through Christ, God says, "Enough already, come out and play. Live large, take risks, let your God-image shine in the world!"

What if we actually lived as if these words were true? What holds you back from living large? Put all that in a bag and imagine giving it to Jesus. Come into an awareness of your body. What does it feel like to be free from your baggage? Come into an awareness of your emotions, and allow them to speak to you.

Loving God, help me to let go and trust in your love. Amen.

Martin Buber, an early twentieth-century Jewish theologian, dedicated his life to understanding relationships. He saw two distinct types—experiences (I-It) and encounters (I-Thou). In I-It relationships we treat people as objects. In I-Thou relationships we see the other as a beloved child of God.

I-It relationships can make us feel demoralized, disempowered, misunderstood, and unworthy. I-Thou relationships offer honor, respect, empowerment, and hope.

Jesus reminds us that learning how to love is our life's work. Through his life and ministry, Jesus shaped people in I-Thou relationships while living in the middle of an empire of I-It relationships. The commandment to love God and neighbor may seem like dropping a pebble in a ocean, but the cumulative effect of the ripples is never-ending.

My teacher friend, Bill, was in a hardware store when he locked eyes with one of the store employees. The young man did a double take and then approached Bill saying, "Do you remember me?" Bill said, "I think I was your third-grade teacher." The young man nodded and then told Bill the story of how important Bill had made this immigrant boy feel by asking him to lead the class one day. As Bill welled up sharing this story with me he said, "You just never know the impact that we have on each other. I don't even remember that day, but this boy still carries it in his heart."

A smile, a hug, deep listening, caring for the earth, being kind and respectful of others—all these simple acts create a ripple of unfolding love in our families and communities to the ends of the earth. To love others remains a radical witness of Christ in the world, for God dwells not only in Christ but also in each and every single human being. No exceptions.

Today look for the Christ in everyone you meet.

From Fear to Freedom

Even though this passage was easy to memorize as a child, it confounded me. How could I love God when I couldn't see, hear, or touch God? Years later as a teenager I discovered that God was love, and if we loved each other we loved God. Now, as an adult I am beginning to understand the beauty and simplicity of this passage.

We are created in God's image—*imago Dei*. As a matter of fact, we see God's imprint on all the created order. The Lord our God is one. All living things are part of that oneness. We are all connected like a body with many parts, all holy and sacred. Think about that. We. Are. All. Connected. The great I Am of God continues in our own small version of I Am. All of creation reflects God's nature and sovereignty.

Loving others begins with our capacity to love ourselves— not in a selfish, egotistical way but with a sense of deep compassion for our own humanity, warts and all. By being tender with ourselves we can be tender with others. After all, we are spiritual beings, one with God, having a human experience. At this moment are you willing to love and accept yourself no matter what?

When I can acknowledge my belovedness, I can recognize it in you as well. That fulfills this commandment: To love God is to love ourselves. To love our neighbors is to love God. In this we live into God's reign.

Breathe the Spirit of love into your heart space. Imagine your heart opening wider as you breathe in. Allow that love to enter every capillary of your body.

Breathe in love; exhale love. Embody love.
You are love. You are loving. You are lovable.
Share that love with others.

Circles of Blessing

NOVEMBER 5–11, 2018 • BILL BARNES

SCRIPTURE OVERVIEW: Ruth's story forms part of the background of the family of Jesus. The son of Ruth and Boaz, Obed, is David's grandfather. The women of Bethlehem rejoice with Naomi at the birth of her grandson, and the psalmist declares that children are a blessing from God. In the scriptures children are spoken of only as a blessing, never as a liability (unlike some narratives in our culture). The Hebrew writer builds upon the eternal nature of Christ's sacrifice, proclaiming that his death was sufficient once for all. In Mark, Jesus warns his disciples not to be fooled by appearances. Those who put on a big show of piety do not impress God. God wants us instead to give from the heart, even if no one but God sees.

QUESTIONS AND THOUGHTS FOR REFLECTION

- Read Ruth 3:1-5; 4:13-17. How has your life been enriched through the diversity of people around you?

- Read Psalm 127. How do you actively ensure the shaping of your household around godly practice?

- Read Hebrews 9:24-28. What spiritual income do you draw upon to keep your faith and hope alive?

- Read Mark 12:38-44. How do you guard against duplicitous living?

Founding pastor of Edgehill United Methodist Church, Nashville, Tennessee; social justice advocate, lover of the city.

At first glance, Naomi's suggestions to Ruth seem a bit daring, even dangerous. But nothing in the text detracts from a genuine concern for her loyal and compassionate Moabite daughter-in-law who, like Naomi, is a widow. Both women face all the uncertainties and hardships of widowhood in their time and place.

As our population ages, as researchers develop medical techniques that further foster longevity for the elderly, few families will be spared the agony of nursing home choices. But today's text reverses the normal concern: Here the older Naomi attempts to secure and fulfill Ruth's future.

Yet do not most of us spend time and invest resources to benefit loved ones who will survive us? We do so through financial planning. The concern expresses itself collectively as well as privately. We will work together to insure the soundness of Social Security for the decades ahead of us. And we will continue to press for health care coverage for the children of the working poor and others left out of our current system of coverage. Compassion is collective as well as individual.

Naomi has many reasons to be self-centered and self-pitying. But she exercises great love in planning for Ruth's future and well-being. Perhaps Naomi helps us care, focus, and plan for the younger as well as the older generation.

Dear God, let Naomi's spirit of remarkable compassion and follow-through be in me. In my own time and place, fill me and make me a good steward in the healing of creation. Amen.

If you tell the story of King David, Israel's most celebrated ruler, and if you describe his ancestry, you have to include a foreign woman, a Moabite named Ruth. Through her selfless devotion, Ruth became an indispensable link in the succession. In Matthew 1, the genealogy finally includes Jesus.

When we read Ezra and Nehemiah, we face a post–exilic attitude of nationalistic exclusiveness ("put away foreign wives"). Ruth and Jonah exemplify the inclusive, universal yearnings of Israel. If we want a story that reflects the way foreigners, outsiders, and immigrants can profoundly bless the life of a welcoming nation, Ruth is a perfect choice.

I pastored a congregation for thirty years in Nashville, Tennessee. Because of the church building's proximity to several universities, families from Africa, Asia, Latin America, Australia, and the South Sea Islands enriched our congregational life!

Having lived in the same city all my life, I have found that the influx of God's children from all parts of the world has wondrously diversified our city's languages, food choices, labor force, and religious traditions. Life is more and more like a wonderful stew into which all the varied ingredients, without surrendering discrete identity, blend into one another and produce a delicious result.

All around us, as in Israel's history, we hear sounds of resentment, fear, nationalism, exclusiveness. But this passage reminds us to approach diversity with anticipation, not fear; with thanksgiving, not competitiveness; with hospitality, not separation. Allow the simple beauty of these verses glow in your heart and mind, creating initiatives of welcome and hospitality. The promise is one of blessing.

Fill me, O God, with a heart and arms that enfold and embrace, so that I too may receive your blessing! Amen.

Circles of Blessing

"Unless the Lord builds the house, those who build it labor in vain." The psalmist does not depict Yahweh as a contractor ready to receive our blueprint for a new house. Rather, the psalmist insists that the occupants of the house welcome and invite the presence and guidance of the gracious Creator. I believe this psalm has intense relevance for households today.

Child and spousal abuse occurs more often than not within houses where families dwell. Our living rooms become dumps where media violence pours into the eyes and ears of family members. We easily allow the gods of violence and consumerism to shape the life of our households. Is the daily life of your household being formed by the God of grace and compassion?

Have you ever staged a house blessing to remind and strengthen the presence and will of Yahweh? Many times I have held the hands of celebrants as we have weaved in and out of the rooms of a newly occupied house. The faith community sings and prays that in that place the sovereignty of Yahweh will continue to hold sway.

Grace at mealtimes that serves as honest, hopeful, and healing communication comes center stage. All present will share in financial decisions and the setting of priorities. The building that the Lord does in a house is ongoing and daily as hearts and minds open anew to One who creates "all things new."

Clearly the words of the psalmist admonish us to take stock. Is the Lord continuing to build our house? Do we daily open doors of discipline through which we invite the Lord of life? The enduring promise is not only one of willing entrance but of blessed result. Thanks be to God.

Show me new ways, O God, whereby I may receive you daily into my household, so that you may fulfill your will to bless and heal. Amen.

These verses provide a wonderful description of Christian faith. Something momentous has happened through Christ. Coming out of the life, death, resurrection, and ascension of Jesus is a marvelous conviction for the writer. He says, in effect, that the risen, triumphant Lord is now in the presence of the creator God. Jesus, in that presence, expresses the same healing grace for us that he lived out in his earthly ministry. In other words, in his transformed state, Jesus continues to promote our healing actively. That truth is dramatized in Jesus once for all.

In the Christ event we discover that we too can live and die in trust and anticipation. What God has done for us in Christ means that we shall encounter the fullness of that grace in the future. And we shall meet Christ, not as a dreadful accuser but as one who will complete his vocation to perfect us in love. So we "are eagerly waiting for him."

But the "once for all" nature of Christ's work doesn't leave us with nothing to do. To live daily with trust and anticipation, set in a history replete with horror, injustice, and cruelty, we must exercise all sources of "spiritual income," including the daily disciplines of prayer and scripture reading. That "spiritual income," which will keep faith and hope alive and growing, will also come through active pursuit of justice, through acts of forgiveness and reconciliation. Faithfulness will replace and replenish weakened or elusive faith. We will be able to receive the grace of Christ and persevere in trust and anticipation, confident that Christ will come to us again in fullness and clarity and, above all, in grace and power. Hallelujah!

Thank you, dear God, for that burst of saving grace in Jesus' death and resurrection. Open me daily to your sources of spiritual income, so that my living may continue to express what I understand of Christ until I see Jesus face to face. Amen.

Jesus is painfully aware that we who compete, consume, and worry anxiously about ourselves may wear more than one face. In our self-identity, do we live our lives as chameleons and weather vanes or do we live faithfully, aware of the sovereignty and will of a gracious creator God? All of us are subject to Jesus' scrutiny and judgment, for we all know the disorienting power of duplicity.

I read about a Nazi commandant of a concentration camp during World War II. Daily the acid clouds of smoke rose into the sky, signaling the burning of Jews during the Holocaust. He organized and oversaw cruelty of a type and scale that surpasses imagination. Yet at the end of the day, this German officer went home to his family where the members of the household moved sanctimoniously through a meal blessing in the hallowed tradition of their Christian denomination. While the chasm between public and private may seem much smaller for us, we constantly struggle for greater integrity.

Jesus describes the appearance of pillars of the community who, like a hungry dog going for a bone, frantically desire admiration, respect, and honor. But their public image conceals their greedy and evil exploitation of defenseless widows. As we turn inward, we see reflections of ourselves in Jesus' words as we obey the contradictory wills of so many gods. Increased integrity and the consequent peace of mind wait for greater diligence in prayer on our part, for honest self-criticism and a calling up of the gifts of the Spirit offered by God. Let us open our clenched fists to receive the blessings of community, scripture, devotional discipline. We not only will be blessed but will become more of a blessing to this broken world.

Come, Holy Spirit. Lead me into the integrity and peace of serving the one true God of justice and healing. Amen.

For anyone looking to the Bible to support laziness, the two phrases "unless the Lord builds" it and "unless the Lord guards" it could serve as a foundation. Our resignation that *only* God can build the house or that *only* God can guard the city can easily result in proverbial hand-wringing that absolves everyone of responsibility. However, to conclude that God is the exclusive actor and that humanity is the debt-free recipient overlooks the critical transformation that occurs when we strive to live as followers of God.

At some level, *everyone* builds and guards. Even establishing a family can help us build and guard for the future. Children provide security and stability for old age. They also provide support during difficult times. But whether building or guarding a physical structure or a family, our labor is futile unless we rely upon God.

During a conversation with a surgeon, I heard him describe occasions during surgery in which he felt that he had exhausted the limits of his knowledge and training. Nevertheless, he could feel God taking over and working through him—guiding his hands and decisions—to complete the procedure successfully.

For all of us, our labor does not focus upon personal goals and achievements; our efforts are for the glory of God. In these efforts, there is no shame.

God of all wisdom, help us always to celebrate you when we labor to build or protect. Amen.

Dietrich Bonhoeffer wrote about "cheap grace," grace without serious cost, grace without a cross, cosmetic sharing and blessing not deeply felt. Charity also can be either cheap or costly. We can contribute without feeling the impact on our checkbooks or credit cards. We willingly share our money "off the top" and maybe even a little volunteer time. But we avoid long-term exposure to or lasting relationships with the disadvantaged of our cities or communities. Charity is fine as long as it leaves the givers in control. Jesus sits, watches, and then teaches his disciples about his observation. The poor widow's sacrifice genuinely foreshadows one who gives all on a merciless cross in the consummate expression of costly grace.

Years ago one of the young girls (call her "Annie") from the nearby "projects" attended the church's after-school program. The mother of her single-parent household struggled with alcoholism (a struggle she finally won). Annie's mother lived a miserable life—especially in light of the poverty and addiction she faced daily. One afternoon before the program began, Annie knocked on my office door. When I opened the door, she handed me a surprisingly heavy small paper sack. The sack contained pennies she had accumulated over months. She wanted to contribute to the church's after-school program, for which she thanked God. I held back tears until she left. Today, some twenty years later, Annie is a full-time member of the church staff and directs its children's ministries program. God is still in the Easter business, transforming the widow's mite or sacks of pennies into concentric circles of blessing. I thank God for Jesus' truth and story. Believe it and do likewise!

Use me, O God, to confirm your power to translate even small but costly sacrifices into joyful blessings for many. Amen.

Looking to the Lord

NOVEMBER 12–18, 2018 • CHRISTINE JOY MARTINEZ

SCRIPTURE OVERVIEW: The inability to have a child brings pain to many today, and this was equally true in ancient times. In that context it was sometimes even worse, for Peninnah openly ridicules Hannah for being unable to conceive. But as a result of her desperate, heartfelt prayer, God blesses Hannah with a son, Samuel, who will become a powerful prophet. Hannah then rejoices in a God who exalts the poor and needy. Hannah provides an example of the boldness with which we also can approach God now because of Christ's sacrifice. The destruction of Jerusalem is the focus of the passage in Mark. Jesus here predicts the demolition of the Temple and the city, which the Romans executed in 70 CE.

QUESTIONS AND THOUGHTS FOR REFLECTION

- Read 1 Samuel 1:4-20. When have you felt trapped by circumstances not of your own making? How did the situation resolve itself?

- Read 1 Samuel 2:1-10. When has a situation in your life changed because you persisted in prayer? What did that experience teach you?

- Read Hebrews 10:11-25. Do you perceive God's remembering your sin no more as encouragement or license? Why?

- Read Mark 13:1-8. What signs make you anxious about the world's future? What helps you rest easier?

Works with the Philippine Bible Society and considers Bible translation her vocation; loves Jesus, coffee, and urban cycling.

In Old Testament times, the high priest entered the Holy of Holies once a year to offer atonement for Israel's sins. The high priest readied himself for the extensive liturgy and performance of rituals. The ceremony involved multiple changes of clothes. The priestly garb included bells on its hem that tinkled with movement as the priest ministered in the holy place. Can you imagine the priestly ranks trembling in rapt attention, listening for the faint sound of bells while they await the conclusion of the rituals? Or the tense silence when they hear nothing and the sigh of relief as the tinkling draws near?

Today's reading continues the contrast between earthly high priests and Christ as high priest. They stand "day after day," while Christ sits, having completed his redeeming and sanctifying work. Verses 11-14 remind us of Jesus' sacrifice for us, we who are unholy and unworthy, a sacrifice that bolsters our confidence to enter God's presence without fear. Jesus—both in sacrifice and as high priest—in his death on the cross became for us the blood sprinkled on the altar to atone for our sins. That atonement is not just for today but also for the sins of our past and our future. We no longer require ritual sacrifices because God remembers our sins "no more."

Jesus Christ assures us that the One who mediates for us is holy and without blemish, the One who has conquered death. We can come freely to the Father because of the Son. We look to Jesus the high priest through whom we have unlimited access to God.

Jesus, thank you for paying the price so I can enjoy God's presence without fear. Forgive me for the times I have forgotten the value of your sacrifice. May I express my gratitude daily and treat your gift with utmost humility. Amen.

When in your life did you feel discouraged and chose to meet with other Christians, to be part of Christian fellowship? Did it result from persecution from people, friends, or family who do not share your faith? Have other Christians hurt your feelings? You're not alone. The readers of the letter to the Hebrews might have felt the same way.

This letter was written to encourage its original readers to persist in the faith especially in the face of persecution and suffering. The writer encourages them to "hold fast to our confession" (4:14), "lift your drooping hands and strengthen your weak knees" (12:12). The believers lack commitment, and worship attendance is dropping. Opposition is so great that many are tempted to abandon their faith.

The author reminds his readers of the hope they have in Christ in moments of difficulty. Believers are saved not only from sin but also from the fear of death because they place their eternal hope in Christ who redeems them. Jesus establishes our confidence to enter God's presence and to approach God "with a true heart." We "hold fast to the confession of our hope," and finally we "provoke one another to love and good deeds."

The author emphasizes the importance of Christians meeting together in support. With one another's help, we endure and are strengthened and emboldened in times of hardship. The meeting together itself bears witness to our faith in Jesus, and we eagerly await his return.

Jesus, help me depend on you when I go through trials. May your life and the lives of others inspire my living that I may bear faithful witness. Amen.

Born in a time when women had no inheritance or birthright, Hannah is the proverbial underdog. Marriage assured and insured a woman's future through male offspring. In spite of Hannah's being the first wife (v. 2) and Elkanah's favorite, her barrenness brings her to a point of desperation. Peninnah, the fertile second wife, makes Hannah's life miserable by irritating her about her inability to bear a child.

Like Hannah's, our lives don't always go as we'd expected. Perhaps people test our patience. We may be at the end of our rope because of circumstances beyond our control. Today's scripture tells us not to despair. God hears the cries of the oppressed and marginalized.

Hannah does not retaliate in anger against Peninnah; that isn't Hannah's way. She cannot change her circumstances or the way people treat her. But one thing she knows: "The LORD had closed her womb." So it is to the Lord that Hannah turns. It is the Lord to whom she looks for hope and for answers. Hannah pours out her soul before the Lord, and the Lord grants Hannah's request for a son.

Whatever barrenness we may be experiencing or however many Peninnahs we encounter in life, Hannah's story affirms God's honoring of prayer and sacrifice. Even Eli grasps the significance of the moment and offers his blessing: "Go in peace; the God of Israel grant the petition you have made."

Teach me to relinquish control of my life to you, O God; may I trust in you especially when I don't understand your will. When everything seems to be falling apart, may I cling to your everlasting love. Amen.

At first reading, we might mislabel Hannah as the ungrateful, entitled wife. True, her husband's second wife gives her a hard time, but she is the favorite. Receiving double the portion she deserves, Hannah is blessed to have a generous husband who pacifies her amidst her tears, "Am I not more to you than ten sons?" What more can a person desire?

However, Hannah's inability to bear a son jeopardizes her life and future; she must depend on her husband's generosity for her daily needs. What will happen when Elkanah dies? We know that when the time comes, Hannah could not trust Peninnah to be partial to her husband's favored childless wife. What Hannah needs to hear from Elkanah is this: "*You* are worth more to *me* than ten sons." But this isn't the case. Sonless, Hannah can turn from blessed to homeless in the blink of an eye.

So Hannah looks to the Lord for help. And Eli, the servant of God who should have been able to look past her condition, quickly brings judgment. The priest labels Hannah a drunkard and advises her to keep away from wine despite there being no bottle in sight! After listening to Hannah's story of anxiety and prayer, Eli blesses Hannah and her petitions.

Like many today, Hannah is a victim of systemic injustice. How many times have we looked at a person experiencing homelessness and thought, *What a bum!* Or perhaps we have smirked at victims of abuse saying, "It's her fault; she didn't fight back!" God's ways are not so. God commands that we look beyond each person's condition and act in kindness toward people's needs. Then we shall find favor in God's sight.

We look to God as we pray to become catalysts of transformation and justice in our communities.

Looking to the Lord   379

Being born a woman in Old Testament times, Hannah knows firsthand her disadvantage. As if this weren't enough, she cannot have children. Insecurity, uncertainty, disappointment, and judgment are aspects of life that she juggles day after day. Yet Hannah looks beyond her situation to the One who holds and keeps her life.

God remembers her persistent dependence. And Hannah remembers the One to whom she owes thanks. Her song of thanksgiving expresses who God is and how God works in her life, despite her difficulties. Hannah's song magnifies the Lord.

A physician once told me that we can magnify something or someone in two ways. First we can magnify something small to make it look big, such as when we look through a microscope to see microbes and viruses. The organisms look big when they are actually undetectable by the naked eye. The second approach to magnification occurs when we look at something seemingly small and see it for how magnificent it really is, such as looking at the moon, planets, and stars through a telescope. We realize that not only are they bigger than they appear but that we can never come to terms with their size, greatness, and beauty.

Hannah's expression of God's reversals in her hymn of thanksgiving reminds us that our God is much greater than our problems. She looked to God and persisted in the knowledge that no situation lies beyond God's intervention and answers.

May I magnify you at all times, O Lord. Help me sing your praise even in difficult moments. Remind me of Hannah's song and your ability to turn things around for your glory. Amen.

The birth of Samuel marks the start of a new age—not just for Hannah's family but also for Israel. Through Samuel, the last judge of Israel, God anoints a king: Saul and later David. We know that through the Davidic line God fulfills the promise of establishing a kingdom that will last forever. Though the theme of barrenness dominates the history of Israel's matriarchs (Sarah, Rebekah, Rachel), it seems to end with Hannah as a culmination of God's agency of reversal from that of despair to blessing, from childlessness to an assurance of Israel's future through the line of David.

Not only does Hannah's life testify to God's faithfulness to her family, her thanksgiving becomes a prophetic voice for Israel's story. Before her, we read of God speaking to the Patriarchs in their narratives. Rarely did prophets speak on behalf of God before kings ruled in Israel. But in this passage we hear God's message of assurance and anointing through one from the margins; one who was oppressed, one who was judged for murmuring, one who was a woman! An unthinkable possibility during her time, but Hannah's God does not stand on predictability.

Hannah looked to the Lord in her time of dire need and expressed her innermost desires. God employs her situation to display divine faithfulness both to Hannah as God's servant and to Israel as God's people. Hannah may have been unaware of the prophetic promise she declares, but God uses Hannah's utmost gratitude to usher in God's reign.

May my praise be evident and my thanksgiving be loud, O Lord. May my declarations profess your promises and your faithfulness in fulfilling them. Amen.

Rattled by Jesus' prediction, the disciples eagerly inquire about the details of the impending threat of the Temple's destruction. "When will this be, and what will be the sign that all these things are about to be accomplished?" Rather than directly answering the questions, Jesus issues further warnings and a staggering prediction of fearful things to come: earthquakes, famine, war, disasters, and messianic imposters. Like the disciples, we may cringe upon reading Jesus' list. But unlike the disciples who tremble in fear of the future, we cringe because the list seems all too familiar in our world.

The disciples await the unfolding of Jesus' pronouncements while today we watch with bated breath to discern if we're truly living in the last days. The warnings Jesus enumerates are just the tip of the iceberg. The chapter continues with a longer list of persecution, political opposition, familial wrath, and betrayal that his followers will have to endure. Jesus warns people so they will not be alarmed but instead remember that these are "birth pangs"—the necessary process of suffering that results in the birth of God's reign.

No matter how intense the persecution, however frightening the world events, those who trust in Jesus can take comfort in knowing that God's plan unfolds according to the word of the Son. Jesus' warning holds true, but the assurance of the resurrected Christ is equally true, "I am with you always, to the end of the age" (Matt. 28:20). And until that day, we look to our Lord Jesus, Author and Perfecter of our faith, our strength and shield, our one true ruler.

Lord, in these times of unrest and natural calamity, may I be a light in this dark world and be a vessel of your gospel of peace as we, your people, await your coming. Amen.

Soon and Very Soon

NOVEMBER 19–25, 2018 • JAMES K. KARPEN

SCRIPTURE OVERVIEW: Second Samuel records the final words of David. David takes comfort in the covenant that God has made with his family, which must be continued by kings who will honor God and rule justly. The psalmist sings of this same covenant with David's family and the same necessity to follow God's decrees in order to rule well. Revelation opens with a vision of Jesus Christ, the fulfillment of the Davidic covenant, the King to rule over all kings for all time. Many expected Jesus to set up a political kingdom. Yet in John, Jesus tells Pilate that his kingdom is not an earthly one. This week let us thank God that the kingdom is based not on the exercise of power but on Jesus' example of serving others.

QUESTIONS AND THOUGHTS FOR REFLECTION
- Read 2 Samuel 23:1-7. Upon your deathbed, what would you like your last words to be?
- Read Psalm 132. What is your vision of Paradise? Who will be seated around your table?
- Read Revelation 1:4b-8. How do you bear faithful witness to "the Alpha and the Omega"?
- Read John 18:33-37. To whom do you pledge allegiance? To whom do you give lip service?

Senior pastor of St. Paul and St. Andrew United Methodist Church, New York City; currently teaching Christian ethics at Drew University in Madison, New Jersey.

Famous last words. Famous people leave behind famous last words. They may be interesting, like Goethe's "Mehr licht!" ("More light!"), or inspiring, like John Wesley's "The best of all is, God is with us." Harriet Tubman left this life singing "Swing Low, Sweet Chariot." Sometimes the last words are remembered only because the speaker was so famous, like Elvis's, "I'm going to the bathroom to read."

The writer of Second Samuel passes on to us the last words of King David. Not as short and pithy as some, but good to remember. David speaks about the need for a ruler to be dependable and fair, to rule with justice. A ruler like that is like the sun rising on a cloudless morning.

When I visualize the end of my earthly life, I picture the sun going down, the end of a long day's journey into night. Not David. For him, the freshness of a new day comes to mind and springs to his lips, the sun "gleaming from the rain on the grassy land." David, a deeply flawed person, is all too aware of his faults and failures. But he goes to his death not counting on his own accomplishments but recognizing the ideal for which he had striven. And, to his credit, David never shied away from a challenge, even that of his own death. Death is, after all, as the German theologian and pastor Dietrich Bonhoeffer put it, the greatest feast on the way to freedom.

Speaking of Bonhoeffer, King David might have approved the last words he reportedly spoke as he prepared to face a rope at the Flossenburg concentration camp: "This is . . . the beginning of life."

God, now I see through a glass darkly, but then I will see face-to-face. Give me the strength to stand up for justice while I live and to face my own death like the sun rising on a cloudless morning. Amen.

King David spends his last breath on those he calls *godless,* a word that could also be translated as "despicable." He doesn't spend a lot of time on them, only two verses, barely longer than a tweet. They're not worth it. They're like thorns—prickly, worthless.

We all have despicable people in our lives. Relatives, colleagues, coworkers, neighbors. People who don't see the world the way we do. People who don't think like us or believe like us or do things our way. Objectionable. Despicable. What to do with all these despicable people?

King David had a lot of enemies. He knew exactly what to do with most of them. He killed them. Jesus also had a lot of enemies. He knew exactly what to do with them. He ate with them, debated with them, challenged them, and listened to them.

It's hard enough to get along with our loved ones, the people who generally want what's best for us. But Jesus asks us to love the people who oppose us, who want to put us down, who want to leave us out. Is that even possible? And if it's possible, should Jesus expect it of us? Or is this just another ridiculous Jesus thing that sounds nice, but we're not going to try to do it?

Surely Jesus knows the only way to avoid making enemies is to be so inoffensive that you never stand for anything and never stand up for anyone. Jesus knows that, because who made more enemies than Jesus? And what did he do with them? He loved them.

Got an enemy? You know what to do. Got a Pharisee who thinks you're a disgrace to your religion? Go eat at his house. Got a disciple willing to sell you for silver? Invite him to your last supper. Got a government putting you to death? With your last breath, ask God to forgive them.

Lord, help me to love even the people who get in my way. Amen.

This psalm speaks to us of the importance of making a place for God. It quotes King David saying that he will not go to his own house, will not get into his bed, and will not sleep until he finds a place for God to dwell.

God needs space. If we don't make space for God, other things will crowd in. That's true in my life and yours. And it's true in our world. We have a choice. We can work to carve out space for the will and way of God, that way of love, justice, and reconciliation, or we can watch the world fill with fear, frustration, despair, and distrust.

On the evening before Thanksgiving, the sanctuary of our church fills with Jews and Buddhists, Muslims and Methodists, Presbyterians and Pentecostals, all trying to make a place for God. One of the songs we sing is an "Alleluia" we borrowed from the synagogue that shares our sanctuary. We sing it in church all the time, and I finally confessed to the rabbi that we'd stolen his song, "Hallelu." He said, "That's okay. We stole it from a Pakistani Muslim group. It's really called 'Allah-hu' ('God Is')." Tonight we'll gather again in that sacred place, that place for God, and God's peoples will pray together, laugh together, listen to one another's sacred texts, and imagine a world of faith, love, and respect.

One year the congregations gathered for a meal together. We tried hard to balance things. We had fifty Jews, fifty Muslims, fifty Methodists. We wanted each table to have a mix to facilitate discussion. So, in the beginning, people were calling out, "We need another Jew! We need another Muslim!" The rabbi got up and said, "This is how Paradise will be; not 'Stay away, you're different; but come here, we need you.'" Amen.

God, help us create a place for you in our lives. Amen.

THANKSGIVING DAY, USA

Do not worry." It's funny to read these words on Thanksgiving Day. Thanksgiving is the one day above all others when I worry. I worry about what the family will eat. I think about what I'm going to wear.

Thanksgiving is a good day to worry. If we're going someplace, we can worry about how it's going to be, how our kids are going to behave, what an annoying uncle might say to set us off. If we're having people over, we can worry about getting the house in decent shape and whether we have the right amount of food, drink, plates, silverware. If we're by ourselves, we can worry about that.

Jesus has a different and simple idea: Relax. Put things in perspective. Will our worrying help us live longer? Trust. Breathe. Live. Focus instead on what's important, Jesus says. Think about God's kingdom, where God's way of love and justice holds sway. It's coming! Soon and very soon! Think about God's righteousness rather than your own.

I ate dinner with a Muslim friend recently, and the subject of holidays came up. She said Thanksgiving is her favorite holiday. Why? Because it's one she can share with her whole extended family, Muslims and non-Muslims, and remember the things they have in common. A love of family. A love of this country. A love of food!

We have so many things other than Thanksgiving to worry about. We're not going to get Thanksgiving right anyway. The only way to get it right is to let it go. Be thankful—very thankful.

God, your blessings surround us. We awaken to your morning. You feed us like the birds. You clothe us like the flowers. Thank you. Thank you. Thank you. Amen.

Restore our fortunes, O Lord, like the watercourses in the Negeb." I once spent several summer days in the Negeb Desert. It was hot; I was thirsty. Even the camels were thirsty. There was no water, but there were watercourses!

Watercourses, streambeds. Wadis, they call them. A wadi is the bed or gully of a stream that's dry most of the time. And these wadis were dry. But my friend, a Bedouin, told me how they erupt with gushing, glorious water when the rains come.

The people of Israel went through many a dry spell, literally and figuratively. At times they felt deserted by God and disconnected from one another. Many times hope was hard to come by, times when the very act of hoping seemed hopeless.

And still the people trusted in God. Still they looked to a time of restoration of their fortunes—a time when they would once again dream, laugh, shout with joy. A time when even the Gentiles would say, "The LORD has done great things" for them.

Every nation has its times of trial. Times when kings and presidents and prime ministers fail the people. Times when the economy fails the people. Times when justice is hard to find; peace is elusive; rights are trampled. Dry spells. Thirsty times. Times when it is hard to hope. And yet, we know that God will never abandon us. The God who may not come when we want but who is always on time. Soon and very soon.

I have had my share of dry spells, frustrating times, times of despair. Times when "even hope seems hopelessness," as the hymn puts it ("Cuando El Pobre," UMH, no. 434). Do I still trust God in those times? Do you?

God, give me hope. Lead me into the future where you already are. Amen.

Soon and very soon. "Look! He is coming with the clouds." Not long ago, I cooked up a series on the book of Revelation, going to people's homes in various neighborhoods around the city to gather with people who lived in those areas to eat and to study. I called it "House Calls: Appetizers and the Apocalypse." I didn't know whether people would be interested, but more than a hundred showed up altogether. Maybe the appetizers drew them: lake of fire nachos and Babylon blintzes. Still, most people expressed curiosity about this strange, final book of the Bible. How can we interpret it? Does it have any meaning for us today?

By reading Revelation we learn that John of Patmos is deeply disturbed about the world as it is. Power and oppression hold sway. Faith is challenged; rights are trampled. Following Jesus and living a life of love and justice can get you into big trouble. In other words, it's a time and a situation not dissimilar from our own. We know that our world is far from the way of Jesus, far from the reign of God.

Jesus is coming! That is the promise. But when can we expect the return of Christ in glory? Soon. Soon and very soon.

Jesus is coming! Beginning next week, the first Sunday of Advent, my faith community will sing the South African song, "Freedom Is Coming": "Jesus is coming, O yes I know." We will pray, in the words of Revelation, the penultimate verse of the whole Bible, "Amen. Come, Lord Jesus!" (Rev. 22:20). And meanwhile, we'll bear faithful witness to "the Alpha and the Omega," who circumscribes our living with the holy.

Lord, your kingdom come. Your will be done. Come, Lord Jesus. Amen.

REIGN OF CHRIST SUNDAY

Today we celebrate the reign of Christ. It's not my favorite liturgical moment in the life of the church. To me it sounds hierarchical and authoritarian. But Reign of Christ Sunday has an interesting history. In 1920s Italy, Pope Pius XI was concerned about the rise of a narrow nationalism at home and abroad. He wanted to mark a day when the church could recognize and affirm that our primary loyalty is not to a political party, or even to the nation we live in, but to Jesus Christ. So Pius took the last Sunday of the Christian year, which before this was called variously "Day of the Last Judgment" or, more cheerfully, "Dooms Day" and changed it to honor the lordship of Jesus, the Reign of Christ.

Today serves as a reminder to us that whoever is in power, whoever occupies the throne or the White House, our allegiance is to the Jesus who was declared a king while standing trial for treason. Today we remember whom we follow and to whom we affirm our allegiance.

Jesus reigns! So Caesar doesn't. Jesus reigns! "Our struggle is not against enemies of blood and flesh, but against the rulers, against the authorities . . . against the spiritual forces of evil in the heavenly places" (Eph. 6:12). Jesus reigns! "Neither death, nor life, nor angels, nor rulers . . . will be able to separate us from the love of God in Christ Jesus our Lord" (Rom. 8:38-39).

And then on the cross, under a sign that mocked his authority—"Jesus of Nazareth, King of the Jews" (John 19:19)—Jesus shows the basis for his power and his authority. Nothing. Nothing but that of love. In the name of the Prince of Peace, the King of kings, the Lord of lords, the Lonely One who ended this life crowned with thorns on a cross of shame.

Lord, may I follow only you. Amen.

Expecting a Loving God

NOVEMBER 26—DECEMBER 2, 2018 • LACEYE WARNER

SCRIPTURE OVERVIEW: As we prepare our hearts for Advent, the celebration of Jesus' first coming, we remember in Jeremiah that the birth of Jesus has a deep background, a background rooted in God's promise to David. Psalm 25, traditionally credited to David, speaks of God's faithfulness to those who follow the paths of the Lord. David asks God to teach him to follow God's paths even more closely. The New Testament readings actually point us toward Jesus' second coming. Paul encourages the Thessalonians to excel in holiness and love while they wait. In Luke, Jesus discusses the coming of the kingdom in a passage that some find confusing. We note that he focuses not on the exact time frame of the arrival of the kingdom but on our need to be alert.

QUESTIONS AND THOUGHTS FOR REFLECTION

- Read Jeremiah 33:14-16. What has been your experience with a promise-making and promise-keeping God?

- Read Psalm 25:1-10. How do you perceive God's instruction in your life?

- Read 1 Thessalonians 3:9-13. How has God's presence buoyed you up in times of persecution or distress?

- Read Luke 21:25-36. What is your Advent posture this year? If "believing is seeing" were true in your life, what would you see?

Associate Professor of the Practice of Evangelism and Methodist Studies, Duke Divinity School, Durham, North Carolina.

This Sunday marks the beginning of Advent, a season of hopeful preparation for and expectation of Jesus Christ's coming. Advent is an ancient Christian tradition and, for most faith communities, it begins the church year with distinctive scriptures, music, and practices to prepare for Jesus' birth, as well as the hope of Jesus Christ's impending second coming. The term *Advent* derives from the Latin word *adventus,* which means "coming." The Latin *adventus* is translated from the Greek term *parousia*, which is often used when speaking of Christ's second coming. This season is characterized by deep hope as the church and the world await the unfolding of God's promises.

Today's passage includes several references to events that foretell Christ's second coming. They create a seemingly detailed account of history both past and future. While scripture consistently refers to similar events and themes, its purpose is not to provide a chronology of God's actions but rather a narrative of God's desire to be in relationship with creation for its salvation. Scripture demonstrates the character of God.

This week we read of God's character, including God's promise-keeping, steadfast love, and forgiveness. God's character and actions in Jesus Christ, both the nativity at Christmas and eventual second coming, invite us and all God's creation into saving relationship and participation in God's reign. These verses suggest an Advent posture: "Stand up and raise your heads." Our "redemption is drawing near."

Reflect upon the many promises God keeps in relationship with us and all creation—and in prayer, give thanks to God.

Our God makes and keeps promises. This chapter begins with God's promises of restoration, forgiveness, and steadfast love to Jerusalem and Judah. The following verses in the chapter remind us of God's commitments to fulfilling promises or covenants. The chapter ends with a reminder of God's faithfulness reaching from Abraham, Isaac, Jacob, and their offspring to demonstrate God's promise-keeping.

Scholars do not consider the book of Jeremiah a messianic text like other books in the Old Testament, for example, Isaiah, in its echoing of God's promises of a messiah or savior. However, these verses resonate with God's promise *of* and God's people's hope *for* a messiah. John Wesley, the founder of the early Methodist revival movement in Great Britain, comments on this text in his *Explanatory Notes upon the Old Testament*. Wesley is particularly interested in the name "The Lord is our righteousness." Wesley states this is a promise relating to Christ to carry on David's failed lineage (33:16-17). The coming of this king, or messiah, as described in Jeremiah will fulfill God's promises to Israel and the house of Judah, facilitating God's justice, righteousness, and salvation.

God promises salvation alongside steadfast love, forgiveness, and restoration. This is God's gift of hope to us and all creation. God promises and acts in the midst of the messy chaos of the world by sending Jesus Christ, God's own Son, fully human and fully divine, to live with us, deeply love us, and fully redeem and save us. In the season of Advent we wait with expectation and hope, faith and confidence in God's promises.

Reflect upon the gift of Jesus Christ, the Messiah, and the implications for our lives and all creation—and in prayer, give thanks to God.

Signs point to the coming of the Son of Man and the kingdom of God: "There will be signs in the sun, the moon, and the stars, and on the earth." Beginning with verse 29, a parable describes the fig tree, like all trees, offering signs that summer is near when it sprouts leaves. "So also, when you see these things taking place, you know that the kingdom of God is near."

Interpreting signs can be difficult and confusing. We find it more difficult to notice signs of God's kingdom if we are not formed to see God's actions in the world. For example, as a middle-class, educated US woman, the lens through which I view the world is mainly informed by modern influences of humanity's perceived control mediated through medicine, technology, and economics—those proven and seen disciplines. Yet, humanity's control is woefully overestimated. Whether natural disasters, deadly diseases, or simply misappropriating wants for needs, human control of the world is, for the most part, impossible. The only constant is the triune God's promises of steadfast love, forgiveness, and relationship.

What would it mean to see the world through our belief and faith in God? Instead of "seeing is believing" what if "believing is seeing"? What if we choose to view the world through God's promises contained in scripture and shared in communities of faith as we participate in God's kingdom? Would we then be alert to the signs of God's coming?

Reflect upon how believing in God's promises reshapes our perceptions of life and the world. In prayer, ask God to give you new lenses to see God's presence and actions.

Expecting a Loving God

This psalm describes God's character and relationship with all creation. Also, God's promises of steadfast love and mercy are not new but long-standing promises "from of old" that continue to be fulfilled. God's characteristics as "steadfast in love" and "merciful" indicate God's desire for relationship with creation. God's character and desire for relationship figure prominently in Psalm 25. Psalm 25 demonstrates two complementary dynamics of God's relationship with creation: (1) God's actions toward humanity and creation and (2) humanity's response and receiving of God's holiness.

The Advent theme of waiting comes into play in verses 3 and 5. The psalmist awaits God's instruction. In verse 5 the psalmist also acknowledges God's promise of salvation. Steadfast love and mercy characterize God's salvation. That steadfast love grants forgiveness for all transgressions. God's desire for relationship is not limited to those able to meet the requirements or maintain expectations of worthiness. Instead, God, with steadfast love and mercy, forgives all sins.

Some Christians refer to God's forgiveness of sin as the doctrine of "justification." As a child I learned this concept with the phrase "just as if I never sinned" as a play on the term *justification*. For John Wesley, the doctrine of justification indicates what God does for us, clothing us with the righteousness of Jesus Christ and forgiving all sins. There is nothing we must do, or can do, to earn God's forgiveness; it's part of the unconditional love God freely offers to us all.

Reflect upon God's steadfast love and mercy for you and for all humankind—and in prayer, give thanks to God.

Expecting a Loving God

Yesterday we reflected on God's actions toward humanity and creation. Today we reflect on humanity's response to God's mercy and our receipt of God's holiness. Psalm 25:4, 5, 8-10 mention the psalmist's desire to know God's paths, truth, and way in order to keep God's covenant. While we can do nothing to earn God's steadfast love and mercy beyond accepting that love, we may desire to grow in love and relationship with God. Growing in love and relationship with God and others as a Christian disciple is often described in relationship to the doctrine of "sanctification."

For John Wesley, the doctrine of sanctification indicates the work of God in us by the Holy Spirit facilitating a new creation by granting us holiness of heart and life. While God solely enacts sanctification, or the granting of God's holiness in us, God invites our participation through love of God and neighbor.

In verses 8-10 we read that God "instructs sinners in the way," "leads the humble in what is right, and teaches the humble his way." This is God's work in us through sanctification: keeping God's covenant by practicing love for God and neighbor and allowing the Holy Spirit to make us a new creation.

Reflect upon the Holy Spirit's work of sanctification in your life. How are you called to love of God and neighbor? How are these practices creating holiness of heart and life in you?

In prayer, give thanks to God and ask for God's leading in your continued efforts to love God and neighbor and to follow God's paths.

The apostle Paul writes to a community of faith that suffers persecution due to their Christian beliefs and practices. Paul expresses gratitude for this community and encourages them to keep the faith. The passage concludes with a prayer for the community. It asks God to strengthen their hearts in holiness that they may be blameless before God at the coming of our Lord Jesus, a reference to the second coming of Christ.

Though young in the faith, this community is distressed and persecuted (verse 7), perhaps provoking Paul's letter of gratitude and encouragement. While they and we acknowledge God's steadfast love and mercy offered to all without requirement or qualification, we also acknowledge the fact that relationship with God does not exempt individuals and communities from persecution and distress.

All Christians (and non-Christians for that matter) will experience persecution and distress in various forms at some point. Some argue Christians may be more susceptible, much like Job in the Old Testament who was God's "favorite." However, persecution and distress is not punishment; it is simply an aspect of the times in which we live: after Creation and the Fall but before Jesus Christ's second coming. The more hopeful news is that in the midst of persecution and distress or joy and celebration, God never leaves us and continues to offer steadfast love, mercy, strength, peace, and hope.

Reflect upon times of persecution and/or distress in your life or the life of your faith community. What was the nature of the difficulty? How did you sense God's presence and love in the midst of those times?

In prayer, give thanks to God and ask for God's continuing presence and love in the midst of times of persecution as well as celebration.

Expecting a Loving God

FIRST SUNDAY OF ADVENT

Throughout scripture we sense a focus on communities rather than individuals. Yet, in my own experience and cultural pattern, the category of individual rather than community receives emphasis. This assumption of individualism is influenced by modernity's being informed by the Enlightenment, including the emergence of democratic governments and capitalist economies. I benefit greatly from these valuable influences. However, concepts and categories related to individualism are not particularly prominent in scripture.

In 1 Thessalonians 3:11-13, the apostle Paul addresses the community of faith. Though suffering persecution and distress, this community receives comfort and encouragement from one another in their Christian faith and practice, as well from others connected to them in faith but at a distance. As members of communities of faith we are baptized into a local congregation as well as a vast network of communities of faith, and, most importantly, the body of Christ. What an amazing gift to share our Christian beliefs and practices in a community not bound by time and place!

Though we prepare and wait for the second coming of Jesus Christ, from scripture we know how the narrative unfolds. Not only does God offer us steadfast love and mercy in relationship, but the joyful fellowship we experience in communities of faith gives a foretaste of the heavenly banquet prepared for all those in relationship with God.

In prayer, give thanks to God for relationship with the triune God and with communities of faith.

Some Assembly Required

DECEMBER 3–9, 2018 • JEREMY SMITH

SCRIPTURE OVERVIEW: The prophet Malachi speaks of a future day when God's messenger will come to prepare the way for the Lord. The Lord will then purify the people and restore proper worship of God. Christians believe that John the Baptizer was this messenger, preparing the way for Christ. In Luke 1, the Holy Spirit fills Zechariah, John's father, who proclaims that the fulfillment of God's promises to their descendants has begun. Luke continues the story of John in chapter 3, describing John's ministry of calling people to repentance. They need to prepare the way of the Lord in their own hearts, thus fulfilling Malachi's prophecy. Paul in Philippians focuses not on the advent of Christ but on the ongoing power of Christ's presence to make us blameless and righteous in God's sight.

QUESTIONS AND THOUGHTS FOR REFLECTION

- Read Malachi 3:1-4. How have you experienced the refiner's fire? What was your experience?

- Read Luke 1:68-79. At home and work, are you usually the first touch, the second touch, or the third touch? How so?

- Read Philippians 1:3-11. How could you make expressing your gratitude to others a habit?

- Read Luke 3:1-6. How are you preparing the way of the Lord? What crooked paths are you helping to make straight?

Senior Pastor, First United Methodist Church of Seattle, Washington.

The minor characters matter in stories seen on the stage and screen. In detective shows, you have to pay attention to the minor characters because one of them may be the criminal. In Disney movies and adapted plays, the minor character often performs one heroic act that turns the tide and saves the day. The major characters get the majority of the screen or stage time, but often the minor characters transform the story.

One such minor character in the biblical story is the prophet Malachi. Malachi is the last of the prophetic books in the Old Testament (Hebrew Bible). It seems like the series ends with a whimper—only fifty-five verses! The New Testament only references Malachi in two unique stories, and the lectionary of commended readings lists only two small sections, including this one today. A "minor" prophet indeed!

And yet Malachi contains a prophecy that neatly dovetails the story of the people of Israel with the future story of Jesus and John the Baptist. The prophet uses the image of a refiner's fire that will burn away all the iniquities and sins of the community. Gold or silver cannot purify itself: It takes an extraordinary action beyond their ability to purify them. The anticipated action of God alone is what will save the Israelites from their impurity and return them to glory.

Malachi sits between the two Testaments, which describe the God to whom all are called; yet only God's future action will save the people. What can that possibly mean to a nation surrounded by the Empire? Maybe this minor prophet matters more than we thought; this week we may discover what that message means for us.

Holy One, help us recognize the everyday people in our lives. Turn our attention away from our phones and toward one another, seeking transformation in the conversations. Amen.

A children's book titled *Love You Forever* by Robert Munsch (2011) always makes me cry. In the book, a mother tells her son, "I'll love you forever, I'll like you for always, as long as I'm living my baby you'll be." The book depicts her repeating this line at many stages of his life until she dies of old age. On the final page, the son repeats the same line to his newborn daughter. The cycle of love and affection continues.

The people beloved by God know God is with them no matter what. In the wilderness after Exodus, God is there. In the warring tribes, God is there. In the strife between nations, God is there. And now, surrounded by an impenetrable and seemingly everlasting Empire, God is there with the nation of Israel. Zechariah gives a prophecy that God will uphold God's end of the covenant and deliver the people from this time of trial as well—and, yes, he's referencing Malachi.

We often view prophecy as tumultuous, an upsetting of the status quo. But to the Israelites, prophecy about God's faithfulness is like a warm blanket, a reassurance in the midst of the storm. A repeated line that says, "I'll love you forever," no matter what.

To live into the prophecies and to embrace the prophets will lead to drastic change to the status quo. But to do so leads the people back into the comfort, care, and concern of their God. How may we see that drastic change also leading us closer to the God we seek?

Holy One, we know you love us forever. May this reassurance give us what we need to share that love with one new person this day. In Jesus' name. Amen.

I love volleyball. After the serve, each team has three touches to get the ball over the net to the opponent's turf. At the competitive levels, the three touches have the same pattern: first, the reaction hit that simply gets the ball into the air after the other side sends it over. Then there's the second touch: the set. This light touch is an easy-up that "sets" up the third touch: the spike, the light tap, or whatever play that will send the ball to an unprotected part of the opponent's turf. The cycle repeats until one team misses.

So often we get stuck in the belief that we are the first or third touches. We really want to be the third touch: the one who gets things done, achieves a goal, has the final word. So often we are the first touches: the light tap to another, the quick response to the ball as it comes to us. I believe the most important touch is the second: the one who sets up what comes next. There's incredible power in this role, but it comes from a place of humility, a knowledge that you aren't going to be the one who scores a point.

In this passage, the long-awaited son of Zechariah and Elizabeth is born into a priestly family. Zechariah has been instructed by God to name the child John—not a family name. Zechariah, unable to speak since questioning the news of the birth, writes the name John—but John will not be a priest. He will be a prophet setting up the final touch for the one who will follow him: Jesus of Nazareth, soon to be born in Bethlehem.

John won't score the point, but John will be the one who sets up the One who is to come.

Holy One, you come to us in unexpected ways. Guide us always to set up your possibilities to your preferred future. In Jesus' name we pray. Amen.

"Thank you so much" is the best way to start a letter or e-mail. Whether you are thanking the recipient for a gift, for their attention to your relationship, or for their action, it is a versatile response. I especially like to say "thank you so much" in response to letters of critique to write that I'm thankful for their obvious concern and look forward to engaging their concerns in the body of the message. It immediately frames the content in gratitude for the relationship the sender and receiver have to merit such a communication.

When we do good things, we feel like we should be the objects of praise; but we see in Paul's letter to the Philippians that we are not the object. Paul says "I thank my God" whenever he thinks of the Philippians acting in charitable ways. He doesn't say "thank you so much" to the Philippians—he says it to God for blessing him with coworkers and siblings in Christ.

Paul eagerly expresses his appreciation for the people in Philippi who "from the first day" have taken the gospel to heart. They have both received and given. Paul chooses to testify in defense of the gospel, calling God to bear witness to his longing for the Philippians. Christ who began a good work in them is the one who will see it to completion "by the day of Jesus Christ." So, like the Philippians, we find ourselves living between "the first day" and "the day of Jesus Christ."

Gratitude and appreciation are the ways of living that can transform a rigid framework. How might you live in gratitude today, and whose relationship could you transform by starting it with "thank you so much"?

Holy One, grant us the willingness to express our thankfulness to one another, even to those who are not friends. May our efforts be appreciated, not by one another but by you. Amen.

In *The Phantom Menace* (1999) Yoda says this: "Fear leads to anger, anger leads to hate, hate leads to suffering." Yoda sees fear as the gateway that leads to other bad qualities. Naming and owning fear, Yoda implies, renders the rest less overwhelming.

In this closing section to yesterday's passage, Paul also names a gateway emotion to myriad other things: love. If Yoda summarized Paul, he might say, "Love leads to knowledge, knowledge leads to insight, insight leads to righteousness."

Love leads to knowledge because if you love someone, you pay attention to them. You notice when they struggle. Knowledge comes only from attentiveness born of love, informed by knowledge of God's love as well.

Knowledge leads to insight ("to determine what is best") because only from accumulated knowledge and fresh perspective do novel ideas come forth. An unjust situation or a seemingly entrenched position can be better named with more knowledge born of love.

Finally, insight leads to righteousness as you live differently than expected but in accordance with your knowledge of God. You live pure and blameless (there's Malachi again with his refiner's fire) because you have the knowledge and love that keep you connected with God and neighbor.

May we also start with love as the gateway habit to a chain of betterment for ourselves and our neighbors. And may that love for neighbors be informed by what God's love looks like in scripture and what it may be calling us to do in the present.

Holy One, guide us to overcome our fears and embrace the new reality of love. May we praise you even when love doesn't prevail, in the knowledge that love will prevail in the end. Amen.

Finally, we get to John—John who was predicted in Malachi, John who was just born in Luke 1, finally arrives in Luke 3. This is the guy! This is who we've been waiting for! What novel idea or message can we expect?

Steve Jobs, the founder and deceased former CEO of Apple technology company, was a master at managing expectations. He would paint a picture of a situation so difficult that it would be impossible to fix—and then Apple would come out with a product that solved the problem. Or they would take away abilities from a newer model of their technology, claiming it's not a defect—it's a feature! You want simplicity, right? Jobs's charisma and ability to generate product by sheer mental force both managed expectations and built anticipation for the secrecy-wrapped novel products, for better or worse.

John the Baptist may have had serious expectations for his life given his father's prophecy. But those expectations may not have been met. John wore strange clothes and ate strange foods, and he had only one sales line: "Prepare the way of the Lord." Even that line came from Isaiah.

Steve Jobs may have been a master at managing individual expectations, but we see that John the Baptist is the master at overwhelming the expectations for who Jesus is to be. Jesus is expected not simply to arrive but to set the world aright, to remove the inequalities, and to humble the self-exalted. We've now spent two millennia understanding that those massive expectations are met only when they are made real in every community's life together across the globe.

Holy One, help us name our expectations for this day, and guide us to wisdom on how to align them with your possibilities. Give us courage to go into the wilderness. Amen.

SECOND SUNDAY OF ADVENT

We return to Malachi to bookend this week, but I invite you to read a bit more. Malachi 3:5 follows today's reading with these words: "I will be swift to bear witness against the sorcerers, against the adulterers, against those who swear falsely, against those who oppress the hired workers in their wages, the widow and the orphan, against those who thrust aside the alien, and do not fear me, says the LORD of hosts."

The goal of the refiner's fire is not to make gold or silver pure. The goal of the fuller's soap is not to make a garment clean and white. The goal of the life of following Christ is not to become what John Wesley would call a "holy solitary" separated by piety from the world's problems.

No, the goal for Malachi is to stand in solidarity with the poor, the widow, the orphan, and the immigrant. We seek refinement in Malachi 3, God's fidelity in Luke 1, love and insight in Philippians 1, and radical reorientation in Luke 3 in order to benefit the marginalized in biblical society and today.

Look around you. Do you know the name of the person experiencing extreme poverty in your neighborhood or on your way to work? Are you aware of how the political structures impact the orphan and the immigrant differently than you?

We can recommit ourselves to all the ponderings of scripture, but if they have no discernible effect on our life alongside the marginalized, then they are noisy gongs or clanging cymbals. We can make a difference in people's lives. Go, and make the paths of the marginalized straight.

Holy One, help us live out the scriptures in action and deed. Fill our lives with interaction with the outcasts, and we shall find the joy of life in you. Amen.

Rejoice, Give Thanks and Sing

DECEMBER 10–16, 2018 • LYNNE M. DEMING

SCRIPTURE OVERVIEW: As I reviewed the scripture passages for this week, a hymn titled "Rejoice, Give Thanks and Sing" kept going through my mind. The writers of this week's texts advise us to do all these things. At this time of year, these responses often seem to come naturally for many of us. The prophet Zephaniah exhorts his audience to sing aloud and rejoice. The prophet Isaiah calls on the people of Judah to "give thanks to the Lord." In the letter to the Philippians, Paul advises his audience to "rejoice in the Lord always." The tone of the Luke passage for this week is more somber; through the words of John the Baptist, Luke challenges his audience to maintain right relationships with God and humanity. Taken together, these passages provide a number of life lessons.

QUESTIONS AND THOUGHTS FOR REFLECTION

- Read Isaiah 12:2-6. Think about the times of uncertainty in your life. What did you fear? Who or what gave you comfort during these times?

- Read Zephaniah 3:14-20. When have you found joy in the midst of trouble? Think back on that time in your life, and give thanks for God's presence.

- Read Luke 3:7-18. Where in your life are you being nudged to do the right thing? How will you respond?

- Read Philippians 4:4-7. At what times is God most present in your life? When do you find yourself searching for God?

Former Executive Director of Publishing, The Upper Room; now retired and living in Nashville, Tennessee.

Today's scripture was spoken by the prophet Isaiah to the people of Judah, who were living in the shadow of the powerful Assyrian Empire at the time. Isaiah prophesied to Judah from roughly 750 to 700 BCE. The eighth century was a time of turmoil and unpredictability in the lives of Isaiah's hearers. Toward the end of that period, Assyria besieged Judah but did not totally destroy the nation, proving to Isaiah that its inhabitants could "trust, and not be afraid." Throughout the first thirty-nine chapters of Isaiah (often called First Isaiah or Isaiah of Jerusalem), the prophet counsels the people of Judah to trust God in the midst of uncertain circumstances.

Like the nation of Judah almost three thousand years ago, many parts of the world today also face an uncertain future. As we reflect on our own lives, we can identify places and feelings of unsettledness. Yet we, like Isaiah, affirm God as the source of our salvation. In our Advent waiting, we affirm God's action and faithfulness in the past and look forward with hope. We know God's deeds and bear witness.

This morning I read the daily entry of one of my favorite wise writers. Her word for today is *trust*. *Trust* is an appropriate word for this time of year, no matter the circumstances. We trust that the coming year will be a good one for us—that God's salvation will bring comfort, hope, and joy.

The prophet Isaiah echoes this theme in today's reading. "I will trust, and will not be afraid." Trusting God and not being afraid is an important life lesson, but it is easier said than done for most of us!

Loving and gracious God, help us trust in you during times of uncertainty and turmoil. May we not be afraid. Amen.

Zephaniah 1:1 dates this prophetic book during the reign of King Josiah of Judah, from 640 to 609 BCE. King Josiah brought about important religious reforms in Judah. (You can read about Josiah's reign in 2 Kings 22–23.) However, most of Zephaniah's prophecy concerns judgment against Judah and its neighbors. After several chapters of doom and gloom in which the prophet actually suggests that the best thing God could do is "sweep away humans and animals" and cut "off humanity from the face of the earth" (1:3), the clouds seemingly part to allow light to break through: "Rejoice and exult with all your heart!" The New Revised Standard Version refers to today's scripture as "A Song of Joy." The prophet encourages his audience to rejoice because God has rescued them from their adversaries and they can now look forward to a future without judgment and oppression. Zephaniah describes that future time using the phrase "on that day," a common theme in these chapters. The message of the text is clear: Salvation is near. God comes to redeem.

Recently I saw a story on television that illustrated the concept of joy in the midst of trouble. The story was about a boy born with autism. His mother was determined to, as she put it, "not change him, but bring out the best in him." Perhaps the most helpful thing she did was to buy him a bird. That boy, now a teenager, said that the bird was a perfect pet because it couldn't talk and neither could he. Currently this boy, who has just graduated from high school, has been awarded a Rhodes scholarship and is on his way to study at Oxford. His mother offers a shining example of finding joy in a difficult situation.

Loving God, we thank you for the joy we find during the times of turmoil and trouble. Make us aware of this joy. Amen.

John the Baptist's harsh words remind us of God's judgment while opening the door for a teaching moment. John gives three pieces of advice when asked, "What then should we do?" First, give your second coat to someone who needs one and leftover food to someone who is hungry; second, collect no more tax than you should; and third, do not extort money and be grateful for what you are paid for your work. Justice is a big issue for the Gospel writer, for John, and for God. These relatively small acts of propriety and generosity can make significant changes in the lives of others.

A number of years ago, I received a cancer diagnosis. As a result I had to go through six months of chemotherapy, which left me sick, exhausted, and bald. One morning during this time I was sitting in a nearby coffee shop waiting for a friend. I was wearing my usual baseball cap; surely it was obvious to everyone that I was in the midst of chemotherapy. A young man approached me while I sat there and asked whether I was in treatment for cancer. I said yes. He then told me his mom was in treatment for lung cancer. He said he hoped things would go well for me—a short conversation, but it meant so much to me for him to wish me well.

Since that experience, I have established a discipline for myself. Whenever I see a person obviously in chemotherapy, I always approach that person and ask whether he or she is in treatment. After hearing the story, I wish the person well. That young man's simple act years ago made a big difference in my life and, I hope, in the lives of others dealing with cancer. May it be so.

God of love and generosity, we are grateful for your presence and guidance in our lives. Help us to live up to your expectations of us. Amen.

Begin today's meditation time by rereading Isaiah 12:2-6. This passage contains a multitude of words and phrases we can take to heart. Choose the one that is most meaningful for you this day, and repeat it to yourself throughout the day. Take inspiration from this prophet's words, uttered so many years ago! My choice today is this: "Give thanks to the LORD."

Despite Israel's waywardness, God bestows mercy. Isaiah urges his hearers to give thanks and proclaim God's name everywhere. His words encourage the people to make God's name known among the nations "on that day," pointing toward a day of salvation and rejoicing. The prophet's verbs are plural here—he speaks to the whole community. Indeed, proclaiming God's name everywhere is a common practice when the community worships together.

In yesterday's meditation I mentioned that I am a cancer survivor. My diagnosis was a number of years ago, but I still see my oncologist at the end of every year. So technically, I am still in remission. Each visit to the oncology center fills me with empathy and gratitude. After seeing my doctor, as I leave the clinic I pass the infusion room. My practice is to go to the door, look inside, and say a breath prayer that expresses both my gratitude for good health and my hopes for similar outcomes for those inside.

Giving thanks and proclaiming God's greatness everywhere in response to divine presence in our lives is a life lesson we can practice as we "shout aloud and sing for joy."

Gracious God, help me remember to express my gratitude to you and to use my life to proclaim your name to others. Amen.

In these two short verses, the prophet Zephaniah accomplishes a major task: He moves from disaster to celebration. Many of the Hebrew prophetic books close with a message of hope and comfort, and this book is no exception. God will vanquish the oppressors, restore the reputation of the people among the nations, restore their fortunes, gather them together, and bring them home. What a joyful conclusion and what an appropriate message for us to hear in Advent! Notice that God speaks in the first person in these verses and speaks directly to the people. God's nearness surely supports an incarnational message for us.

Reading these verses brings back a poignant memory for me. About a year ago, my brother and I lost our mom after her health steadily declined for a number of years. After her death we decided to celebrate her life at the facility where she lived by singing her favorite hymns and songs, telling stories about her life and contributions, and offering prayers—and God was in our midst. That helped us move from heartache to celebration. Among her friends and those who cared for her, we were able to make the transition from disaster to celebration, and we sent her home.

Some scholars believe these two verses are a later addition to Zephaniah's prophecy because of their post-exilic overtones (such as gathering of the exiles and returning to their land of origin). Nevertheless, they provide a fitting conclusion to this song of joy and serve us well in our Advent waiting. We too anticipate God's presence and salvation.

Ever-present God, we pray that you help us learn how to move from disaster to celebration during the trying times in our lives. Amen.

One of our sons works for the US State Department, and his position requires him—and his family—to move somewhere in the world every two years. Their current post is in the Philippines. Either my husband and I must travel long distances to see them or wait until they have home leave and can come here to see us. Because our son and family travel such long distances, I always track their flights while they are in the air. As I do so, I pray a prayer asking God for their safekeeping. I taught our five-year-old grandson how to track flights, and together we tracked the flights of family members who traveled here and gave thanks for their safe arrival—and rejoiced.

Paul offers advice to the entire community, and it begins with rejoicing: "Rejoice in the Lord." Then he suggests that they "let [their] gentleness be known" and "do not worry about anything." We may consider that third piece of advice the hardest to deal with given our anxiety-producing times. Notice the sentence right before this injunction: "The Lord is near." So, near to the believer? Near in terms of the second coming? Perhaps both meanings encourage the Philippians not to allow anxiety to consume them. Paul has no doubt about the ultimate outcome of all events.

Paul writes this epistle while in prison. He writes to reassure the people of Philippi that he remains full of joy and confident despite his situation. So we, with our families of origin and families of faith, acknowledge God's presence, rejoice always, and give thanks. Whether traveling long distances or enduring hardships in life, we rejoice in the fact that God is near, desiring the best for us.

Ever-present God, we are grateful that you are near to us. We carry your peace in our hearts, and we rejoice. Amen.

THIRD SUNDAY OF ADVENT

During Advent, we often find ourselves thinking warm and comforting thoughts about Christmas and babies and manger scenes and carols. Some of us think warm thoughts about families gathering to celebrate the season. However, today's scripture confronts us with prophetic words that are neither warm nor comforting. John the Baptist sounds angry when he calls the people gathered before him a "brood of vipers." That condemnation doesn't help us get into the Christmas spirit!

However, we need to keep reading. After John speaks about trees being cut down and thrown into the fire and burning chaff with fire, the Gospel writer concludes this section with these words: "With many other exhortations, [John] proclaimed good news to the people." So John's message isn't all negative.

We may wonder why the people stay and listen to John given his strong judgmentalism. When does judgment become good news? Perhaps the people perceive a word of truth in what they hear. His hearers, rather than walking away or arguing with John, respond by posing a simple question: "What then should we do?" And John's response is equally simple: Do the right thing. Be generous. Don't steal from others. Do not take advantage of people. And so it comes to us: Volunteer in our communities. Be honest in our dealings with friends and colleagues. Go above and beyond to offer help.

And perhaps beyond the good life lessons, John turns their attention to the coming One who baptizes with the Holy Spirit and fire—a foretaste of Pentecost.

Loving God, we need your help to do the right thing. Be with us as we try to do our best. Amen.

God's Surprising Presence

DECEMBER 17–23, 2018 • MAX O. VINCENT

SCRIPTURE OVERVIEW: As Christians we understand that our faith is rooted in the ongoing story of God's faithfulness to God's people. Micah celebrates this story, prophesying that the true king of Israel will one day come from the small village of Bethlehem, Jesus' birthplace. Luke features women prominently throughout his Gospel. The two readings from Luke this week highlight the prophetic insights of Elizabeth and Mary. Mary visits Elizabeth, who is pregnant with John, God's messenger. After Elizabeth identifies Mary as the mother of the Lord, Mary breaks into song, understanding that her story is tied to the fulfillment of God's promises going back to Abraham. Little does she know that her son will one day offer his body as a sacrifice for all, as Hebrews tells us.

QUESTIONS AND THOUGHTS FOR REFLECTION
- Read Micah 5:2-5a. What "small" beginnings have yielded great results in your life?
- Read Psalm 80:1-7. How does this psalm of lament speak to you? When has God restored you and shone the light of divine love on you?
- Read Hebrews 10:5-10. What do you believe God desires from you? In what ways does Jesus' life of obedience help you understand God's intention for you and the world?
- Read Luke 1:39-55. When have you been stopped in your tracks by meeting unexpectedly an old acquaintance? How did God speak to you in that encounter?

An elder in the North Georgia Conference of The United Methodist Church; coauthor of *Another Bead, Another Prayer* with his wife, Kristen.

Walking into the sanctuary one Sunday morning, I was stopped in my tracks when I saw the face of an old friend. We had not seen each other in ten years. He is a Lutheran pastor in Louisiana. I serve a United Methodist congregation in Atlanta, Georgia. We met in graduate school almost twenty years before this Sunday reunion. Though we stayed in contact with each other through the years, we were seldom together in person.

In that moment of recognition, I was flooded with a series of emotions. When another pastor takes time off to come worship with me, I consider it an honor. When an old friend goes out of his or her way to pay a surprise visit, I am reminded of the intimate bonds that have united us across the years. But mostly I am just surprised.

Elizabeth greets Mary with a similarly surprised response. Elizabeth is six months pregnant at this point. She may have had many visitors during that time; but when Mary greets her, something different happens. The baby within Elizabeth leaps for joy at the sound of Mary's voice.

Elizabeth is surprised. She is delighted. After Mary's greeting, she responds, "Why do I have this honor, that the mother of my Lord should come to me?" (1:43, CEB). Mary's surprise visit stops Elizabeth in her tracks as she realizes that God has come to visit her through the presence of her pregnant cousin Mary.

Advent invites us to be ready for God's appearance at unexpected times, in unexpected places—even through unexpected voices and faces.

Lord, surprise me with your presence today. Amen.

In a communications class in college, my professor made a comment that has stayed with me for nearly thirty years now: "News happens where we place reporters." She did not mean that important events happen only where news reporters are stationed. Rather, the news we hear or read comes to us because someone is there to tell the story. News happens every day, but we do not hear about it because no one is in that location to report the events. If the story is big enough, we may hear about it several days later because it takes time for a reporter to travel to the location. We frequently hear the news from places where governments are located or from large cities because these are the locations where news agencies place their reporters. We expect the news to come from London, Tokyo, or New York.

Granted, this situation has changed drastically in the last thirty years with the invention of cell phones and the Internet. Now anyone with a camera and a network can create a story to share with a large audience around the world. However, most of us still look to the major news centers, the large cities, the places of power and prestige to get our news.

Micah tells of a redemption that will come from an unexpected place. Micah says, Do not look to Jerusalem, the large city and center of government. Look instead to Bethlehem, that tiny place among all the towns and hamlets of Judah. From this often overlooked little spot, one will emerge who will be great over all the earth.

Advent reminds us that no place is too small for God's presence.

Lord, there is nowhere I can go to escape your presence. Make me mindful of your presence wherever I am today. Amen.

God's Surprising Presence   417

Serving as a guest minister in a congregation one Sunday, I closed the service with the blessing from Numbers 6:24-26: "The LORD bless you and keep you. The LORD make his face shine on you and be gracious to you. The LORD lift up his face to you and grant you peace" (CEB). As I spoke this benediction, I noticed one woman's demeanor change as she heard the words. It did not surprise me when she came to greet me immediately after the service. This woman shared with me her memories of attending church youth meetings while growing up and how the group always ended their gatherings by saying together the blessing from Numbers 6. She had not been attending worship for over ten years. She came to worship on this particular Sunday because of her awareness of a sense of longing that made it difficult for her to feel joy and peace. She had sat through the service hoping that the words of the hymns, the prayers, or even the sermon might speak to her about the longing she felt. As the service came to a close, she thought she was going to leave disappointed. But those familiar words of benediction reminded her that God wanted to shine God's face upon her.

In this lament from Psalm 80, the people cry to God to save them. Twice in this brief passage, the psalmist pleads for restoration, for God's face to shine upon the people. In good times and bad times, the people turn to God. After addressing the sense of separation the people feel between themselves and God, the psalmist equates this turning of God's face to the people with salvation.

Throughout this final week of Advent, remember that God desires to look graciously upon you.

Lord, shine the light of your face upon me. Amen.

God's Surprising Presence

What does God want? As Christmas approaches, we can easily focus on what *we* want. Some of us may compile "Wish Lists" for others to purchase for us. Even when we turn our attention to God, we can quickly zero in on the things we want from God—not simply material things but requests like these: "God, grant us joy. Give us peace. Bring us hope."

The Bible does indeed teach us to bring our cares and concerns to the Lord in prayer. And I do not want to dissuade requests for joy, peace, and hope. But this passage from Hebrews raises the question, "What does God desire?"

Our reading notes that God does not desire sacrifice and offering. If you have read the books of the law in the Old Testament, this may sound strange. Entire chapters are devoted to the offerings and sacrifices of the Israelites. God goes into great detail about when to bring sacrifices, what constitutes an offering, who is to offer which sacrifice, when to bring your offering. Later, in verse 8, the author of Hebrews even points out that these offerings and sacrifices were required by the law.

Today's passage opens with Christ himself quoting the words of Psalm 40, which set aside ritual and sacrifice in favor of doing God's will. The incarnation of Christ ("offering of the body of Christ" in life and death), who lives in complete obedience to God, fulfills God's intention for humanity.

So what does God desire from us? If it is not sacrifices and offerings, which are commanded, what does God want from us? We will return to this passage tomorrow to see what the writer of Hebrews says, but for today spend some time with this question and see what God is speaking to you.

God, what do you desire from me today?

Regulations for sacrifices and offerings fill the Old Testament. How can the author of Hebrews say, "Sacrifices and offerings you have not desired"? The Bible I am reading lists Psalm 40:6 as a cross-reference for this verse in Hebrews. Indeed the two verses are almost identical. The tradition of the Old Testament prophets is that of calling out to Israel, saying God desires more than ritual observance. Samuel, Isaiah, Amos, Hosea, and others all speak out against those who concern themselves only with rote observance of the Old Testament offerings and sacrifices. These prophets call for social justice alongside ritual observance of the law.

But there is more to this statement in Hebrews than the Psalms and the prophets. Jesus also uses this idea that God desires more than rote observance of the law to defend his ministry. Indeed the author of Hebrews places these words on Jesus' lips: "Consequently, when Christ came into the world, he said, 'Sacrifices and offerings you have not desired, but a body you have prepared for me.'"

The point of this passage is not to disparage the offerings and sacrifices. The author is trying to remind us that God's true desire is the living out of God's will in our lives. So Jesus comes in a human body to live out God's will among us. Through his life of obedience, Jesus brings to us the gift of holiness that we too may live according to God's will.

God surprises us with the gift of holiness when God visits us in Jesus.

God, give me grace to live your will today. Amen.

Micah speaks of little Bethlehem suddenly becoming great. The greatness will come about not because Bethlehem suddenly grows, develops a great advertising campaign, or is discovered to be the center of a natural resource like gold or oil. No, the little town of Bethlehem will become great by the visitation of the Lord, what the Lord causes to happen there.

Many of the places the Bible commemorates are small, seemingly insignificant. Judah is not a large country. Even Israel under David and Solomon was no vast, expansive empire. Many towns and villages mentioned in the Bible are hard to locate today. The Jordan River, so significant in the biblical narrative, is a small river when compared to the Nile, the Euphrates, or the Mississippi. What makes any of these places important, what leads to their being mentioned in the Bible, is that they are places where encounters with God occur.

Any place takes on special meaning in our lives when we view it as a site where we have encountered God. It may be in a sanctuary during worship, on a retreat with other Christians, sitting on a bench in the park, in a corner of a coffee shop; but when it suddenly becomes a place where God's presence has visited us, our "little Bethlehem" becomes a center of peace in our lives.

Like Bethlehem, the places of our God-encounters may seem tiny and the least noticeable, but they become great places in our lives. Today many travel each year to the small Judean town of Bethlehem because God once visited it in the birth of God's Son.

Shepherd, thank you for the places in my life that have been filled with your presence and where I have experienced your peace. Amen.

God's Surprising Presence 421

FOURTH SUNDAY OF ADVENT

Elizabeth is surprised that the child within her leaps for joy at the sound of Mary's voice. Elizabeth's greeting in return surprises Mary. Elizabeth, "filled with the Holy Spirit," confirms Gabriel's message to Mary, who surprisingly breaks out in song.

Mary's singing may not surprise those of us who read Luke 1 and 2 every year at Christmas. Once we reach the part where Elizabeth greets Mary, our minds may race forward to Mary's singing about the greatness of God. Seriously, when did you last open the door to your house, greet someone, and have that person start singing? But it seems like everyone starts singing at Christmastime. Luke tells the Christmas story in such a way that we think singing has always been a part of Christmas.

The beginning of Luke's Gospel reads like a musical. Visits are suddenly interrupted by someone breaking into song: Zechariah at the naming of John, the angels telling the shepherds about the birth of Jesus, Simeon in the Temple at Jesus' dedication, and Mary when she visits Elizabeth.

Mary sings about being caught up in God's visitation of Israel, a visitation that alters the status of the poor and the proud, the hungry and the rich. She does not sing of future promises but of promises fulfilled. God's redeeming work is already active. And God's visitation is more than a blessing for Mary's life; it is a blessing that extends far beyond her.

When God surprises us with a visitation, it not only blesses our lives but the lives of others by God's work through us. So join voices with Zechariah, Simeon, the angels, and Mary. Rejoice in God's surprising work in and through you.

God, my spirit rejoices in your surprising presence among us. Amen.

From This Time Onward

DECEMBER 24–30, 2018 • PAMELA C. HAWKINS

SCRIPTURE OVERVIEW: The boy Samuel worshiped and served God from a young age. He grows in stature and favor, the same description that will later be applied to the young Jesus in this week's reading from Luke. The psalmist praises God for raising up a "horn" for the people. This "horn" is referred to elsewhere in the Psalms as being the True King from the line of David, identified later by Luke (1:69) as Jesus. Paul encourages the Colossians to let love rule in their community and to praise God with songs and hymns (such as the Psalms). The additional readings for this special week focus our minds on the Advent of the Lord, the amazing truth that "the Word became flesh and lived among us" (John 1:14), as the prophets had prophesied long ago.

QUESTIONS AND THOUGHTS FOR REFLECTION

- Read Isaiah 9:2-7. Where in your world do you see darkness? What lies within your power to dispel it?

- Read Psalm 148. How have you witnessed creation praising the Creator?

- Read Colossians 3:12-17. With what qualities from this list do you clothe yourself daily?

- Read Luke 2:41-52. When has a not-as-usual occurrence generated anxiety in your life? How was it resolved?

Writer and artist, living in Nashville, Tennessee.

CHRISTMAS EVE

In our time, we have a keen awareness of lurking darkness as close as family secrets and as distant as tribal genocide across the globe. As we approach Christmas and read the season's scriptures about God's promised light soon to be revealed, we are often even more aware of many shadows of darkness and despair in the world. Although our lives may be rooted in the joy and hope of Advent and Christmas, as God's beloved people we are called to bear God's light to others who walk the earth in places where that light seems absent.

This Christmas Eve, we who seek to follow Jesus receive profound clarity about how we are to live as children of God; in Jesus, God's light shines for all to witness. And we, created in God's image, have been given life so that this light can confront and lift the death-dealing darkness that threatens to snuff out life. As Christ-followers, we believe that if one of God's children lives in "deep darkness," then, in solidarity, we all do. Together we all must bear God's light until life breaks through again.

The prophet Isaiah tells of this God-light, which is no longer a promise but now a reality that breaks through paralyzing, community-wounding darkness. If we, on this Eve, dare to open our eyes and hearts to this life-changing light, we will be witnesses "from this time onward" that there is no darkness too deep or thick to keep the Light of the world from breaking forth.

Beacon of love, Light of the world, may my heart, on this holy night of your birth, burn with such brightness that I radiate your love and light to others. Amen.

CHRISTMAS DAY

Nestled against Mary's heart, her arms still awkward with first-time mothering, this newborn squirms against the cloth that binds him. He whimpers a bit, to which his young mother responds with gentle words and soft strokes. He hears her heartbeat intensify, a familiar sound to him, and his heart replies with a quickening of its own.

Mary draws in a deep breath, her body quickly remembering the soreness from last night's labor. She flinches for a moment, fearing her sudden movement might disturb her son; yet he just frowns a little and settles into the curves and contours of her body all the more. It is as though he wants to bring comfort to her as much as she does to him, and slowly their breathing settles into each other's.

Here begins the first day of the life of God's Son, the first incarnate act of love between the Creator and created. Here the "exact imprint of God's very being" rises and falls in breath's intimate rhythm with humanity. Here the "reflection of God's glory" can be first seen in the anxious eyes of a young, vulnerable woman who wants nothing more than to love her child well. In a few brief hours, the love of God-With-Us has already changed one life on earth.

At the birth of Jesus Christ, humankind receives the first indelible image of what God intends human love to look like—the love between mother and child. And from that moment forward, God-With-Us reveals how love can take hold of and change us for the rest of our lives if we dare, like Mary, to make ourselves vulnerable to God's love that is unexpected and unimpressive in worldly ways. May we dare to love like this.

Creating God, in Jesus you show me how I am to love and to be loved. Help me pay attention. Amen.

From This Time Onward

From Creation's first breath, we are reminded through the poetry of the Psalms that every single part of life imagined, formed, and spoken into being by God is imbued with the capacity to respond to God in praise. Not only can everything praise God, but according to Psalm 148, everything in creation is called to do so. Praise of the Lord is not an option for creation but is creation's innate expression of gratitude and awe for having been created at all.

Praise of God is essential to our living as God created us to live. Praise resides in our DNA, and, like breath, is a life-giving force of our nature by which we remain in ongoing communion with God beyond our consciousness or control. Like breath, praise enters our spirits as we take in the wonders that God places around us, and praise leaves our hearts as we respond to the mysteries and beauty of God.

And if we ever begin to walk down the thorny path of human self-importance, believing ourselves to be the most significant source of praise, the psalmist's words remind us that our praise is but a refrain in the chorus of all creation. Long before we found our voice, all of heaven and earth was already singing praise to the Lord. Stars, moon, and sun; mountains, hills, and oceans; "creeping things," fish, and birds—even the trees from which birds sing have been sharing the magnificent inhale and exhale of praise since the beginning of time.

Let us remember that the chorus of praise on the night of Jesus' birth, from all heaven and earth, did not begin then, but welled up at the beginning of creation and continues as we now join our voices for all time.

O Lord of heaven and earth, of sweeping wind and falling stars, teach me to listen and notice; teach me to sing and be silent. I long to praise you with my whole being. Amen.

The story of Samuel begins one chapter before our reading. In the scriptures we first meet his father, Elkanah, and mother, Hannah, and learn that Hannah is barren. Year after year she goes with her husband to the temple at Shiloh and prays to the Lord for a male child, promising, if her prayers are answered, to consecrate her son to God's service.

The Lord grants her request, and she and Elkanah conceive a son and name him Samuel. As promised, when Samuel is old enough to be weaned, Hannah takes him to the temple and presents him to the old priest Eli to be raised in the priesthood. From that time onward Samuel lives in God's service, growing "both in stature and in favor of the LORD and with the people" (2:26) and will one day become one of Israel's most influential prophet-judges.

But today we focus on Samuel's childhood years, noticing a particular thread that weaves through his story: the author's repeated emphasis that Samuel's formation as a servant of God begins at a very young age. Chapter 1 reveals Samuel as barely weaned when Hannah consecrates him to God's service. Then three times in today's brief passage, Samuel's youth is confirmed, twice as a "boy" and once because the robe his mother brings each year is "little." If we read further, this vein of Samuel's childhood formation and calling continues, detailing God's work in the life of this young man.

Scripture affirms God's commitment to the spiritual value of children who, like Samuel, become an example of faithfulness. Perhaps our task, then, is to grow in attentiveness to the children around us, joining God's formational work already begun.

God of every generation and age, teach us your ways of wisdom and love that we may serve you all the days of our lives. Amen.

By the time Jesus turns twelve, Mary and Joseph have carved out life-as-usual routines and traditions for their household, including the annual Passover pilgrimage from Nazareth to Jerusalem and back again. Jesus travels with his extended family "every year," going "up as usual for the festival," and returning home together.

But this year, without his parents' knowledge, Jesus stays in Jerusalem after the festival instead of going home. A whole travel day passes before Mary and Joseph discover their son is missing. Immediately they retrace their steps to Jerusalem. Three anxious days later, they find Jesus in a place they never thought to look—"in the temple, sitting among the teachers," amazing everyone with his unsettling maturity of presence and understanding.

Mary and Joseph are also astonished and unsettled, but for different reasons. Their twelve-year-old son is not where he's supposed to be. From their perspective, Jesus, perhaps for the first time in his life, has disobeyed his parents. Mary interrupts the teachers by confronting her son: "Why have you treated us like this?" Knowing already that his answer will not be understood, Jesus replies that he "must be about my Father's business" (KJV). Jesus tells his mother that he *is* home, just not where she expected him to be.

For the rest of his life, Jesus continued to surprise, even disappoint, people by being where they thought he should not be. Jesus continues to be about his Father's business, spending time with the poor and the forgotten of our day. If we are seeking him, that's where we'll find him.

Holy Jesus, may I search for you unceasingly. Remind me every day to turn to you and to trust that I will find you and you will find me even in uncertain and unlikely places. Amen.

How are we to live in the waning light of the Christmas star? Our hearts and lives quickened in breathless anticipation as we prepared to receive the Christ child. But here in the slow unfurling of days beyond Bethlehem, what can prepare us to face the headwinds swirling toward us from every direction, pressing us to conform to everyday routines?

Mary, the mother of Jesus, offers a helpful image. From the first earthly breath drawn by her son, Mary is aware of risks that he will face when exposed to the threatening ways of the world. Carefully, with great tenderness, she takes cloth, binding the tiny, vulnerable body of Jesus against immediate dangers, remembering her promise to God to give this life a chance. In what seems now to us so small a gift—a few bands of cloth in the hands of a loving parent—the future of love finds life.

How much more, then, are we prepared to receive God's gifts that can, through us, continue to keep love alive in the world? As followers of Jesus, we will face harsh and threatening winds of our times, forces that can overwhelm and confuse us along the way of discipleship. But the writer of Colossians reminds us that we, like Jesus, have a loving parent who will not leave us stripped bare and alone to face worldly dangers. God our parent offers spiritual cloth to us, cloth that, if worn, can sustain us as we move forward in faith. Our task is to clothe ourselves in these gifts of compassion, kindness, humility, meekness, patience, and love and also to accept the bindings of forgiveness and peace.

May we seek and accept these gifts from God, and may we wear them in life-changing ways.

Loving God, I come to you this day with deep gratitude for all that you provide for me in this life. May I become humble like Jesus so my dependence on you continues to be revealed. Amen.

A new calendar year stretches before us, stirring up fresh resolve in many of us to change our circumstances or ourselves during the next twelve months. Some will write official New Year's resolutions, making lists of goals to accomplish. Others will not be so formal, writing secret New Year's longings on our hearts.

Our reading from Colossians also reveals the hope of living a better life. But it is God's hope for our lives that is recorded in this passage, not a list of resolutions that we have created. In these verses, we find some of God's deepest hopes for us: hopes for changes needed in the world from this moment onward and hopes made all the more possible by following Jesus.

How might this new year be different from years past if we resolve to grow in compassion, kindness, humility, meekness, and patience? If this day becomes a day of forgiveness, a day that we set our intention either to offer or to accept forgiveness— not in general terms, but with someone in mind—what new life possibilities will open up for us and for others? And even better, what if we set a new-year intention to make forgiveness a spiritual life practice, a daily pattern of prayer and response for which God has already given us an example in Jesus?

And finally, what if our night prayer from this time onward —a prayer to guide our resolutions and hopes, whatever they may be—could rise out of God's word:

Through this night, O God, and in every waking moment, clothe me with your love. Bind me in perfect harmony to everything you love, and open my heart more and more each day to carry the peace of Christ. Amen.

Prince of Peace, I lift my heart in thanksgiving that you are my guide into the coming year. May I follow you in the ways of love. Amen.

Following the Light, Being the Light

DECEMBER 31, 2018 • J. MARSHALL JENKINS

SCRIPTURE OVERVIEW: As we approach Epiphany Sunday, we think of the coming of God into the world as the coming of a brilliant light—a light that shines into dark corners, a light that shines on people who dwell in darkness. The light of God brings with it the power of restoration to a people in exile. It shines transforming power on forgotten ones who will now arise and shine. God's presence brings light and well-being. At this time of year, we may desire God's light to shine upon us.

QUESTIONS AND THOUGHTS FOR REFLECTION

- Read Isaiah 60:1-6. When have you lived your way into being what you most desired?

Author, spiritual director, and licensed psychologist, living in Rome, Georgia.

Israel, long acquainted with darkness, still awaited daybreak. Remembering invasion, dispersion, and exile, a recently returned remnant felt homesick in their homeland where they faced much rebuilding amid suspicious neighbors. As a weak political player, God's chosen nation dwelt in darkness. But through the prophet, God offers a new vision of power: The weak nation rises, not through intrigue or violence but through attracting others to divine blessing.

In that vision, powerful nations realize that they too dwell in darkness. Weary of paranoia, wall-building, and war-mongering, they find that darkness surrounds them even in victory. For winning the day means defending it tomorrow until finally another wins and jumps on the same defensive treadmill.

Then the nations see the light. God's glory shines through the chosen people. Their simple being, without sharpening a sword or seeking any advantage, pierces the night.

Finally, the nations realize the incompatibility of domination with peace, and they want peace. So they turn to the nation whose God is love. The priestly nation becomes the great power not by locking gates but by opening them, not by intimidating but by welcoming, not by hoarding but by sharing. God's love not only fills them but forms them into a nation that loves as God loves. A world that realizes that only God can bring daybreak gladly pays homage to the people who rise in morning light.

As God's beloved, we let God's love fill and form us. By nonviolent love that mirrors God's mercy, we light the night and beckon the world. "You are the light of the world," Jesus said (Matt. 5:14). In God's time, we become the daybreak that first awakened us and that will invite the world.

Lord, as your love in Christ illuminates us, may we share your light that draws the world out of darkness. Amen.

The Revised Common Lectionary* for 2018
Year B – Advent / Christmas Year C
(Disciplines Edition)

January 1–7
Isaiah 61:10–62:3
Psalm 148
Galatians 4:4-7
Luke 2:22-40

> **New Year's Day**
> Ecclesiastes 3:1-13
> Psalm 8
> Revelation 21:1-6a
> Matthew 25:31-46

January 6
EPIPHANY
(may be used for Sunday, Jan. 7)
Isaiah 60:1-6
Psalm 72:1-7, 10-14
Ephesians 3:1-12
Matthew 2:1-12

BAPTISM OF THE LORD
Genesis 1:1-5
Psalm 29
Acts 19:1-7
Mark 1:4-11

January 8–14
1 Samuel 3:1-20
Psalm 139:1-6, 13-18
1 Corinthians 6:12-20
John 1:43-51

January 15–21
Jonah 3:1-5, 10
Psalm 62:5-12
1 Corinthians 7:29-31
Mark 1:14-20

January 22–28
Deuteronomy 18:15-20
Psalm 111
1 Corinthians 8:1-13
Mark 1:21-28

January 29—February 4
Isaiah 40:21-31
Psalm 147:1-11, 20c
1 Corinthians 9:16-23
Mark 1:29-39

February 5–11
TRANSFIGURATION
2 Kings 2:1-12
Psalm 50:1-6
2 Corinthians 4:3-6
Mark 9:2-9

February 12–18
FIRST SUNDAY IN LENT
Genesis 9:8-17
Psalm 25:1-10
1 Peter 3:18-22
Mark 1:9-15

February 14
ASH WEDNESDAY
Joel 2:1-2, 12-17 (*or* Isaiah 58:1-12)
Psalm 51:1-17
2 Corinthians 5:20b–6:10
Matthew 6:1-6, 16-21

February 19–25
SECOND SUNDAY IN LENT
Genesis 17:1-7, 15-16
Psalm 22:23-31
Romans 4:13-25
Mark 8:31-38 *or* Mark 9:2-9

February 26—March 4
THIRD SUNDAY IN LENT
Exodus 20:1-17
Psalm 19
1 Corinthians 1:18-25
John 2:13-22

March 5–11
FOURTH SUNDAY IN LENT
Numbers 21:4-9
Psalm 107:1-3, 17-22
Ephesians 2:1-10
John 3:14-21

March 12–18
FIFTH SUNDAY IN LENT
Jeremiah 31:31-34
Psalm 51:1-12
(*or* Psalm 119:9-16)
Hebrews 5:5-10
John 12:20-33

March 19–25
PALM/PASSION SUNDAY
Liturgy of the Palms
Mark 11:1-11, 15-18
(*or* John 12:12-16)

Psalm 118:1-2, 19-29
Liturgy of the Passion
Isaiah 50:4-9a
Psalm 31:9-16
Philippians 2:5-11
Mark 14:1–15:47
  (*or* Mark 15:1-47)

March 26—April 1
HOLY WEEK

   HOLY MONDAY
   Isaiah 42:1-9
   Psalm 36:5-11
   Hebrews 9:11-15
   John 12:1-11

   HOLY TUESDAY
   Isaiah 49:1-7
   Psalm 71:1-14
   1 Corinthians 1:18-31
   John 12:20-36

   HOLY WEDNESDAY
   Isaiah 50:4-9a
   Psalm 70
   Hebrews 12:1-3
   John 13:21-32

   MAUNDY THURSDAY
   Exodus 12:1-14
   Psalm 116:1-2, 12-19
   1 Corinthians 11:23-26
   John 13:1-17, 31b-35

   GOOD FRIDAY
   Isaiah 52:13–53:12
   Psalm 22
   Hebrews 10:16-25
   John 18:1–19:42

HOLY SATURDAY
Easter Vigil
Exodus 14:10-31
Isaiah 55:1-11
Psalm 114
Romans 6:3-11
Mark 16:1-8

EASTER SUNDAY (APRIL 1)
Acts 10:34-43
Psalm 118:1-2, 14-24
1 Corinthians 15:1-11
John 20:1-18
  (*or* Mark 16:1-8)

April 2–8
Acts 4:32-35
Psalm 133
1 John 1:1–2:2
John 20:19-31

April 9–15
Acts 3:12-19
Psalm 4
1 John 3:1-7
Luke 24:36*b*-48

April 16–22
Acts 4:5-12
Psalm 23
1 John 3:16-24
John 10:11-18

April 23–29
Acts 8:26-40
Psalm 22:25-31
1 John 4:7-21
John 15:1-8

April 30—May 6
Acts 10:44-48
Psalm 98
1 John 5:1-6
John 15:9-17

May 7–13
Acts 1:15-17, 21-26
Psalm 1
1 John 5:9-13
John 17:6-19

May 10
ASCENSION DAY
Acts 1:1-11
Psalm 47
Ephesians 1:15-23
Luke 24:44-53

May 14–20
PENTECOST
Acts 2:1-21
Psalm 104:24-34, 35b
Romans 8:22-27
John 15:26-27; 16:4b-15

May 21–27
TRINITY
Isaiah 6:1-8
Psalm 29
Romans 8:12-17
John 3:1-17

May 28—June 3
1 Samuel 3:1-20
Psalm 139:1-6, 13-18
2 Corinthians 4:5-12
Mark 2:23—3:6

June 4–10
1 Samuel 8:4-20
Psalm 138
2 Corinthians 4:13–5:1
Mark 3:20-35

June 11–17
1 Samuel 15:34–16:13
Psalm 20
2 Corinthians 5:6-17
Mark 4:26-34

June 18–24
1 Samuel 17:1a, 4-11, 19-23,
  32-49
Psalm 9:9-20
2 Corinthians 6:1-13
Mark 4:35-41

June 25–July 1
2 Samuel 1:1, 17-27
Psalm 130
2 Corinthians 8:7-15
Mark 5:21-43

July 2–8
2 Samuel 5:1-5, 9-10
Psalm 48
2 Corinthians 12:2-10
Mark 6:1-13

July 9–15
2 Samuel 6:1-5, 12b-19
Psalm 24
Ephesians 1:3-14
Mark 6:14-29

July 16–22
2 Samuel 7:1-14a
Psalm 89:20-37
Ephesians 2:11-22
Mark 6:30-34, 53-56

July 23–29
2 Samuel 11:1-15
Psalm 14
Ephesians 3:14-21
John 6:1-21

July 30—August 5
2 Samuel 11:26–12:13a
Psalm 51:1-12
Ephesians 4:1-16
John 6:24-35

August 6–12
2 Samuel 18:5-9, 15, 31-33
Psalm 34:1-8
Ephesians 4:25–5:2
John 6:35, 41-51

August 13–19
1 Kings 2:10-12; 3:3-14
Psalm 111
Ephesians 5:15-20
John 6:51-58

August 20–26
1 Kings 8:1, 6, 10-11, 22-30,
  41-43
Psalm 84
Ephesians 6:10-20
John 6:56-69

August 27—September 2
Song of Solomon 2:8-13
Psalm 45:1-2, 6-9
James 1:17-27
Mark 7:1-8, 14-15, 21-23

September 3–9
Proverbs 22:1-2, 8-9, 22-23
Psalm 125
James 2:1-17
Mark 7:24-37

September 10–16
Proverbs 1:20-33
Psalm 19
James 3:1-12
Mark 8:27-38

September 17–23
Proverbs 31:10-31
Psalm 1
James 3:13–4:3, 7-8a
Mark 9:30-37

September 24–30
Esther 7:1-6, 9-10; 9:20-22
Psalm 124
James 5:13-20
Mark 9:38-50

October 1–7
Job 1:1; 2:1-10
Psalm 26
Hebrews 1:1-4; 2:5-12
Mark 10:2-16

October 8–14
Job 23:1-9, 16-17
Psalm 22:1-15
Hebrews 4:12-16
Mark 10:17-31

>**OCTOBER 11**
>**THANKSGIVING DAY, CANADA**
>Joel 2:21-27
>Psalm 126
>1 Timothy 2:1-7
>Matthew 6:25-33

October 15–21
Job 38:1-7, 34-41
Psalm 104:1-9, 24, 35c
Hebrews 5:1-10
Mark 10:35-45

October 22–28
Job 42:1-6, 10-17
Psalm 34:1-8, 19-22
Hebrews 7:23-28
Mark 10:46-52

October 29—November 4
Ruth 1:1-18
Psalm 146
Hebrews 9:11-14
Mark 12:28-34

>**November 1**
>**ALL SAINTS DAY**
>Isaiah 25:6-9
>Psalm 24
>Revelation 21:1-6a
>John 11:32-44

November 5–11
Ruth 3:1-5; 4:13-17
Psalm 127
Hebrews 9:24-28
Mark 12:38-44

November 12–18
1 Samuel 1:4-20
1 Samuel 2:1-10
Hebrews 10:11-25
Mark 13:1-8

November 19–25
THE REIGN OF CHRIST
2 Samuel 23:1-7
Psalm 132:1-18
Revelation 1:4b-8
John 18:33-37

November 22
THANKSGIVING DAY, USA
Joel 2:21-27
Psalm 126
1 Timothy 2:1-7
Matthew 6:25-33

November 26–December 2
FIRST SUNDAY OF ADVENT
Jeremiah 33:14-16
Psalm 25:1-10
1 Thessalonians 3:9-13
Luke 21:25-36

December 3–9
SECOND SUNDAY OF ADVENT
Malachi 3:1-4
Luke 1:68-79
Philippians 1:3-11
Luke 3:1-6

December 10–16
THIRD SUNDAY OF ADVENT
Zephaniah 3:14-20
Isaiah 12:2-6
Philippians 4:4-7
Luke 3:7-18

December 17–23
FOURTH SUNDAY OF ADVENT
Micah 5:2-5a
Luke 1:46-55
  (*or* Psalm 80:1-7)
Hebrews 10:5-10
Luke 1:39-55

December 24–30
FIRST SUNDAY AFTER CHRISTMAS
1 Samuel 2:18-20, 26
Psalm 148
Colossians 3:12-17
Luke 2:41-52

December 24
CHRISTMAS EVE
Isaiah 9:2-7
Psalm 96
Titus 2:11-14
Luke 2:1-20

December 25
CHRISTMAS DAY
Isaiah 52:7-10
Psalm 98
Hebrews 1:1-12
John 1:1-14

December 31

New Year's Day
Ecclesiastes 3:1-13
Psalm 8
Revelation 21:1-6a
Matthew 25:31-46

EPIPHANY
Isaiah 60:1-6
Psalm 72:1-7, 10-14
Ephesians 3:1-12
Matthew 2:1-12

A Guide to Daily Prayer

These prayers imply worship time with a group; feel free to adapt the plural pronouns for personal use.

MORNING PRAYER

"In the morning, O Lord, you hear my voice;
    in the morning I lay my requests before you
    and wait in expectation."

—Psalm 5:3

Gathering and Silence

Call to Praise and Prayer
God said: Let there be light; and there was light.
And God saw that the light was good.

Psalm 63:2-6

God, my God, you I crave;
my soul thirsts for you,
my body aches for you
like a dry and weary land.
    Let me gaze on you in your temple:
    a Vision of strength and glory
    Your love is better than life,
    my speech is full of praise.
    I give you a lifetime of worship,
    my hands raised in your name.
    I feast at a rich table
    my lips sing of your glory.

Prayer of Thanksgiving

We praise you with joy, loving God, for your grace is better than life itself. You have sustained us through the darkness: and you bless us with life in this new day. In the shadow of your wings we sing for joy and bless your holy name. Amen.

Scripture Reading

Silence

Prayers of the People

The Lord's Prayer (see Midday Prayer for text)

Blessing

May the light of your mercy shine brightly on all who walk in your presence today, O Lord.

MIDDAY PRAYER

"I will extol the LORD at all times;
    God's praise will always be on my lips."
                                        —Psalm 34:1

Gathering and Silence

Call to Praise and Prayer

O LORD, my Savior, teach me your ways.
    My hope is in you all day long.

Prayer of Thanksgiving

God of mercy, we acknowledge this midday pause
of refreshment as one of your many generous gifts.
Look kindly upon our work this day; may it be made
perfect in your time. May our purpose and prayers
be pleasing to you. This we ask through Christ our
Lord. Amen.

Scripture Reading

Silence

Prayers of the People

The Lord's Prayer (ecumenical text)
    Our Father in heaven,
        hallowed be your name,
        your kingdom come,
        your will be done,
        on earth as in heaven.
    Give us today our daily bread.

Forgive us our sins as we forgive
   those who sin against us.
Save us from the time of trial,
   and deliver us from evil.
For the kingdom, the power, and the glory
   are yours, now and forever. Amen.

Blessing

Strong is the love embracing us, faithful the Lord from morning to night.

Evening Prayer

> "My soul finds rest in God alone;
> my salvation comes from God."
> —Psalm 62:1

Gathering and Silence

Call to Praise and Prayer

From the rising of the sun to its setting,
let the name of the LORD be praised.

Psalm 134

Bless the Lord,
all who serve in God's house,
who stand watch
throughout the night.

Lift up your hands
in the holy place
and bless the Lord.

And may God,
the maker of earth and sky,
bless you from Zion.

Prayer of Thanksgiving

Sovereign God, you have been our help during the day and you promise to be with us at night. Receive this prayer as a sign of our trust in you. Save us from all evil, keep us from all harm, and guide us in your way. We belong to you, Lord. Protect us by the power of your name, in Jesus Christ we pray. Amen.

Scripture Reading

Silence

Prayers of the People

The Lord's Prayer (see Midday Prayer for text)

Blessing

May your unfailing love rest upon us, O Lord, even as we hope in you.

This Guide to Daily Prayer was compiled from scripture and other resources by Rueben P. Job and then adapted by the Pathways Center for Spiritual Leadership while under the direction of Marjorie J. Thompson.